The Politics of Reading

Power, Opportunity, and Prospects for Change
in America's Public Schools

The Politics of Reading

Power, Opportunity, and Prospects for Change in America's Public Schools

Jo Michelle Beld Fraatz

Foreword by Seymour B. Sarason

TEACHERS COLLEGE PRESS

Teachers College, Columbia University
New York and London

Published by Teachers College Press, 1234 Amsterdam Avenue,
New York, NY 10027

Library of Congress Cataloging-in-Publication Data

Fraatz, Jo Michelle Beld.
  The politics of reading.

  Bibliography: p. 223
  Includes index.
  1. Socially handicapped children—Education—United
States—Reading.   2. Educational equalization—United
States.   3. Education, Elementary—United States—
Aims and objectives.   4. Education and state—United
States.   I. Title.
LC4091.F678   1987   371.96'7   87-9937
ISBN 0-8077-2858-6
ISBN 0-8077-2857-8 (pbk.)

Manufactured in the United States of America
92 91 90 89 88 87   1 2 3 4 5 6

For
Bill and Tommy

Contents

Foreword

In his presidential address to the American Psychological Association in 1899, John Dewey explicitly stated that education is, and had to be conceived as, part of the social sciences. This was not a matter of theory but of the obvious fact that education as a field was an endeavor intimately related to the central concerns and goals of the social sciences; Dewey took this position because of the role of education in a society committed to a democratic ideology. It was clear that to the extent that education remained or became isolated from the social sciences, both would be impoverished, with the consequence that the commitment of the society to foster the intellectual, social, and political development of its citizens would not be met, except in small measure. His dictum that schooling was not a preparation for life but life itself—a place and ambience where intelligence was nurtured in the context of group living—encapsulated Dewey's position. And what he saw in our schools was nothing less than a context in which conformity and stultifying routine were outstanding features. In that presidential address Dewey's observations led him to a use of language atypically passionate and derogatory for him.

The unhappy fact is that education never became part of the social sciences. Through the decades there were always a few social scientists who focused on education from the vantage point of sociology, anthropology, or political science. But they were few and what they wrote had no effect on their fields. Indeed, as I can attest from decades of observation of academia, any social scientists, especially young ones, whose central scholarly and research interests were in education, were looked upon as oddities and their chances for tenure were thereby reduced. Education remains outside the mainstream of the social sciences: an ignored and even a rejected field willingly left to the educators.

When Dr. Fraatz asked me to read her manuscript, I was both pleased and concerned. Pleased because she is a fully credentialed political scientist—who my counterintelligence had told me was unusually gifted as an observer and thinker—and yet concerned with how she would treat the complexity we call schools. In regard to schools it is so easy to be glib and superficial, to oversimplify, to scapegoat, to blame the individual motivation of students, teachers, and administrators as if they consciously and deliberately are intent on subverting efforts to improve schools. I did not have to get far into the manuscript for my concerns to disappear. When I was finished, my overall judgment did not have to be formulated; it had already been made: Dr. Fraatz has illuminated in a quietly compelling way (but with cumulative impact) the subtleties of how the processes of program implementation have the unintended consequence of defeating the goals of the program; more correctly, perhaps, how the goal of "enrichment" of the school experience of disadvantaged children gets unwittingly interpreted and implemented in ways that simply are not enriching. When I finished reading the manuscript I agreed completely with one of Dr. Fraatz's opening statements: "My argument is straightforward: A close look at the ways in which people in schools negotiate the tasks of providing opportunities for learning can go a long way toward explaining the persistently lower educational outcomes of poor and minority children; furthermore, it can also suggest strategies for improvement."

Of the many facets of Dr. Fraatz's presentation that I found so seminal and compelling, the one that I wish to mention here is that which emerges with unusual clarity from the interviews with teachers, administrators, and special personnel. It is the "pursuit of routine," a most felicitous phrase that allows Dr. Fraatz to weld together a wealth of statements given by the interviewees. Here, too, I can do no better than to quote Dr. Fraatz: "The pursuit of routine requires teachers to identify some categories of behavior as disruptive or inattentive . . . the pursuit of control requires teachers to be in such constant interaction with so many students that they have to limit the things they will notice and respond to. Both these coping strategies force teachers to rely on the same standards to assess everyone, both in testing and in observation. This is an ironic outcome because *teachers were unanimous in identifying low-income children as those least likely to adapt well to the routines of instruction*" (italics in original). Dr. Fraatz did not dream up that conclusion. It is an interpretation of interview responses that any fair-minded reader would come to. In the culture of the school, as in any complicated social organization, the need for routine too easily becomes an end in itself and individual needs and differences go by the boards. This tendency, Dr. Fraatz makes clear, is not a function of stupidity or callousness. Her interviewees are a dedicated, highly motivated group struggling to make a difference in the lives of disadvantaged youngsters. There are no villains here. There is a culture of the school that, when not understood, works against outcomes consistent with stated goals.

One other facet of Dr. Fraatz's presentation requires mention here, a facet to which as a political scientist she is quite sensitive: that "relationships of power and influence between people in schools affect dramatically the kinds of opportunities available to low-income children learning to read." It is easy to nod assent to that in the abstract but when you have finished reading this book, that abstraction will have concrete significances which will be difficult to forget.

This book is a major contribution to our understanding of the culture of the school and the problem of change. We have been witness in the past several years to scores of reports about what is wrong with schools and how they should be improved. I wish the writers of these reports had had the opportunity to read this book. It would have reduced the degree of the irrelevance of these reports to the truly basic issues of life in schools. John Dewey was a voice crying in the wilderness. I hope that Dr. Fraatz does not meet the same fate.

Seymour B. Sarason

Acknowledgments

It is with a profound sense of gratitude that I reflect on the many debts I have incurred in the writing of this book. Chief among them is my debt to Edward Pauly, the political scientist who convinced me that school politics is *real* politics, who spent endless hours reading and responding to several drafts of this manuscript, and whose thoughtful suggestions, sound advice, and unwavering support are in large measure responsible for whatever success this book may enjoy. I am similarly obliged to Robert Dahl, friend, mentor, and model of scholarship, whose faith in this project from its inception has been a constant source of encouragement. The sustained enthusiasm of Audrey Kingstrom at Teachers College Press, coupled with her friendship and forbearance in the face of the innumerable, if inevitable, delays we encountered, was nothing less than inspirational. Having admired Seymour Sarason's work for several years, I was delighted at the interest he took in my own fledgling attempts, and several portions of this manuscript are considerably better as a result of his suggestions. Finally, a number of my colleagues at Saint Olaf College, particularly Jim Farrell and Jack Schwandt, have generously offered both professional and personal support. This book has been greatly enriched by the contributions of each of these persons. Undoubtedly, it would have been even better had I taken all of their good advice, but since I did not, I must acknowledge any remaining sins of omission or commission to be strictly my own doing.

In a class by themselves are the many educators whose experiences and reflections are the substance of this book. The issues I raised with them were not easy ones, often touching on deeply felt ambivalences and frustrations. Yet their honesty, thoughtfulness, and consideration made the fieldwork for this book not only possible and profitable, but enjoyable. I am grateful for the gifts of time and talent that they offered me, even though I represented still another demand on their all-too-scarce resources.

I also have incurred many debts in the lengthy process of manuscript preparation. I am grateful for the financial support provided for this purpose by Saint Olaf College, and for the technical support provided through the College's Academic Computer Center, especially that of student assistant Eric Voth. The staff members of Rolvaag Memorial Library, particularly Patricia Lewis and Connie Gunderson, were indispensible. The political science department secretary, Patricia Christiansen, should probably be canonized. Her unfailing patience and good humor in the face of computer catastrophes, copy machine malfunctions, and simple human error (usually mine), were matched only by her apparent ability not only to do the impossible, but to do it well. In addition to her considerable talents at the keyboard, Pat displayed remarkable administrative prowess in her supervision of a small army of capable Saint Olaf student assistants. Scott Biehle, Eric Blegen, Tom Christensen, Elizabeth Grygo, Rod Jensen, Scott Kueppers, Susan Nyhus, Kari Nyline, and Mark O'Sell spent many long hours at the computer, in the library, and at the copy machine on my behalf, and I thank them all for their hard work.

My gratitude to my husband Bill is inexpressible; his unwavering encouragement, support, faith and love sustained me; his attention to the home front freed me; his criticism and advice challenged me; his willingness to relinquish the upstairs study for an entire year astonished me; and his capacity to tolerate endless discussions about "The Book" amazed me. I cannot imagine what more he could have done to smooth my way, short of writing the book himself. My small son Tommy has been equally tolerant and good natured, partly because of his extraordinary father and partly because he doesn't know yet that most moms don't live in the study. I am thankful to Bill and Tommy, treasures of my heart and guardians of my spirit; and I hope they never call in the debt I owe them, for I cannot repay it.

Introduction
Politics, Policy, and Equal Educational Opportunity

A few years ago, while attending the Annual Meeting of the American Educational Research Association, I decided to track down a professor of educational administration from a nearby university, in hopes that he could offer me some advice on the research I was then conducting for Chapter 6 of this book. Noticing a woman wearing a name tag from the same university, I approached her and explained my mission. In the process of introducing myself I mentioned that I was a political scientist. She drew back, looked at me as one might look at a lost child, and said, "Well, what are you doing here then?"

Nonplussed at the time, I reflected later that it was a fair question. What business *does* a political scientist have in a world populated mainly by scholars and practitioners in education? The answer to this question is at once simple and complex. Simply put, educators are public employees, acting as agents of the state implementing an important set of public policies; and as such they merit the attention of political scientists and policy analysts concerned about this arena of government activity. A small but growing number of social scientists has begun to approach the analysis of public policy "from the bottom up." I count myself among them, believing with researchers such as Weatherley and Lipsky (1977) that program outcomes are largely determined by the discretionary decisions of the "street-level bureaucrats" who are in face-to-face contact with program clients in the delivery of services, who confront on a daily basis the inadequacy of program resources to meet all the needs of program clients, and who make subtle but major choices about who will receive public resources, how, and why. Their agendas, their struggles, their resources, their frustrations, their hopes and dreams shape their understanding of the tasks they take up every day. In fact, *their experiences and exchanges are the substance of public education policy.* Legislators may legislate and administrators may administer, but it is the educators in the schools who make sense out of legislation and administration, who translate laws, regulations, mandates, and directives into educational services for American school children. To be sure, policy makers on school boards, in legislatures, and in state and federal education agencies help to set the legal and fiscal parameters within which educators must operate. But the decisions of policy makers *outside* the schools are always mediated by the day-to-day decisions of policy makers *inside* the schools—the classroom teachers, the school principals, the federally funded specialists and the district officials. A complete picture of the educational policy process and its outcomes requires systematic attention to the contributions made by those who actually deliver services to children in public schools.

A more complex answer points to the political as well as the policy implications of the daily choices faced by these grassroots policy makers. The observer who looks beyond the apparent rhythms and regularities of the classroom, the principal's office, and the administrative offices "downtown" will see an enterprise that engages its participants in constant negotiation, bargaining, persuasion, and compromise. In short, people in schools establish and maintain relationships of power and influence that dramatically affect the policy choices they make. These relationships are conditioned by the complicated context in which they are conducted, a context marked by mystery, paradox, and uncertainty. Confronted by multiple demands, hampered by finite resources of energy, time, and money, people in schools must negotiate the terms on which they will work together to define and carry out their publicly mandated tasks. School policy and school politics are intimately related, and a clear picture of each requires that they be examined together.

This book assesses the relationship between policy and politics in a specific set of educational practices, those designed to promote equality of opportunity. My argument is straightforward: A close look at the ways in which people in schools negotiate the tasks of providing opportunities for learning can go a long way toward explaining the persistently lower educational outcomes of poor and minority children; furthermore, it can also suggest strategies for improvement. The perspective supporting this argument is somewhat different from that adopted in most educational policy analyses, which treat specific educational programs, such as Title I/Chapter 1, Head Start, bilingual education, and special education, in isolation from the larger systems of public schooling in which they are situated. In contrast, my purpose here is to describe and analyze the operation of public schools as *whole systems* with respect to economically disadvantaged children. Such an "ecological perspective" (Cremin, 1976; Goodlad, 1984; Sara-son, 1982) permits a comprehensive picture of the ways people in schools work together to provide schooling for the poor. Accordingly, the chapters which follow describe and analyze the joint contributions of classroom teachers, reading specialists, school principals, parents, and district officials to the provision of opportunity in the context of the public school. My intent is to highlight the close connection between policy and politics that characterizes the uncertain enterprise of schooling the poor.

In order to focus my research agenda, I limited my fieldwork to an examination of equal opportunity in reading programs in grades 1 through 4. Reading instruction serves as a good vehicle for the analysis of educational opportunity in several respects. While elementary schools obviously do a great deal more than teach reading, a major portion of their efforts in the early grades supports the acquisition and development of reading skills (Eder, 1981). Reading programs provide a microcosm of school life both inside and outside the classroom, and they affect the transactions that take place between almost everyone connected with instruction: children, teachers, principals, reading specialists, parents, and district administrators. The policy research that attempts to assess how well schools do in providing equal opportunity frequently relies on the results of standardized achievement tests, usually in reading, to measure, evaluate, and compare student performance. More importantly, schools treat the opportunity to learn to read both as a means to other opportunities and as an end in itself. Although the debate about the impact of success in reading later in life rages on,[1] it is clear that children who do *not* learn to read with some degree of competence remain disadvantaged in the options available to them after their years of schooling are completed. And whether or not success in later life depends on success in reading, it is undeniable that success in *school* depends on success in reading. As several of my respondents said, "If a kid can't read, he can't do anything." Reading programs thus do not tell the whole story about power and opportunity, but they tell a good part of it.

The field research reported in the chapters that follow attempts to describe, analyze, and interpret the conduct of reading programs in elementary schools, using patterns in the delivery of services in reading instruction to assess the relationship between power and opportunity in American elementary education. During the 1981–1982 school year, I conducted 103 open-ended interviews about reading instruction with people working in four different school districts in a northeastern state. The respondents included 49 classroom teachers, 15 reading specialists (Title I/Chapter 1 teachers and district reading consultants), 12 building principals, and 25 district administrators. The districts I visited varied greatly in the populations they served. Two of the districts were urban, and two were suburban. Trade City served a high proportion of black students, while Factory City served many Hispanic and foreign-born students, and the average income of Factory City residents was lower than that of Trade City residents. Blue Collar Suburb was a working-class neighborhood with many Italian and Eastern European families, and teachers there reported that a number of the parents in that district could not speak English. The schools in White Collar Suburb served a middle and upper-middle class population of university, professional, and business families. Four schools were sampled in Trade City, four in Factory City, two in White Collar Suburb, and two in Blue Collar Suburb. A more complete description of my respondents, the conduct of the interviews, and the procedures used to analyze the data is included in the Appendix.

This approach to educational policy analysis offers several important benefits. By viewing public schools through a wide-angle lens, we can see more clearly how transactions between one set of individuals (e.g., teachers and children) affect, and are affected by, transactions between others (e.g., principals and reading specialists). Several researchers have commented on the extent to which teachers, for example, are constrained by school-level demands and available resources in their day-to-day classroom decision making (Doyle & Ponder, 1977; Lieberman, 1982). What is true for classroom teachers is also true for reading specialists, principals, and administrators. Individual decisions are shaped by the social organization which defines the alternatives and provides the resources, and the perspective advanced in this book is faithful to this reality of educational policy making.

Second, an ecological perspective sheds new light on the nature of power and influence in the public school. It treats the business of education as "a social event of shared meanings" (Gowin, 1981, p. 10) and permits the observer to draw out the significance of both the social events and the shared meanings—not only the ones in the classroom, but also those in the principal's office, the specialist's reading lab, and the administrative offices downtown. I concur with Gowin's observation that "the social setting of education is a governing influence that controls meaning"—and I treat the control of meaning as an important feature of organizational power (Nyberg, 1981). The chapters that follow provide insight into the meanings people in schools ascribe to the objectives and activities of schooling, suggesting some of the ways that the negotiated transactions between school people influence the meanings they share.

Finally, an ecological perspective helps to keep the difficult questions we need to be asking about schools, power, and equality in the limelight. It prevents us from limiting the inquiry to the effects of special program treatments which are added on to the regular school program, and from concluding that because some children "do better" with special programs than they would without them, the demand for equality of opportunity is being satisfied.[2] An ecological approach requires us to examine, not isolated programs, techniques, teachers, or schools, but rather the total package which constitutes schooling for the poor. This is especially important in view of the fact that, according to a recent federal study of compensatory education, approximately 60% of all economically deprived students in elementary schools do not receive compensatory education services (Carter, 1984, p. 6). For the majority of poor children, equality of opportunity is determined by what goes on in the regular school setting. An ecological perspective on educational policy thereby focuses our attention on the characteristics of *schooling* rather than on the characteristics of school children (Oakes, 1985, p. 73). This keeps our approach to the goal of equality consistent with—one might say, on an equal footing with—our approach to the goal of excellence. After all, when parents, educators, and researchers started worrying that middle-class children were not performing in school as well as they should, they looked at what might be wrong with the schools, not at what might be wrong with the children. An ecological approach allows us to do the same with respect to schooling for economically disadvantaged children.

The chapters which follow examine the provision of opportunity in the day-to-day operation of public school reading programs. Chapter 1 introduces the conceptual frameworks used to describe and analyze "power" and "opportunity" as school people understand and experience them. Chapter 2 analyzes the classroom setting, describing the social and instructional demands teachers must try to meet, the strategies they use to cope with the paradoxes and uncertainties that characterize their tasks, and the consequences of these strategies for equality of opportunity. Chapter 3 examines the services provided by school and district reading specialists, describing how relationships of power and influence between specialists and classroom teachers produce remedial services which replicate and reinforce the mobilization of bias in the classroom setting. Chapter 4 describes the limited impact of school principals on equality of opportunity, arguing that even the contributions of "effective" principals are constrained by the essentially autonomous choices of classroom teachers. Chapter 5 probes the home-school connection, suggesting that "cooperation" between parents and teachers is in fact a subtle form of cooptation, limiting parents' ability to influence how teachers define, interpret, and respond to children's educational needs. Chapter 6 examines the politics of "downtown," showing how the district official's search for legitimacy with subordinates precludes attention to problems of inequality. Chapter 7 summarizes my findings and briefly suggests their implications for educational reform. Each of these chapters speaks to the close connection between power and opportunity in the public school setting, and each relies on the voices and experiences of teachers, specialists, principals, and district administrators to define the issues they must confront and how they confront them. In the portrait of schooling offered in these pages, my aim is to be as faithful to their professional realities and obligations as I am to my own, in the hope that scholars and practitioners alike will find this analysis authentic and compelling, even if they take issue with its conclusions.

1

Schooling the Poor

Frameworks for Analysis

I wonder if we ever *teach* reading. Because reading is so complicated, and it's *not* complicated, that sometimes I don't know what I'm doing. Am I just laying out the material for them, hoping for it to go through by osmosis? I mean, I know that you need to know how to syllabicate, and how to do this and that . . . [but] I don't know what reading *is*, after all these years, after a masters' degree in reading. It becomes more and more complicated to me. I find that I'm just a person that . . . gives [the students] a variety of ways to approach something, just hoping that it all fits together. (*Blue Collar Suburb teacher*)

The day-to-day enterprise of public education engages people in the creation of meaning. Why people do what they do in the schools is rarely self-evident. Those who educate and those who are being educated must work together to develop and sustain a shared sense of purpose, order, direction, and control in their daily activities, "hoping that it all fits together." Analyzing the "subjective meanings" (Fullan, 1982) that people ascribe to the work of schooling is not the only way to describe and interpret the business of education; but these meanings are important contributions to educational policy making.

This chapter examines the meaning of "opportunity" and "power" in the public schools for the educators who work there, using school reading programs as a vehicle for analysis. While the frameworks I will try to develop to analyze these concepts are my own, they are grounded in the "subjective realities" and "shared meanings" (Gowin, 1981) that characterize the delivery of services in reading instruction. These frameworks are also informed by the work of other social scientists who have wrestled with the

7

meaning of power and opportunity, not only in the context of educational policy but in other social contexts as well.

A CONCEPTUAL FRAMEWORK
FOR EQUALITY OF EDUCATIONAL OPPORTUNITY

Deciding what constitutes equality of opportunity is a formidable task. The past twenty years of scholarly and professional debate is, if nothing else, a testimony to the intractability of the problem of definition. The accumulated wisdom on equal opportunity now includes a multiplicity of goals, concepts, programs, and policies, impressive in both scope and substance. The following is a representative, although by no means exhaustive, sample:

A common curriculum providing equal access to knowledge (Goodlad, 1984);

Equal distribution of cognitive outcomes, without respect to social class (*Barriers to Excellence*, 1985, p. x; Oakes, 1985, p. 11);

Development of the maximum potential of each student (Hallinan, 1984, p. 229);

Compensation for preschool disadvantages (Hunt, 1982; Gowin, 1981, p. 176);

Equal distribution of financial resources within a given school district or state (Wise, 1979, p. xiii);

Equal distribution of equally good human resources (effective teachers; low student-teacher ratios) (*Barriers to Excellence*, p. 37);

Equal psychosocial conditions through integration (Hallinan, 1984, p. 231);

Equal time available for learning (Goodlad, 1984, p. 97ff);

Equally good standards and curricula in different schools (Persell, 1977, p. 12);

Minimum achievement standards for all (Gowin, 1981, p. 176);

Equal attention to individual needs through within-class ability groups (Hallinan, p. 229);

Equal years of schooling (Burton & Jones, 1982, p. 10);

Equal vocational outcomes (Bowles & Gintis, 1976);

Equal noncognitive outcomes, e.g., self-concept, aspirations (Hallinan, 1984, p. 235).

This list reveals a number of tensions in the concept of "equal educational opportunity," broadly understood. First, "equal opportunity" suffers from the same semantic problem as the term "public policy": it can refer both to outcomes (ends) and to inputs (means). Equality of means involves matters such as instructional time, financial resources, and effective teachers. Equality of ends involves such things as cognitive and noncognitive outcomes, years spent in school, and vocational choices. Some policies even seem to be ends and means simultaneously, such as integration and equal years of schooling. A second tension has to do with the problem of human diversity. Equality involves some policies where students need exposure to the *same* treatment (common curriculum, minimum achievement standards, time-on-task, psychosocial conditions) and others where the treatment should be *different* (compensation for preschool disadvantages, differential ability groups). Finally, there are conflicts over who should assume the major share of responsibility for equal educational opportunity. Some of these policies seem to imply school- or classroom-level alternatives (time-on-task, ability groups, effective teachers), while others assume externally imposed standards and resources (school finance equalization, minimum standards, integration, mandated curricula).

The array of potential policies to promote equality, coupled with the tensions inherent in the multiplicity of these approaches, makes the task of assessing where schools are, where they are heading, and how they ought to change a knotty problem indeed. Moreover, this list points to a major problem in equal opportunity policy that this book is intended to address: the need to examine *how people in schools themselves perceive the goal of equal opportunity and the tasks required to promote it*. Their perceptions matter a great deal, since it is their choices which frequently carry the most weight in determining the educational services a child will actually receive. While it is true that their choices may be constrained by decisions far removed from schools—by decisions concerning the level of state and federal resources schools will receive, the proficiency requirements for new teachers, or the textbooks schools may use—it is the responsibility of school-level and district-level employees to assign the teachers, group the students, buy the texts, apply for grants, assess students' needs, establish criteria for receiving special services, and decide which children meet the criteria. We cannot hope to assess what schools have done and are currently doing to promote equality of opportunity without a clear understanding of how school-level policy makers view the educational problems and the policy alternatives at stake in the pursuit of equality.

The first step in constructing a framework for understanding is to distinguish ends from means. In the context of school reading programs, a clue to this distinction is evident in the ways educators respond to the question, "What do you think your job is with respect to reading instruction?" Many respondents explained only the specific tasks for which they were responsible; but several also discussed the overall purpose of the program. And when the conversation shifted in that direction, the degree of consensus on the goals of reading instruction was remarkable. Teachers, specialists, and administrators alike portrayed the overall goal of the reading program as insuring that each child is reading "to the best of his or her ability at that level of development."

> I think the most important thing is to take the child where I find them—not to complain about what he hasn't had, what skills he hasn't acquired—and take him along as far as he possibly can go. (*Blue Collar Suburb teacher*)

> [Our goal is] stated right in the philosophy of the reading program . . . in that basically you take the youngster from where he or she is and you bring that youngster along according to his or her skills potential. (*White Collar Suburb Director of Instruction*)

> My job is to make sure all the children in this school are reading up to their level—and if they're not, to find out why and to get them some help. (*Factory City principal*)

The "shared meanings" associated with the goals of school reading programs are remarkable in several respects. First, the consensus prevailed across all four districts and at every level of the school system. Second, it reflected an unspoken assumption that "ability" and "potential" are fixed, measurable, almost tangible human characteristics that everyone can recognize and act on. And finally, this grassroots version of the purpose of reading instruction parallels a widely shared social scientific perspective on equality of opportunity, which insists that the ability to learn is normally distributed among and within socioeconomic classes, and that the outcomes of learning (usually measured by achievement scores, assignment to reading groups, and assignment to remedial reading or learning disability programs) ought to be similarly distributed (Oakes, 1985). While no educator made this claim explicitly—in fact, they often found open discussion of unequal outcomes upsetting—their assertion that "each child should be reading at the best of his or her ability at that level of development" is nevertheless quite consistent with Oakes' perspective on equality.

The next step is to determine how schools try to fulfill this obligation. How do they try to carry out the purpose of reading instruction as articulated by these respondents—a purpose which most educators would undoubtedly affirm? This question addresses the means schools use to pursue the end of "each child reading to the best of his or her ability." The educators I spoke with provided one general answer and many specific ones. The general answer was given in all districts and by people in all positions, and can be summarized in a single phrase: meeting individual needs.

I believe strongly that you look at their needs nightly. I think about them every night—where is he, what is he doing? And I try to meet their needs as best I can. (*White Collar Suburb teacher*)

[My job is to provide] more individualized reinforcement . . . on certain skills that these kids just haven't been able to pick up when it was given as a group lesson. (*Blue Collar Suburb Title I teacher*)

The classroom teacher [makes] provision for individual differences and individuals [who] fall on the low level of the structure . . . are picked up by our Title I people. . . . We have many, many special programs, and where the child would fit, the service is definitely there. (*Trade City principal*)

The remainder of this book will accept as given the general formulation of equal educational opportunity suggested in these comments: With respect to reading instruction, the end of equal opportunity is for each child to be reading to the best of his or her ability at any given time; and the means schools use to promote this end require instruction which meets individual needs. While it is difficult in principle to define and measure "ability," this formulation of ends is consistent with the belief that educational outcomes (in this case, reading achievement) should not be distributed according to class, race, or sex; and the formulation of means is consistent with policies such as Title I/Chapter 1 which are intended to provide for the "special educational needs" of "educationally deprived children."

By itself, however, this formulation is not very informative. How do we know when a child is "reading to the best of his or her ability"? What constitutes an "educational need"? What kind of instruction "meets" such needs? These questions point to still another step in developing an appropriate conceptual framework for equal educational opportunity: identifying and analyzing the specific programs, policies, and perceptions that constitute the public school's approach to "meeting individual needs." Such an enterprise requires an examination, not only of the policies themselves, but also of how schools are organized to identify and provide for the individual educational needs of the children they serve. Borrowing from a classic work by political scientist E. E. Schattschneider (1960), I will refer to this dimension of public education as the school's *mobilization of bias* with respect to equal opportunity. By "mobilization of bias" neither Schattschneider nor I intend to refer primarily to individual attitudes and opinions. Rather, this phrase refers to the way in which *organizational structures and processes condition the ways people interpret their goals, alternatives, resources, and personal contributions to the "mission" of the institution.* While it is true that individual attitudes can affect organizational structure itself, as well as the discretionary choices people make within the constraints of that structure, it is equally true that patterns of influence run in the other direction as well. How schools are organized and administered affects dramatically the attitudes of the individuals who comprise the organization; it affects the way they view the "clients" of the organization and the nature and range of the choices they see. This is a very different claim than the one which argues that the most important obstacle to equality of opportunity is the prejudice or hard-heartedness of educators—attitudes I hardly ever saw in my respondents.

An analysis of the school's mobilization of bias can focus attention on the range of options schools pursue—as well as the options they do *not* pursue—in seeking to meet individual needs. Schools are organized in ways which promote some kinds of alternatives and which fail to promote (and in some cases actually rule out) others; and as Schattschneider (p. 66) also observes, "the definition of the alternatives is the supreme instrument of power." By interpreting the choices of educational "street level bureaucrats" in terms of the mobilization of bias, we are able to maintain appropriate connections between the distribution of power and the distribution of opportunity. It is also entirely consistent with an ecological approach to schooling; it sets our sights, not so much on the qualities of the individuals who make up public schools, but rather on the organizational framework that directs and constrains individual perceptions and behavior.

My respondents described a number of different policies, programs, and practices designed to meet individual needs. Based on their descriptions, it is possible to sort out the alternatives for individualization that schools can pursue along three dimensions: first, there are activities designed to *identify educational needs*; second, there are activities designed to *provide educational resources*; and third, there are activities which *structure educational interactions*. Moreover, my respondents' remarks also suggest that there are three criteria which the activities in each of these dimensions ought to meet in order for schools to provide truly individualized instruction. Criterion 1 requires that these activities must be provided in sufficient *amounts*; Criterion 2 requires that they be of sufficiently high *quality*; and Criterion 3 requires that they be *appropriate* to the child in question. Figure 1.1 is a conceptual framework illustrating how these dimensions and criteria can be combined to describe and evaluate school practices. I have included examples to illustrate the various combinations the framework makes possible.

This conceptual framework serves a number of purposes. Probably the most important is that it permits us to clarify the nature of the debates that surround different public school practices and policies—both actual and proposed—intended to promote equality of educational opportunity. Struggles over textbook adoption, for example, can revolve around questions of

FIGURE 1.1   Alternative Approaches to Individualized Instruction

DIMENSIONS	CRITERIA		
	1 *In sufficient* *amounts*	2 *Of sufficient* *quality*	3 *Appropriate* *to the child*
Identifying *educational* *needs*	Frequent diagnostic testing	Improving teacher observation for diagnosis	Removing cultural bias from standardized testing
Providing *educational* *resources*	Minimum quantities of supplies per pupil	Periodic replacement of texts with new editions	Requiring that textbooks use children's language patterns
Structuring *educational* *interactions*	Ceilings on class sizes	Professional development for teachers	Matching teachers' instructional styles with children's learning styles

quality (e.g., the extent to which textbooks, workbooks, and test materials are coherent and integrated) or around questions of appropriateness (e.g., the population to which a text is designed to appeal) (Bowler, 1978, p. 515). Principals trying to promote time-on-task often frame their proposals in terms of "quality education"; but what they are really emphasizing is the *quantity* of educational interactions between teachers and children. And for their part, teachers struggling to meet time-on-task standards are confronted in the realities of classroom life with a permanent tension between spending a minimum amount of time with all students while reserving extra time for children who "need" it more—that is, balancing sufficient amounts with appropriateness.

A second purpose of this conceptual scheme is to stimulate new thinking about avenues schools *could* pursue in the search for equality of opportunity. As we begin to look more closely at the kinds of opportunities schools currently provide, we will also begin to see more clearly the kinds of things they are *not* doing. More specifically, we will see which dimensions are more likely to characterize present practices and which criteria schools are more likely to use in evaluating those practices. This scheme thus identifies the possible standards against which the performance of public schools (by which I mean its activities, not just its outputs) *can* be evaluated, as well as those against which it *is* evaluated. And to the extent that we find fewer options being pursued in one of the dimensions than in the others, then we have the beginnings, at least, of an agenda for reform.

A final purpose of this scheme is to highlight the ways in which these various means of providing opportunity interact (Alexander, Cook, & McDill, 1978). A teacher's observations of a child's classroom behavior (assessing educational needs) affect the "level" of reading materials she will make available to the child (providing educational resources) and the amount of independent work she will expect the child to do (structuring educational interactions). A child in a remedial reading class (interactions) may use different worksheets (resources) and take different tests (assessment). A particular basal series (resources) may include more vocabulary tests (assessment) and may require teachers to spend more time giving instructions and less time listening to children read (interactions). The connections between the different kinds of activities surrounding the provision of opportunity in and out of the classroom are important, and this conceptual scheme permits us to examine them.

The chapters which follow do not give equal attention to all three dimensions of equal opportunity, primarily because my respondents were not equally attentive to all three. In the end, this selective attention is itself an indicator of the school's mobilization of bias—that is, the way school organization constrains individual perceptions and choices. The day-to-day operation of the school commands attention to some issues rather than others, elevates some purposes and goals over others, and capitalizes on some resources while ignoring others. As the remainder of this book will show, a close look at the "mobilization of bias" is a useful way of naming and analyzing the grassroots policy choices that constitute schooling for the poor. It reveals nondecisions as well as decisions (Bachrach & Baratz, 1962, 1963); both are important for assessing the degree to which schools help to promote equality of educational opportunity.

A CONCEPTUAL FRAMEWORK
FOR POWER AND INFLUENCE

Unlike the debate on the nature of equal educational opportunity, the debate about power in public schools is not rooted in a rich theoretical or empirical heritage in the scholarly literature on education. Systematic analyses of power and influence in public schools are rare. In one of the very few theoretical treatments of power in public schools, David Nyberg assesses the state of the art in no uncertain terms:

The idea of power has lain more completely neglected in educational studies than in any other field of thought that is of fundamental social interest. Power talk is consistently absent from schools and from educational literature. There is no theory of power that contributes much at all to understanding education and its importance in American society. . . . One is more likely to hear singing in a bank than serious talk of power in relation to education. (1981, p. 535)

This is not to say that no one ever refers to the existence of power in schools. Nyberg's point is that the kind of power talk educators and scholars engage in is not very enlightening, nor does it draw on the growing and highly relevant literature of organization theory (Barnett, 1984). Scholars who refer to power in schools—if they refer to it at all—fail to define exactly what they mean by "power" (Nyberg, 1981, pp. 535–36), and tend to assume that power is something people at the top of the school hierarchy have that people at the bottom don't (Weick, 1976, 1982; Wise, 1979). When educators refer to power, they generally discuss who *doesn't* have power, not who *does*; and in their view, the one who doesn't is usually the person at the bottom of the heap—the classroom teacher. Lieberman and Miller (1979, p. 64) and Sarason (1982, pp. 193–94) point out that one of the salient features of the classroom teacher's professional predicament is the feeling of powerlessness he or she experiences both inside and outside the classroom. Yet the practitioner's interest in power has failed to spark a similar interest in the scholarly community.

A final problem in the relatively thin literature on power in public schools is that it tends to treat power as a generalized, rather than situational, phenomenon. It is by now a commonplace among political scientists that the distribution and exercise of power resources vary from one policy arena to another (Lowi, 1964). While debate continues over the particulars of those arenas, and on the precise ways they shape the politics they produce, Lowi's general point is conventional wisdom in political analysis. It is surprising that, to my knowledge, no one has ever applied this analysis to power in public schools. Yet it seems intuitively obvious that the "power structures" surrounding such matters as textbook adoptions or teacher evaluation procedures, for example, would differ from the power structures concerning recess schedules, workshop topics, or eligibility criteria for Title I/Chapter 1 services. The portrait of power that will emerge in this book is thus restricted to the policy arena of reading instruction. I believe such a treatment is faithful to the policy-specific nature of power described above; yet it will also promote speculation about the distribution of power with respect to other school policies, given the centrality of reading instruction and its connectedness with other important aspects of life in schools. I also hope to establish a common language of power and influence in schools that may prove useful in examining how power is exercised in other educational policy arenas.

Since both the theoretical and the empirical cupboards are bare, so to speak, my intent is to be as descriptive and straightforward as possible in my examination of school power and influence. I cannot yet offer a theory of power, but I *can* offer a set of concepts, grounded in the ecological realities of life in schools, that will help to lay a foundation. The first step is to establish consistency in my use of the related terms "power" and "influence." I will take as my working definition of "power" a modified version of that proposed by political scientist Robert Dahl (1984). Under this definition, Person A may be said to exercise power over Person B in two ways. First, A exercises power when A gets B to do something B probably would not have done otherwise, and when that "something" is in accord with a plan A wants to put into effect (Nyberg, 1981, p. 540). A second form of power is for A to prevent B from doing something B otherwise would have done, again in accord with A's wishes. Thus, a principal exercises power over a reading consultant when the principal asks the consultant to go observe a teacher the consultant had been avoiding, and the consultant complies. At the same time, the teacher in question may be said to have exercised power over the consultant in making the latter feel unwelcome and avoid visiting that teacher's classroom.

Influence is somewhat different than power. Person A may be said to have influenced Person B when A causes B to do something different, but B's actions need not be in strict accord with A's plans (Nyberg, 1981, p. 540). As I will use these terms in the chapters which follow, *the main difference between power and influence has to do with the extent to which people in schools can get others to follow plans those others did not themselves devise.* Thus, a reading consultant may be said to exercise influence over a classroom teacher when the consultant gets the teacher to try some new technique or book in her class—but not necessarily a technique or book that the consultant had suggested specifically to the teacher. The exercise of influence, as we shall see, is far more common than the exercise of power, but both are affected by organizational constraints and resources.

Although power and influence may be distinguished from one another for the purposes of analysis, they share a number of empirical characteristics. Many of the resources and strategies a person might employ in exercising power are the same as those she might use to exercise influence; the main difference is whether the changes she effects in others' behaviors are in accord with her plans. The following conceptual scheme defines several terms associated with three aspects of power and influence in the public school setting: the *resources* people draw upon; the *strategies* guiding their use of those resources; and the *characteristics* of the school setting that affect their transactions.

1. Resources
    a. *Access to information.*   Knowledge about instruction, district rules, educational resources, and so forth (Barnett, 1984, p. 44). Example: Principals who use data from the literature on instructionally effective schools to defend their procedures in teacher evaluation.
    b. *Control over the distribution of human or material resources.* Ability to determine who gets what books, equipment, room assignments, teacher aides, etc. (Barnett, p. 44). Example: Reading consultants who decide which teachers will get which supplementary materials.
    c. *Control over rewards and sanctions.*   Ability to identify and manipulate consequences others view as desirable or undesirable (Nyberg, 1981). Example: Teachers who decide whether children will sit near their friends in reading groups.
    d. *Planning.*   Ability to design and communicate effectively a course of action requiring the cooperation of others. Example: A principal who begins a schoolwide emphasis on reading by requiring the reading consultant to visit classrooms twice a month.
2. Strategies
    a. *Threat of sanction or promise of reward.*   Straightforward enough. Example: A Director of Elementary Instruction who tells a principal that until the school's reading scores improve, the principal will be evaluated twice as often as everyone else.
    b. *Persuasion.*   Person A convinces Person B that it is in B's own best interests to change his behavior, by appealing to common values or goals, or by showing how B's behavior hurts B's ability to reach his own goals (Nyberg, p. 544). Example: A classroom teacher who convinces an overworked reading teacher to take an additional remedial student by pointing out the likelihood that the child's parents will protest if he doesn't receive services.
    c. *Bargaining and negotiation.*   A gets B to change by offering compromises that suit B's interests as well as A's. Example: Teachers who work with principals in establishing the criteria on which the teachers will be evaluated.
3. Contextual features
    a. *Dependency relationships.*   The extent to which A and B rely on each other, and what they rely on one another for (Barnett, p. 44). Example: Teachers who depend on principals for favorable evalua-

tions and principals who depend on good teachers to maintain their reputations.

b. *Autonomy.* The extent to which B is free from A's scrutiny or intervention. Example: A teacher who uses a different text in his classroom without anyone finding out.

c. *Incentives.* The structure of values people pursue and the amount of time and energy they spend in pursuit of their values. Example: Teachers' desire for good relationships with their students.

d. *Proximity.* The number of opportunities for contact between A and B. Example: A principal of a smaller school who is able to make classroom visits more often than a principal in a larger neighboring school.

This list of concepts is not meant to be exhaustive; it does not include all the terms social scientists have used to describe the nature of power and influence. However, it *does* include the concepts that proved most relevant and useful in analyzing the school setting. My purpose here is to uncover features of power and influence common to most elementary schools; I will not compare the power exercised by teachers in large schools to that exercised by teachers in small schools, or the influence of a Trade City principal to the influence of a White Collar Suburb principal. The focus will be primarily on patterns, not on deviations. Each of the chapters which follow will draw on this framework to describe and analyze the typical exercise of power and influence in the various "behavior settings" that constitute schooling for the poor—classrooms, reading labs, the principal's domain, and district offices. Perhaps most important, these concepts will help demonstrate the special connections between power and opportunity in the school. Organization is, after all, a matter of influence relationships, so a careful analysis of the school's mobilization of bias and its effects on opportunity requires, by definition, a careful analysis of school power and influence. This dual enterprise begins in the following chapter, which examines the nature of power and opportunity in classroom reading instruction.

2

The Tail that Wags the Dog
Power and Opportunity in the Classroom

For most elementary school children, rich and poor alike, the school's provision of opportunities to learn to read begins and ends with the classroom. Here is where the majority of activities related to opportunity occur: children's needs are assessed; they are provided with tangible learning resources; and they interact with one another and with their teachers. It is true that these activities are partly shaped by outside resources and constraints, such as district directives, community expectations, school budgetary politics, classroom assignment processes, and textbook purchases. What many educational policy analysts overlook, however, is the extent to which the day-to-day demands of classroom life shape the opportunities schools do— and do not—provide. Teachers' responses to the internal dynamics of the classroom context are at the heart of the mobilization of bias in reading instruction. This chapter examines the paradoxes, problems, and power struggles reflected in the tasks of reading instruction; describes the strategies teachers use to cope with the complicated social contexts of instruction; and contends that these strategies produce patterns of opportunity which penalize low-income and minority children and paralyze the teacher's incentives to innovate.

THE TEACHER AS EDUCATIONAL POLICY MAKER

When most people (including teachers) think of educational policy makers, they think of federal, state, and local officials at the top of the most visible legislative or bureaucratic hierarchies: members of Congress, federal or state agency bureaucrats, district superintendents, and so forth. Only recently have scholars begun to recognize that government employees at the bottom of the hierarchy are important policy makers in their own right. Confronted with demands that exceed their human and material resources, these "street level bureaucrats" (Lipsky, 1980) daily make discretionary choices that dramatically affect policy outcomes. We cannot hope to understand the shape of equality policies in American education without a careful analysis of the policy-making role of the classroom teacher, who exercises enormous discretion in using the resources allocated by other federal, state, and local decision makers.

Although they recognize that others' decisions affect their options, classroom teachers are very aware of the discretion they themselves exercise. When I asked my respondents to identify who had the most influence over reading instruction in the classroom, I usually got the following kind of response:

> Me. No one else is really significant, because there's not that much outside influence. It's basically what I feel is important. I cover everything that's in the workbooks, and we go through the stories, but my emphasis is what *I* think they're really going to need, for next year and for later on. (*Trade City teacher*)

The discretionary policy-making role of the classroom teacher is evident in all three dimensions of opportunity, beginning with the assessment of educational needs. While standardized tests are certainly one indicator of "need," teachers' observations of children's behavior in the classroom context also figure heavily. In fact, a child's classroom performance affects the way a teacher interprets a child's test performance.

> [The children are] tested and everything, but that doesn't tell you that much. When we actually get down here and work with them, that's when we find out that this one can't do this or that one can't do that. . . . When I see a kid on the floor, or he's talking or out of his seat, that's a sure hint that he doesn't know what he's doing. Because usually, if they are behaving well, they know what they're doing. (*Trade City teacher*)

> The reading readiness scores may give you some indication [of needs], but let's face it, that's only one judgment. You can't go by just testing per se. These children had trouble following directions; for instance, if I would tell them to underline a word, they wouldn't know where to start. Or I would say, "We're ready for reading group—put your pencils down," and the pencils would go down but you knew they weren't ready to learn. They're looking all over the room, easily distracted, just couldn't concentrate at all. (*Blue Collar Suburb teacher*)

The provision of tangible resources also depends on the teacher's discretion, not only in districts where teachers can be flexible in choosing the materials they use, but also where the reading series is mandated. A first-grade teacher in Blue Collar Suburb, which used a single basal series, noted:

> If I need something—if I have a group and I feel they're not ready for the next level, I might call [the district reading consultant] and say, "Look, I'm looking for something between the first reader and the second reader. What's available?" . . . Basically I have to decide what should be used and what should be left out.

Similarly, a Factory City first-grade teacher said that, in spite of the regimentation of the mandatory Distar series:

> Anything I want, the reading teacher will get the materials I need; if I want to use any other program in addition to what I have, [I] feel free. I feel I can go in any direction I want and handle it any way I want, after I get the Distar in.

Even the choices of the K–2-teacher in the White Collar Suburb Integrated Day program, modeled on an "open school" system and intended to encourage self-directed learning, still influenced the materials her students used:

> I have a little stack of paperbacks right over there, with a wide range of interests [represented], and I know the collection well enough, and hopefully have it arranged well enough, so that if a topic comes up I can find a little book that says something about it, [and] the information gets put into the child's hands. I do help the children choose books, and some I find with particular kids in mind. I consider level first and interest second.

Although most teachers reported that they relied primarily on the basal readers they were assigned, they still affected how much exposure children received to the content and skills the texts were intended to promote, no matter how "rigid" or "flexible" the series:

> In the beginning of this school year, when we were issued the new [Harcourt-Brace] series, we were told to go step-by-step with the teachers' guide suggestions. . . . However, I found that with my experience, and what I feel very comfortable with, I sort of keep that in the back of my mind, but I do what I want to do. Not that I'm not [using the series], but I have my way of doing it. (*Trade City teacher*)

> I'm a Follow Through teacher, so I have to follow the Distar reading program. I have to stick exactly to the program. . . . [But] I sometimes

present words before they're presented [in the series], or I'll skip some lessons if I feel their strength is there and they don't need it. One particular skill might be presented for a two-week period—I cut it shorter if I feel they can handle it. (*Factory City teacher*)

Teachers are clearly central to the provision of tangible reading resources.

Finally, teachers make most of the important decisions about the kinds of educational interactions children will encounter both inside and outside the classroom. Although we think of the ability-based reading group as *the* interactional context of classroom reading instruction, reading actually takes place, not just in a group context, but in many group contexts, virtually all of which the teacher determines. In addition to the homogeneous reading group, there are whole-class instructional periods; seatwork sessions with workbooks or worksheets; ad hoc instructional groups centered on a particular skill or interest; individualized free reading or "research project" periods; and one-on-one help sessions between the teacher and individual students (Harris & Sipay, 1980, pp. 101–4). Teachers play the leading role in deciding which children will participate in which contexts. They are the final arbiters in the assignment of their students to classroom reading groups, whether they actively participate in the pre-September assignment process or simply adjust the composition of the groups in their classrooms after observing student performance (Hallinan, 1984, p. 230). The teacher decides whether to supplement her basic three reading groups with ad hoc groups, and she selects the students who will work in those groups. "Individualized" projects, seatwork, and whole-class reading activities occur at the behest of the teacher. Teachers also decide when and to whom they will offer individual help. This is not to suggest that teachers ignore children's preferences and behavior in making these social context decisions; I will give more attention to children's influence on teachers' choices later in this chapter. What is important here is to recognize that these decisions are policy decisions that affect educational outcomes—and they are decisions teachers are expected to make.

Classroom teachers also play a central role in deciding which students should participate in supplementary remedial reading programs offered by the Title I/Chapter 1 teachers and district reading consultants, who provide additional social contexts for instruction outside the classroom. To be sure, a teacher's recommendation that a child receive extra services does not by itself guarantee the provision of those services, since there are often more needy children than special programs can support; but all of the districts I sampled included teacher recommendation as one of the criteria by which children were to be selected for additional help, and children were never taken from the classroom without the teacher's consent. In fact, one teacher in Blue Collar Suburb told me:

> I have one boy who was taken out of his classroom quite a lot last year, for special help here, special help there, so when I knew I was getting this child, I went to the principal and asked if it was possible, since I only had 15 children, if he could just stay with me all day. Sure, we have these marvelous special programs, but this child needs the security of one-to-one. . . . So he stays with me, and the two programs he was to be in, I have asked that he not go to them.

The preferences and choices of classroom teachers thus shape the contexts in which children are instructed, the materials they use, and the ways their needs are determined. Given this discretion and its impact, it is essential to understand the kinds of choices teachers perceive and why they make the choices they do. This, in turn, requires a careful examination of the social forces at work in the classroom, for these internal social forces are as much a constraint on the teacher's policy decisions as are the external resources and demands of the school or district in which the teacher works.

THE SOCIAL CONTEXTS
OF OPPORTUNITY IN THE CLASSROOM

For teachers and children alike, the most important feature of classroom instruction is the fact that it is a *collective* social enterprise. Teachers trying to help each child learn to read "to the best of his or her ability" are, in the words of Dan Lortie (1975, p. 137), "constrained by the fact of 'classness.'" Their tasks are further complicated by the daily changes within and among the varied social circumstances that comprise a typical classroom day. Teachers' instructional decisions in pursuing the tasks of opportunity are not made in an "empty classroom" (Duffy, 1982), but in a complex, paradoxical, and dynamic combination of group settings. The varied social contexts of reading instruction significantly affect the ways teachers as policy makers interpret and pursue the goal of equal opportunity in the classroom.

The Paradox of Collective Instruction

In order for each child to be reading "to the best of his or her ability" in a collective context, teachers must do two things: first, they must provide reading instruction for everyone; and second, they must address individual differences among their students. The conflict between these two demands produces a tension I will call the *paradox of collective instruction*: In order to provide reading instruction for everyone, the teacher must treat students similarly; but in order to address their differences effectively, the teacher must treat students differently. This paradox is the first important characteristic of the social contexts of classroom opportunity; indeed, it is one of the reasons teachers try to provide multiple contexts.

The demand to teach everyone, with its accompanying pressure to deliver uniform services in reading instruction, is evident in the perspectives of educational scholars and practitioners alike. There is, of course, the legal backdrop of the 1954 Supreme Court ruling in *Brown v. Topeka Board of Education*, which required, among other things, that education "be made available to all on equal terms" (Oakes, 1985, p. 172). Exposure of all children to a common curriculum is one way of accomplishing this mandate (Goodlad, 1984); so is exposure to equal teacher time (Hallinan, 1984). Several teachers in my sample drew a direct connection between the need to teach everyone and a degree of enforced uniformity in instruction:

> I actually have five levels [of reading groups], but we pushed [the lowest level] up because I couldn't have four levels in one room. Three is actually too many instructional groups, but I have three. (*Factory City teacher*)

The most telling comment came from the K–2-teacher in White Collar Suburb who was part of the school's Integrated Day program.

> What I usually do with the younger children, even though they come in at all levels, I still take them much more as a larger group, and make sure that all of them have had phonics sheets, all of the consonants, all of the blends. It's like when I teach handwriting—theoretically I'd love to take each of the children and teach them, alone, say, the letter *Q*. But it's easier, it's faster [to teach them as a group]. And there's something to be gained from waiting your turn, working as a group.

Despite the necessity of group-based instruction, even in an open-school setting, teachers are highly sensitive to the demand to address individual differences and the resulting pressure to treat children differently. My respondents frequently remarked not only on the fact that their students differed but that they differed in multiple and complex ways:

> Children differ in self-motivation, in their maturity, in their work habits, in their listening habits, and abilities. With some children, if you go

over it once or twice, they'll get it; with others, you can go over it ten times and they still won't get it. (*White Collar Suburb teacher*)

Some children just use their eyes—they are visually oriented. You show them a word once, and they know it. Others are using their ears; they need auditory approaches. And others use patterns. I've also noticed a difference between boys and girls. The boys like stories that are factual, full of information—this is how cars are made, that sort of thing. The girls like more make-believe, fairy-tale kinds of things. (*Blue Collar Suburb teacher*)

Their backgrounds are different. I have some children who are Follow Through children, and that means that they've come up through the ranks of preschool and so forth. They have, I find, as a general rule, more background. I also have children who are non-Follow Through, which means most of them did not attend any preschool, that kindergarten was their first experience in a school situation. You find them lacking readiness skills—for instance, color words, number words, sounds, and even basic language development—syntax and so forth. (*Factory City teacher*)

The pressure to respond to these differences by adjusting instruction is articulated in theory as well as in practice. Individualization is recommended by theorists who take a child development approach to instruction (Zigler & Kagan, 1982); those who support a "schema" approach (R. C. Anderson, 1984; Farr, 1984); those of the "teacher effectiveness" school (Hoffman & Rutherford, 1984); and those who advocate mastery learning (Good & Stipek, 1983). While there is fundamental disagreement over which learning differences are the important ones and how teachers should address them,[1] there is widespread scholarly agreement that individualized instruction, however defined, is essential to effective teaching.

My respondents echoed these sentiments. Not only did they recognize differences among children, they believed that these differences should affect the kind of instruction that children receive.

Each child is different; we just have to look at each child and see how we could help each one. They all learn differently, and they're all starting off at a different place, even though they all may be on the same level according to what we're told—"This kid is in Rainbows." But actually they're not; one has more vocabulary, one can do something that the other one can't do. You find out these things in working with them every day. (*Trade City teacher*)

The basic thing [I try to do] is to meet all the approaches [my students need to learn]. So I use flashcards—it's a visual approach. And I use dictation of words—one of my groups [uses] a reading series that is a linguistic approach, everything is phonetically done. So that group will have dictation, to see if they can hear the sounds. The two other children that need a tactual [*sic*] approach go to the resource center. (*Blue Collar Suburb teacher*)

This pressure to provide diverse learning experiences for children with diverse needs thus stands in dramatic contrast to the pressure to provide adequate instruction for upwards of 25 children at a time. A certain degree of sameness is inevitable if instruction is to be provided efficiently—especially since there are so many things to do besides teach reading—yet a degree of diversity is essential if instruction is to be effective. Teachers trying to guarantee that each of their students is "reading to the best of his or her ability" thus cannot escape the paradox of collective instruction in the different social contexts of the classroom.

The Problem of Professional Uncertainty

A second feature shared by the different contexts of reading instruction is the *problem of professional uncertainty*: Despite decades of research and reflection, no one is sure exactly how children learn to read, or how best to teach them. Teachers confront this problem daily on both a theoretical and a practical level. Uncertainty and inconclusiveness in the theoretical scholarship on learning and instruction is a fact of life for educational practitioners. Debate continues on the broadest of questions, such as whether differences among teachers matter for student achievement (Goodlad, 1984; Oakes, 1985) or whether differences in instructional methods matter (Silvernail, 1979). Even assuming that variations in teaching styles and methods do make a difference, it is unclear which variations are the important ones or how to control them (Farr, 1984, p. 42). Debate continues on many narrowly defined issues as well, such as: the nature of letter and word recognition; the relationship between skill in spoken language and skill in reading; the acquisition of left-to-right correspondence; the relationship between decoding and comprehension; and the order in which reading skills should be learned (Carroll, 1984). Compounding the mysteries of individual learning is the fact that reading skills are usually acquired in a group context of one sort or another, and the technology of group instruction is still underdeveloped and poorly articulated (Lieberman, 1982). Finally, the teaching profession continues to be characterized by uncertain links between research and practice (Davy, 1983; Zumwalt, 1982). In short, Dan Lortie's observation that teachers lack a "technical culture" has, unfortunately, stood the test of time; it is still true that individual teachers "must solve recurrent problems largely unaided by systematic, relevant knowledge," a fact that contributes to the "endemic uncertainties" they face daily in the classroom (1975, p. 155).

Lortie goes on to observe that the theoretical uncertainties of learning and teaching are exacerbated by the structure of life in classrooms (pp. 159ff.). My own respondents provided ample evidence supporting Lortie's observations; moreover, they provided some very specific descriptions of the ways classroom life can create its own uncertainty. To begin with, individual children change. One teacher observed:

> Some kids don't always need [individual attention]; they might need it now, but two weeks down the road they might not, because by then they might be comfortable enough with the concept that they won't need the reinforcement. (*Blue Collar Suburb teacher*)

The problem for teachers, however, is not so much the fact of change itself— that's what education is supposed to bring about—but rather its unpredictability. What worked last year (or last week, or yesterday, or five minutes ago) may not work today (Lieberman, 1982, p. 251)—and worst of all, it's rarely clear why.

> Sometimes, nothing works! Or else you find that, after a period of time, all of a sudden they know what they haven't known in some strange way, and you're not really sure how they figure it out. All of a sudden it clicks, and they're able to do that which you have been struggling with for some time. (*Factory City teacher*)

> Even in a small, almost individualized group of four or five children working at this table with me, some kids are just not getting it, and some kids are having trouble focusing on it. . . . I'm sure there are reasons; they are not always apparent. (*Blue Collar Suburb teacher*)

Much of the uncertainty surrounding reading instruction thus derives from the fact that individual children change in unpredictable and mysterious ways, and it is difficult for teachers to gain systematic access to the dynamics of each child's transformation. The whole business is enormously complicated by the intrinsically collective nature of reading instruction. The various classroom contexts engage teachers and students in a joint enterprise which is as much social as it is cognitive and intellectual. Reading in public schools is carried out in complex and dynamic webs of relationships, and those relationships condition the ways teachers and students alike think about the purposes, tasks, and results of reading instruction. It is particularly important to think about the "classness" of instruction with respect to reading, because virtually all instructional activities take place in some kind of group context (even, as I will show later, when the reading activity is to be carried on "independently").

Of these contexts, the best known and most widely used is the "ability-based" reading group, and there is a growing literature describing how the grouped nature of reading instruction complicates the teacher's tasks of assessing needs and providing resources. Eder and Felmlee (1984), for example, have demonstrated convincingly that children's reading can be both positively and negatively influenced by the behavior of other children during reading group instruction. My own respondents confirmed these varied effects.

> Interaction among children is important. Sometimes a child will tell me he doesn't understand something I'm trying to say, and another child will explain it and he'll get it right away. (*Trade City teacher*)

> I have found that unless a class is socially together, you can't teach academics. If you have two kids fighting, the group isn't going to listen; the fight's certainly more interesting than the "short A" sound! (*Factory City teacher*)

> I have suspected . . . that in listening to other children, children become very word-by-word readers, and they begin to mimic that, because they think that's the way they're supposed to read. I'm sure that happened in one case . . . she just thought that a young reader should read like that, even though she had started out smoothly. (*White Collar Suburb teacher*)

This last example suggests that the social contexts of instruction can influence children's perceptions as well as their behaviors. Children evaluate themselves, and the whole enterprise of reading, *in relation to* the behavior of other children in the classroom (Simpson, 1981). They learn to ask questions about themselves such as, "Am I fast or slow?" "Is this book easy or hard for me?" "Am I smart or dumb?" "When am I supposed to read?" "What don't I know that everyone else already seems to know?" "What do I know that most of the other kids don't?" "What can I read that most of the other kids can't?" A White Collar Suburb teacher gave a particularly good illustration of how the social contexts of instruction can influence a child's conception of what it means to be a reader:

> Most children have a level predetermined in their heads that means, "Once I can read that, I don't have to worry any more." Until they get to that level, they're anxious about it, or they're wondering. And what counts for some children won't count for others. Reading isn't Dr.

Seuss, it's Hardy Boys. One second grader came to me and wanted to know if *The Littles* wasn't as hard as *The Hardy Boys*; I asked him why he wanted to know, and he said, "Well, if I can read *The Littles* I'll be as good as _____" and then he named another child in the room. I said, "And you want to be as good as he is?" and he said, "Well, he's the best!"

The uncertainty inherent in the social dynamics of reading instruction affects the perceptions and behaviors of children and teachers alike; it is not surprising that this uncertainty shows up in teachers' descriptions of their evaluative and instructional practices. One problem is the lack of time in the course of the typical classroom day to sort out who needs what and why—a normal consequence of the social dynamics of reading instruction:

Often there is not time to focus sufficiently on the individual student to really determine what they need, because with the clerical work we have to do, the record-keeping, the accountability stuff that we have to do every day, it just does not allow time . . . which means that in the end it's not always possible to determine what causes these differences in the rate at which they are picking up the skills. (*Trade City teacher*)

Teachers discussed the absence of a reliable instructional technology in similar terms, pointing to the uncertainty inherent in their day-to-day activities.

Teaching reading is such a complex skill. We just don't know why some things work and why others don't. One teacher told me once that she thinks that for some of her kids she could stand on her head and speak Swahili, and they would still learn to read. We just don't know how youngsters put together the skills necessary to learn to read. Our best efforts seem to be to instruct children in the skills that have some obvious relevance to learning to read. (*White Collar Suburb teacher*)

Sometimes I wonder if I'm really getting through, lesson by lesson. It's hard to see progress that way. You can see it over a long time, but it's hard to see day by day. I have success, say, in getting them to read more books; by the middle of the year, there are more kids going to the library center in the room than there were at the beginning. Exactly how it happens, I'm not sure. (*Blue Collar Suburb teacher*)

Professional uncertainty, then, permeates both the assessment of reading needs and the provision of reading instruction, not simply because the teaching profession is predicated on a weak knowledge base but because these activities take place in socially dynamic contexts. Teachers are often unsure about the effects of past actions as well as the potential consequences of present choices; there are few reliable guides available to help them make the "right" decisions. Clearly this problem is exacerbated by the paradox of collective instruction discussed earlier; even if teachers felt confident in deciding what to do for each child, it is difficult to find the time to do it. The problem of professional uncertainty pervades all the social contexts of reading instruction and makes life considerably more difficult for the teacher trying to make effective educational policy in the classroom.

The Complications of Power and Influence

Still a third important feature of the social contexts of classroom reading instruction involves the *complications of power and influence.* Students and teachers have available a number of resources they can use to exert influence over one another, and they rely on a variety of strategies in exercising those resources. These influence relationships are made possible by a number of characteristics most classroom settings share. Both the paradox of collective instruction and the problem of professional uncertainty are affected by three sets of complicated influence relationships: students' influence over one another; teachers' influence over students; and students' influence over teachers.

It is clear from the preceding discussion that children influence one another in reading instruction. Above I suggested that students' perceptions of the task of reading itself, and of their own abilities, are affected by their observations of and interactions with other students; and as I proposed in Chapter 1, when one person affects another person's thinking, the former may be said to exercise influence over the latter. The social contexts of instruction supply many opportunities for students to influence one another. A child working at her seat may help her neighbor or model good work habits—or, conversely, may distract her neighbor, give him a wrong answer, or model bad work habits. Likewise, reading groups norms for attentiveness and participation are partly established by peer influence processes (Eder, 1981; Hallinan, 1984). The main resource students use to influence their peers is their ability to control a number of classroom rewards. Having an interesting day is more rewarding than having a dull day, for example, and students can certainly engage in behaviors which make the classroom more interesting (although not necessarily more orderly). Students also give and withhold approval for one another's behavior; the child who chastises his neighbor for fooling around, as well as the child who looks with envy at the book another child is able to read, are both employing this resource. The contextual feature which makes these exchanges of influence between classmates possible (perhaps inevitable) is proximity. This is especially so in reading group structures, where students have opportunities to observe one another closely and for extended periods of time, and where they also watch one another's behavior being assessed by the teacher. Peer influence, then, is an important dimension of the distribution of power and influence in the classroom.

Equally important is the teacher's ability to exercise power and influence over students. Teachers have a number of resources at their disposal. They almost always have access to and control over information the students do not have, and they exercise a great deal of discretion in distributing material and human resources in their classrooms. Teachers certainly control a number of rewards for students—approval, good grades, free time, interesting lessons—as well as sanctions—extra homework, scoldings, calls to parents, recess cancellations. Of all their resources, however, the most important is teachers' ability—indeed, their responsibility—to plan. It is the teacher's job to set the instructional agenda for his or her class in all its varied social contexts. Certainly students work hard to influence their teachers' plans; but the very fact that teachers *have* instructional schemes for which they try to gain student consent and cooperation gives them a measure of power their students lack. The teacher's right to plan is at the heart of the structure of power in the classroom.

Teachers have a variety of options in exercising their power resources. The most obvious is probably the promise of rewards ("If we get through the end of this story today, we'll have time to play Hangman tomorrow") or the threat of sanctions ("If you kids don't have these words learned by the end of this week, I'll have to give homework on Monday"). Teachers also engage in persuasion ("Susie, you have to give yourself a chance to learn; if you're patient and work hard, you'll be able to read *The Happy Hollisters* by yourself in a couple of weeks") and bargaining ("Okay, Rainbows, if you do well on your worksheets today we can skip the ones I have ready for tomorrow"). Sometimes they engage in outright coercion, such as calling a reading group together in spite of opposition from some of its members; but there are few sanctions on which to base frequent coercion, and teachers are more likely to cajole or compromise in the face of student recalcitrance.

A number of features in the classroom context make this kind of teacher power and influence possible. First, students depend on their teachers to tell them what to do, when to do it, how long, and how well; and as suggested in Chapter 1, dependency relationships permit the exercise of power resources. Moreover, students depend on their teachers to help them see the *meaning* of the work they do in the classrooms. Gowin offers an important insight on this point:

> Controlling the *meaning* of what is valid information is a powerful control
> over others. Concepts found in adult life to control others are (1) concepts
> created to evaluate others and (2) concepts that attribute motivation to
> others. . . . Teachers perform these acts in the line of duty. They give
> grades or gold stars to pupils, and in judging the pupil's worth they keep
> the pupil in place. Pupils are told: "You want to be quiet and line up for
> lunch now, don't you?" The teachers never wait for a reply. The teachers
> must control the class. (1981, p. 59)

As a consequence of this dependency relationship, teachers can create
classroom-specific student incentives, a second feature of the classroom
context that gives teachers influence. The power to ascribe meaning to
events that take place in the classroom context makes the structuring of
student incentives possible. Without the teacher to help students make sense
of it all, experiences like "getting up to purple" in an SRA (Science Research
Associates) series, advancing to the Bluebirds reading group, getting worksheets back with happy faces on them, or answering comprehension questions orally in complete sentences (something we hardly ever do in normal
conversation) would never assume the significance children ascribe to them.
A first-grade teacher in Factory City provided an especially apt illustration
of the way reading instruction can structure students' incentives:

> The Distar [reading series is] kind of regimented, you have a certain ap-
> proach that you work in. They encourage you to say, for instance,
> "Oh, I like the way Johnny is sitting," and so you get the whole group
> to [behave that way]. And they love it, they absolutely love that—they
> all sit up and they want to sit [that way].

Students will go to great lengths in order to achieve these experiences, and it
is their teachers who turn these somewhat artificial indices of "ability" and
"progress" into events of shared meaning. Once again, it is the existence of a
plan which permits teachers a modicum of power over these matters. Instructional planning turns the acquisition of purple reading cards and
Bluebird-level texts into goals students want to reach and provides a variety
of means for reaching those goals.

While teachers do most of the overt agenda setting in the classroom,
they are nevertheless very susceptible to the influence their students attempt
to exert. When most educational researchers discuss power or influence at
the classroom level, they tend to assume that power is essentially unidirec-
tional—something teachers exercise over students. We would leave out a
very important dimension of classroom decision making if we failed to
examine the reciprocal influence students exert over their teachers. The
main resource students have at their disposal is their ability to reward their

teachers with attention, interest, cooperation, and appropriate signs of progress (Pauly, 1980). That teachers recognize students' influence on classroom decision making is evident in the results from Goodlad's Study of Schooling, in which he reports that over 75 percent of the teachers he sampled "indicated that they were greatly influenced in what they taught by two sources—their own background, interests, and experiences; and students' interests and experiences" (1984, p. 186). My own sample corroborated Goodlad's findings with concrete examples of student influence in shaping instructional decisions. One second-grade teacher talked about tailoring the reading materials she provides to student topic interests: "My class this year seems to like quiet, nature-type, gentle books, rather than explosive, rockets-and-things books." Other teachers described their "flexibility" in response to classroom dynamics—cutting a lesson short when the students got bored, or keeping a reading group that is finally "clicking" longer than usual. These illustrations suggest that teachers cooperate with students' exercise of influence.

The main way students exercise direct influence on their teachers is by the actual application of classroom rewards and sanctions; but they also exercise *indirect* influence as teachers learn to anticipate students' reactions to teacher-made plans and to adjust instruction accordingly. And as many political scientists point out, getting leaders to anticipate reactions is a potent form of influence (Dahl, 1984, p. 25). Teachers base their anticipations not only on their general experience in the teaching profession, but also on their particular experiences with a particular class:

This year, the children that are slower children—they cannot sit still for a whole half an hour. The last group I had, I could probably go for 45 minutes with that group alone, and they'd keep at it, whereas the lower group cannot. You've got twenty minutes and they've had it— you have to go on to something else. (*Trade City teacher*)

If the attempt to implement a plan distinguishes the exercise of power from the exercise of influence, the ability of students to affect the shape of a teacher's plan is a highly significant factor in their exercise of influence. Students rarely substitute their own conscious and collective plans for those of their teachers, so it is improper to speak of anticipated reactions in terms of student power. But the recognition of student influence on teachers is essential to a clear picture of the distribution of power and influence in classroom reading instruction.

The contextual features of classroom instruction that make it possible for students to influence teachers are similar to those that allow students to influence one another and teachers to influence students. Proximity supplies

teachers with the data they need to anticipate reactions. A related consideration is the incentive structure of the teaching profession, which focuses on
getting rewards from students. Cohen and Murnane put the matter exceptionally well:

> Teachers' work consists largely in efforts to improve other humans, or to
> help them improve. Teachers cannot succeed unless the people on whom
> they practice try to do well in pursuit of the teacher's objectives. Unlike
> surgeons or dermatologists, teachers need active cooperation and engage-
> ment from their students, not just passive acceptance of a treatment.
> Students therefore hold the keys to teachers' success. (1985, p. 21)

This incentive structure engages teachers in an ongoing enterprise of antici-
pating and adjusting to student responses in the search for instructional
effectiveness. The exercise of student resources for influence thus interacts
in complex ways with teachers' attempts to exercise their own resources.

Considered together, the resources, strategies, and contexts that shape
the distribution of power and influence in the classroom complicate enormously an already complex social dynamic. The teacher's susceptibility to
student influence and students' susceptibility to one another make the
paradox of collective instruction and the problem of professional uncertainty that much more difficult. Indeed, the paradoxes and uncertainties
teachers confront in collective instruction are potentially overwhelming;
House and Lapan (1978) are right to call the business of teaching "survival
in the classroom." What is amazing is not that many teachers are in fact
ultimately overwhelmed and choose to leave the profession, but rather that
so many more are not, and choose to stay. How do they do it? How do they
manage to provide opportunity in the face of unrelenting mystery, change,
and paradox? The answers to this question are crucial to understanding the
classroom mobilization of bias.

COPING STRATEGY NUMBER ONE:
THE PURSUIT OF ROUTINE

One strategy that helps teachers manage the paradox of collective
instruction, the problem of professional uncertainty, and the complications
of power and influence, is the attempt to rely on routines in carrying out the
tasks of providing opportunity. Of course, there is no such thing as a
completely routine instructional session; classrooms are too dynamic and
changeable for standard operating procedures to prevail for very long.
Nevertheless, the same social context that thwarts attempts to impose

routine also makes routine an attractive means of reducing complexity and paradox in classroom decision making. In fact, instructional routines are so appealing that they end up dominating what goes on even in nonroutine settings. Temporary and irregular social contexts, like ad hoc instructional groups and brief individual help sessions, are generally used to support the routines of reading group instruction. As a result, routine is pursued in most contexts of reading instruction, and this affects the nature of classroom life and the teacher's ability to cope with it.

The Pervasiveness of Instructional Routine

While there are many contexts in which children learn to read, the major portion of oral reading instruction occurs in ability-based reading groups (Hallinan, 1984, pp. 229–30; Harris & Sipay, 1980, p. 103). Despite presumed differences in ability among and within the reading groups into which a given classroom may be divided, a long list of routines gives shape and meaning to the transactions that go on in all of them. The children assemble and sit in a semicircle or around a table, usually in a designated order of the teacher's choosing, with their textbooks open to the same page. They take turns reading orally, either by following a round-robin order or by waiting for the teacher to call on them. The teacher directs evaluative comments primarily to individual students (Stodolsky, 1984, p. 113); when a child makes an error, the teacher will either correct it or ask another child to supply a correct response. When the textbook reading has been completed, the teacher will evaluate comprehension by asking the students questions, usually about the story's literal content (Durkin, 1978–79, pp. 490, 499). At the conclusion of the group lesson the teacher often gives an assignment, which the students will be expected to complete during seatwork time.

Throughout a lesson the teacher will rely on a variety of behavioral signals to manage the behavior of disruptive or inattentive children, who may be "looking away from the group, watching other group members [rather than the text], playing with objects such as book markers, [or] talking about something other than the activity of reading" (Eder & Felmlee, 1984, p. 192). Such regularities like pointing or question-asking may serve only a management function ("Jeff, stop playing with Lisa's pigtail!"), or they may serve both academic and management functions ("Jeff, can you help Lisa with that word?") (Eder, 1981, p. 154). While working in the group, the teacher may also send management signals to students outside the group ("Mary, please stop talking to Sue," or "Frank, have you finished your worksheet?"). Different teachers may use different kinds of signals, depending on their own teaching habits and the makeup of the particular class or group they are working with. It only takes a few weeks at the beginning of the school year to negotiate an efficient working code that both the children and the teacher understand; the significance of the code is its effectiveness in maintaining the continuity of group instructional routines. The energy teachers devote to the containment of disruption attests to the importance of routine in helping teachers decide what should happen in reading group instruction.

Routine also characterizes a second context of reading instruction, that of "seatwork." If research on within-class ability grouping in elementary schools is a relatively young enterprise (Eder, 1981, p. 151; Hallinan, 1984, p. 229), research on the effects of seatwork is in its infancy (Osborn, 1984, p. 46). But seatwork is an important social context, partly because it occupies a great deal of instructional time, and partly because both the content and the routines of seatwork support the instruction provided in reading groups. Osborn suggests that "in most classrooms . . . students spend as much time reading and writing in their workbooks as they do interacting with their teachers" (p. 51), and she observes that these patterns in workbook usage persist across variations in classroom organization, teacher style, and student ability (pp. 51–53). Furthermore, most of the work children are assigned to do at their seats consists of the commercially produced workbooks and worksheets that accompany the basal series in use in the classroom.[2] Although seatwork may also involve self-selected long-term reading projects, "free reading," or reading games, students usually take up these activities only after they have completed their basal series assignments. For the most part, the content of seatwork assignments is clearly intended to support reading group instruction. In the words of a Blue Collar Suburb teacher, "All their seatwork is a reinforcement of whatever skills they have been taught." And according to a Trade City teacher, "Their seatwork is related to the reading group; there are some things that are already made, that you purchase at the teacher's store, and others I just make up myself."

The routines of seatwork also help to support what goes on in reading groups. Seatwork generally requires teachers to act as assignment-givers and children to act as assignment-doers (the latter with varying degrees of concentration, effort, success, and consistency) (Durkin, 1978–79). Students turn in their workbooks or worksheets at regular intervals or at the teacher's request; the teacher checks the assignment; the students get their papers back; and, depending on the time available, the students get help from the teacher in examining the results of their performance. These transactions parallel those in reading groups which encourage children to rely on their teachers for instructions and evaluations. They also resemble reading group routines that require waiting, following directions, paying attention, and responding to individually directed feedback (Osborn, 1984). One first-grade teacher noted that she had arranged her classroom to facilitate seatwork routines that complement reading group instruction:

> We're just getting in to left-to-right. Turning a page, you have to start on the left. That's why the room is set up this way—I hate rows, but it's to get them used to left-to-right, so they know how to pass papers [and] how to collect things. (*Blue Collar Suburb teacher*)

Another teacher used the chalkboard rather than worksheets because it improved her students' ability to follow directions:

> [My students] need to learn how to read directions from the board and follow them. . . . So I continue to provide it—as you can see, all the boards in my room are filled with skill work. (*Trade City teacher*)

Seatwork routines thus help to support the routines of reading group instruction, not only because seatwork frees the teacher to work with reading groups by giving the rest of the students something to do, but also because the activities themselves train students in behaviors they need for reading group work.

Still another social context of reading influenced by reading group routines is the ad hoc instructional group. Some teachers base their ad hoc arrangements on particular skills needed by children from different ability groups:

> When I get test results, I write up a list of exactly what each child got wrong, and then I would pull them out [of their groups] for skill teaching. This might mean working on commas, alphabetizing, or silent consonants. (*White Collar Suburb teacher*)

Others refer to perceived differences in the children's learning styles:

> I don't always take the same reading groups; on Fridays I try to variate (*sic*), and what I'll do is take some of the kids that I know use their eyes more than their ears, and work on . . . auditory things with them, and take some of the kids that I know rely a lot on hearing and do some visual things with them, to kind of balance it out with them, so they get all their senses in. (*Blue Collar Suburb teacher*)

A few teachers group children according to their interests:

> On Fridays, I try to spend a lot of time one on one, or two on one, and I try to pair kids mostly by interest when I do that small group kind of thing. There's a bunch of guys who are interested in cars, so I

try to pull stories that are about hot rods or whatever, and work that way. (*Trade City teacher*)

The instruction students receive in these groups, however, is always supplementary to the instruction they receive in their ability groups. For one thing, only 10 percent of my sample of teachers reported the use of ad hoc groups, which suggests that in the teacher's view, these groups are clearly subordinate and of secondary importance. For another, the content in ad hoc groups, like that of seatwork, is intended to help the children function better in their primary reading groups. One White Collar Suburb teacher used ad hoc groups specifically to help her achieve a manageable number of ability-based groups:

When I pull children to work on specific skills, I might pull children from different groups—today I had three kids from Level 4 and two from Level 3 working on silent consonants together. . . . When the year began and the children first came into my class, they were all over the place—I had seven levels of children! But by teaching the skills they needed, and by reteaching, I have managed to get them to only three levels.

Moreover, the social context of ad hoc groups is presumably similar to that of ability groups in a number of important respects. Particularly when the groups are based on skill needs or learning styles, the routines that prevail are likely to resemble and reinforce the routines of ability-group instruction.[3] Thus, ad hoc groups serve very much the same functions that seatwork serves.

Teachers occasionally present reading lessons to an entire class at once. Harris and Sipay (1980, p. 102) list a number of instructional activities that can take place in a whole-class context:

1. Student presentation of an oral reading selection, previously rehearsed;
2. Instruction in skills likely to be new to all the students, such as alphabetizing, the use of the dictionary, new vocabulary, and phonics;
3. Reading sessions with common, non-textbook materials, such as current events clippings, newsletters for children, or experience stories;
4. Content-area textbook reading, usually accomplished in a round-robin fashion;
5. Choral reading of poetry or simple prose.

To their list I would add:

6. Oral reading by the teacher from children's novels or short stories in order to interest children in reading and to model good skills.

There was surprisingly little reference to whole-class reading instruction in my sample of teachers. When they did refer to it, their comments suggested that whole-class instruction is useful primarily as a supplement to ability-group instruction. For example, one teacher's description of a typical session in which she introduced common new skills sounded very much like a reading group writ large:

Every morning we do language skills; I have a morning story, and I can kind of tell [how the students are doing] from that. I'll have someone go up and try to find a certain word, and see if they can remember what it looked like, or if they can tell by the beginning sound. . . . Also in that we work on our capitalization, punctuation, all kinds of language skills, and I can see how they listen during that part, how they watch the other children, and when it's their turn I can see which skills they've picked up and which they're lacking in. (*Factory City teacher*)

Whole-class activities can also reinforce the routines associated with comprehension instruction:

I'm always tying reading in to the other curricular areas, such as social studies. The *Weekly Readers* are very helpful there; they have good comprehension questions, and the kids are increasing their language development as they respond to the questions. (*Trade City teacher*)

In short, the routines of large-group instruction are, at least for the teacher, clearly subordinate to the routines of small-group instruction.

The same can be said of the patterns evident in the individual help teachers offer students. It is hard to describe the one-on-one social context of instruction as "routine," because it is by nature highly unpredictable. Some teachers save more time for individual help than others; some students are more likely to ask for it than others; and some days have more "openings" than others. What most of these one-on-one help sessions have in common is that they are intended to support the pursuit of routines in reading groups. When group routines are frequently interrupted by disruptive or inattentive children, or when they are not adequate modes of instruction and a child starts to fall behind, teachers often turn to the one-on-one social context to supplement the ability-group context; and the purpose is ultimately to help the child perform better in the group.

> Very often, if a particular child is having a problem in the group, you can sometimes take that child by himself for five minutes or so—keep him with the group but work with him alone sometimes. (*Trade City teacher*)

Thus, while not "routine" in themselves, individual help sessions do support routines in the other contexts of instruction, particularly in reading groups.

These patterns, together with my earlier discussion of the other social contexts of reading, suggest that *teachers see reading instruction as taking place primarily in the ability groups into which their students are sorted.* The routines of seatwork and ad hoc groups are designed to "reinforce" what goes on in reading groups; whole-class instruction and individual help sessions will take place only when it is efficient to provide them (as in the case of instruction on common new skills) or when they are likely to reinforce behavioral or cognitive skills acquired in reading groups (following instructions or answering comprehension questions). This reinforcement of reading group routines is important. It suggests that the patterns of behavior adopted by teachers and students in reading groups carry over into other social and instructional contexts, while at the same time the patterns that show up in other contexts reinforce the patterns of reading group instruction. The purposes of less routinized contexts, such as ad hoc groups or one-on-one contacts, become subordinated to the routines of reading groups. Thus, routines are pursued even in nonroutine instructional settings.

Some Consequences of the Pursuit of Routine

The pervasiveness of the teacher's pursuit of routine has a number of important effects on classroom life and the teacher's ability to cope with it. The first of these effects is that teachers evaluate individual performance and progress only in the context of group performance or dynamics. In fact, as several interviews cited above suggest, teachers go out of their way to make sure that students display their reading skills alone, without depending on other children. Observational studies like that of Au and Mason (1981) support the claim that it is unusual for teachers to encourage reading group behaviors oriented toward group, rather than individual, performance. The irony is that the standard against which individual behavior is assessed is the performance of the group as a whole. Nonroutine settings like one-on-one help sessions or ad hoc groups are used primarily to help children "fit" better into the reading group. When that fails, the child is simply put into a different group:

> Usually if there's somebody that really doesn't fit in, we try and find another class for them, or another situation to put them in. We have some kids that don't fit in at all that are in learning lab. I have a couple of children that go into the second and third grade because they're way ahead of everybody else. (*Factory City teacher*)

Teachers' incentives to pay attention to individuals are thus conditioned by the demands of the routines associated with group contexts—even when they give help in an individual setting.

A second effect of the pursuit of routine is that, regardless of which social context they are in, children must master specific behavioral "forms" in order to display their mastery of content. A reading readiness teacher in Trade City, who was responsible for children who had finished kindergarten but were judged "not ready" for first grade, provided an especially good description of the relationship between "form" and content for her students:

> I'm dealing with children fresh out of kindergarten who need more time before they go on to first grade. . . . These children are certainly not limited in their ability; they're limited by their own social and emotional capacity to settle down to a first-grade reading program. . . . When they're in the room, you [will] see them moving around, talking, forgetting to be considerate of others—it's just a hodge-podge. Whenever they want, they'll just pick themselves up, come up to me, and none of them would understand that they have to wait and listen to the others to talk.

This teacher's remarks are consistent with the observations of Hugh Mehan:

> Students have a repertoire of academic information and social knowledge available to them. When the teacher initiates action, they must be able to choose a reply from their repertoire that is appropriate for the occasion. When the teacher is allocating the floor to students, they must recognize the turn-allocation procedure that is operating and provide the behavior that is consistent with these normative expectations. Once students have gained access to the floor, they must know what to do with it. That is, they must synchronize the appropriate form of their reply with the correct content. (1982, p. 75)

Equally important, teachers use the same behavioral standards to assess everyone, regardless of which group they are in. It's assumed that not everyone in a class will live up to these standards equally well, as suggested in the comments of the readiness teacher reported above, and as noted in the observational studies of Eder and Felmlee (1981, 1983, 1984). It's also assumed that violation of these behavioral standards will be more frequent in lower reading groups and in the younger grades:

> I like to take my slower group first, because they're fresher, the room is more quiet, and you have a little bit more flexibility with your time. It takes them a long time to find the page; they can't find their pencils. . . . How many times does the first group say "I forgot my pencil, my barrette is coming out, my shoe is untied"—all these things that are interruptions. (*Trade City teacher*)

> Third grade is a tremendous jump from second grade. The academics are much harder. So they have to face an immediate change in their heads about how things are going to be. There is not going to be a lot of printing on the board that they have to copy, there's not going to be a lot of picture drawing, there's not a lot of coloring. They have to adjust to more writing, more working by themselves. (*White Collar Suburb teacher*)

The implication of these remarks is that the behavioral norms that students must follow to demonstrate cognitive achievement are the same for everybody. In terms of performance, the achieving student at any level is one who pays attention, follows directions, gets her work done, doesn't distract or interrupt others, is not easily distracted herself, can work on her own, comes prepared to reading group, and generally abides by the classroom constitution with respect to conversation, movement, and so forth. There is evidence from other studies (Eder, 1981; Felmlee & Eder, 1983) suggesting that teachers may relax these standards for lower achieving reading groups; but even here, the presumption is that the standards apply unless the teacher chooses to relax them. And it's very clear that teachers view such relaxation, not as an alternative form of running a reading group, but rather as an undesirable adjustment to the students' behavioral limitations; the teacher's hope is that student behavior will improve so that relaxed standards will no longer be necessary.

Probably the most important effect of the pursuit of routine is that it helps teachers cope with the tensions of life in classrooms discussed earlier. Routines assist teachers in their attempts to respond to the imperatives of collective instruction by providing ways of making sure that everyone has access (i.e., receives exposure) to similar services. Establishing reading groups of roughly equal size helps to equalize the amount of teacher time each child receives (Hallinan, 1984). The members of a reading group generally use the same text or series. Children must follow the same behavioral rules in getting the floor to speak, interacting with their neighbors, and displaying their cognitive skills. At the same time, teachers use routines to pay attention to individual differences among their students. The emphasis on individual performance is intended to do that; occasional switches to other social contexts of instruction (ad hoc groups, free reading) are also intended to promote individualization. Teachers often described seatwork not only as a reinforcement of skills acquired in reading groups, but as a way to provide for individual differences; they also mentioned reassigning students to new reading groups as a response to individual needs. In short, the routines of reading instruction based around ability groups provide room to maneuver on common ground.

The pursuit of routine also helps teachers cope with the uncertainties and complexities of influence in the multiple social contexts of instruction. Routines tell teachers and students what to do; routines set the classroom agenda, thus reducing the number of decisions teachers will have to make in the course of the day. A teacher may still have to decide how to tell Jeff to quit bothering his neighbor or how long the middle group should meet today; but at least he won't have to decide *whether* Jeff should stop bothering Ted or *whether* the middle group should meet. Providing rules, schedules, and orderliness is no mean feat; it helps reduce the unpredictability that characterizes the social contexts of instruction. Routinization can also help teachers manage and contain change, another dynamic that produces uncertainty in collective instruction. When a child's needs change, the teacher can give her a new worksheet, put her in a different ability group, or instruct her in a specially created ad hoc group. Routine thus makes the effects of "classness" on individual behavior more manageable; it is no exaggeration to conclude that routinization is an important route to "survival in the classroom." Contrary to the claims of some critics, teachers do not choose routine out of a preference for monotony, hostility toward children, or lack of imagination; rather, they choose routine as the alternative that stands between chaos and paralysis. Routine permits a sense of order, predictability, and direction in a world of paradox and ambiguity.

COPING STRATEGY NUMBER TWO: THE PURSUIT OF CONTROL

A second strategy that helps teachers manage the paradox of collective instruction, the problem of professional uncertainty, and the complexities of classroom influence relationships, is the pursuit of control in the classroom. Control permits teachers to deliver both uniform and diversified instruction and helps to contain the unpredictable dynamics of group life. Like routine, control is never completely achieved, but teachers are constantly engaged in a struggle to achieve it. Their struggle takes two somewhat contradictory directions. On the one hand, teachers actively cultivate friendship and intimacy with their students; on the other, they seek the right of command. Both approaches help to mitigate the complexities and paradoxes of teacher decision making.

The Teacher as Confidant

Teachers treat intimacy with students both as an end in itself, in that it can improve the quality of life for everyone in the classroom, and as a means to more effective instruction.[4] Teachers believe that if they really get to know their students, they are in a better position to assess student needs accurately and to choose appropriate materials and instructional modes. The findings reported by Brookover and colleagues connect higher-than-expected achievement in low-income schools with teacher behaviors encouraging close relationships with students:

> The teachers often touched the students, hugged them, and demonstrated patience in attending to the individual needs of their students, both personal and academic. It was not unusual to see one of the teachers who taught in the upper grades sitting with one of her students on the back steps of the school discussing the student's personal problems. (1979, p. 99)

The teachers in my sample provided a number of illustrations suggesting that the "teacher-as-confidant" approach helps them to cope with the tensions and uncertainties specific to reading instruction. Some, like the following White Collar Suburb teacher, talked about reading instruction as a means to furthering intimacy for its own sake:

> I love to read, and I'm always sharing books that meant a lot to me. I tell the children, "Now, I read this when I was eight years old," or "My mother read this to me." I've written many stories about when I was a child, and they have those to read.

More often, though, intimacy was discussed as a means to better instruction and improved student performance; in this sense, it was treated as a way to reduce the guesswork of teaching.

> You have to depend on feedback from the children [in order to tell when someone is having trouble], with the comprehension questions or

during discussions. Of course, some kids are just shy, and you have to tell the difference between someone who is shy and someone who doesn't understand. So I try to develop a closer relationship with them to help them get over being shy. I smile at them, I change my tone of voice, I put my arm around them, I tell them personal things about when I was in school. (*Blue Collar Suburb teacher*)

The biggest thing is to get the kids to talk to you, about everything and anything; not only reading, everything. When they begin to trust you, they'll try to explain to you what they don't understand, then you've got it made. You can teach them anything then. But if they won't talk to you, if there's no communication, you can't teach them anything. That's it with every subject, but especially reading. (*White Collar Suburb teacher*)

Intimacy is also a way of maintaining attention to children's individuality in the face of the collective imperatives of classroom life:

In the back of my mind, there's always been this thought: Every day, I should be able to talk with every child at least for four or five minutes, alone, one-to-one. I don't care what it is, whether we sit and chat, or I work with him silently, but they have that right [to] my undivided attention at least that long during the day. (*Blue Collar Suburb teacher*)

Establishing a close relationship with students thus permits teachers to elicit information that helps them to meet individual needs and to dispel some of the ambiguities of instruction. It is particularly helpful as a way of mitigating the multiple influences to which a student is susceptible. By establishing intimacy, the teacher is in a better position to bargain with students and gain their consent to the teacher's vision of classroom learning. David Nyberg points to the power inherent in the development of "fealty," or "faithfulness or loyalty that is based on trust and mutuality":

As power takes on forms that more and more closely approximate balanced trust, shared understanding, and a mutual plan for action, then more and more of one's available resources can be directed to the plan itself since they will not be needed to guarantee the enforcement of consent. (1981, pp. 578–79)

As teachers strive for this "shared understanding" with their students, they hope that the influences of students who are not in accord with the teacher's agenda can be reduced relative to the influence of the teacher. Intimacy is thus consistent with the structure of rewards that characterizes the teaching profession and the nature of the demands teachers confront on a daily basis.

The Teacher as Commandant

Coupled with this image of the teacher-as-confidant is a second very different image, that of the teacher-as-commandant. What is interesting about the teacher's position here is not her actual success as commander, but rather the universal imperative that she try to command. Certainly this imperative derives in part from societal and professional expectations that teachers will "control" their classrooms (see, for example, House & Lapan, 1978, pp. 58–59). Teachers in every grade and at every school I visited appeared to have internalized these expectations. They devoted an impressive amount of energy to formulating and enforcing the rules of the classroom in order to facilitate reading instruction. Even when teachers differed in the standards they articulated for student behavior in their classrooms, they struggled to make *their* norms the ones that prevailed, as the following two teachers with very different classroom norms made apparent:

When [the children] come here, they definitely have an idea of what I am, what I stand for. Some come in and feel very frightened—they don't know how it will be, because I'm strict and firm, and have certain rules, and won't allow a lot of carrying on. And they know it. They may have had someone a previous year who was very light and easy on talking, and they know they're coming to a different environment, so they're prepared for that. (*White Collar Suburb teacher*)

Children at this age, I think it's too much to expect them to sit at their desks and keep quiet all this time. But I told them I don't mind if they whisper—a busy noise, but I don't want a noise where they're not working, or disturbing the groups. They have learned how to walk around; if they want to converse, they know how to whisper. The trick is, they have to move around and talk so that I do not look up at them; if I look up at them, they know that they're disturbing me. So they try to move quietly so I don't look at them. (*Factory City teacher*)

Teachers also try to communicate and enforce different rules for "appropriate" behavior during different kinds of reading instruction (see Erickson & Schultz, 1976):

I think the biggest thing is to get them used to the idea that there is a certain time called "reading time," where, if they are in the group, the teacher's available. But if they're stuck or they have a question, they have to wait for somebody else. It's a big adjustment. (*Trade City teacher*)

Even in the individualized, open-classroom approach of the Integrated Day program, teachers worked hard to gain student consent to their rules and expectations. A K–2-teacher explained that she spent a good portion of the first weeks of school:

> . . . explaining what a writing assignment was, what a reading assignment was, what I meant when I said things that I knew I would just naturally be saying. . . . It's terms that I use constantly in the room that I want them to have a good handle on. . . . I don't want them to begin to have bad habits in the room—not knowing what to do with a paper when they were through with it, or not knowing what standards I expected, whether to print letters with crayon or pencils.

The teachers I interviewed tried to "command" the social contexts of reading instruction not simply by establishing rules for their own interaction with the students, but also by establishing rules for students' interactions with one another. The following comment from a White Collar Suburb teacher is instructive:

> I only respond to [students'] positive behavior with each other; I don't give them any input for negative behavior . . . [such as] making comments on other peoples' papers. . . . I'll say to someone who has criticized someone else's work, "I thought I heard you criticizing someone else's work, and you hand me *this*!" They finally get the impression that you're paying attention to everyone all the time—and you are.

This teacher's message is clear: *she* is the only person in the classroom with the legitimate authority to offer criticism or assistance when it is not asked for. She models and encourages a cooperative attitude, but only to a point; the children are to support the behaviors the teacher approves of (like paying attention) and they should cooperate when asked for help, but they should not "interfere" with one another's work either by criticizing (that is not their job) or by actually doing someone else's work (answering a question directed to another child or writing on another child's paper). The point here is not that teachers actually succeed in controlling children's influences on one another, but that they work so hard in an attempt to do so. It is one of the ironies of life in classrooms that children are put into a crowded social setting where privacy is impossible and public performance inevitable, and then are told not to judge one another's work. The teacher's attempt to act as classroom commandant, even with respect to students' relationships with one another, is a necessary complement to her role as confidant; both images attest to the importance teachers attach to the maintenance of control.

Why Teachers Pursue Control

It would be easy to see the teacher's struggle for control in the classroom simply as a consequence of external expectations. Teachers who cannot "control" their classes get low marks from their peers, their principals, and the parents of their students. But this explanation alone does not account for the amount of energy teachers expend in search of classroom control. Rather, the search for control must also be seen as a response to the paradox of collective instruction, the problem of professional uncertainty, and the complexities of power and influence in the classroom. Teachers who are on intimate terms with their students can treat them as individuals despite the crowded and busy setting to which most of their interactions are confined. That "five minutes alone" with each child is the teacher's chance to demonstrate concern for, and perhaps to gain insight into, that child's particular needs, wants, preferences, and learning patterns. Intimacy can also reduce the pressures of uncertainty. To the extent that teachers make instructional use of insights gained from one-on-one encounters with their students and then get to "see the light bulbs go on," they can achieve the psychic rewards that accompany professional success. Intimacy thus affords a welcome walk beside the still waters for the teacher who usually feels at sea. And even if the light bulbs are dim, or don't go on at all, the other potential rewards of intimacy—students who feel good about their teachers and teachers who feel good about their students—can make the complexity and the confusion of the classroom much more tolerable. Teachers can cope with the demand to individualize in a crowded, uncertain instructional context by befriending the children they serve.

At the same time, they can respond to the demand to teach everyone in these same circumstances by trying to command the children they serve. Teachers believe they would face an enormous task if they tried consciously to harness the power and energy of community dynamics in some systematic or structured way relevant to reading instruction. If everyone in the class was authorized to assess reading needs, to select reading materials, or to propose the structure and process of reading groups, the confusion would be intolerable—or so teachers believe. It was very clear that, in the teacher's view, the way to keep order, structure, and predictability is for the teacher to bear alone the burden of command. The sense of control a teacher achieves by attempting to make and enforce behavioral norms may be sporadic, short-lived, and occasionally illusory; but it is a way to overcome the sense of helplessness which would otherwise ensue. At the same time, teachers who attempt to maintain control can meet the demand for universal instruction. They can verify that every child in the class has had access to reading services, since they have personally provided them. It is a way of making sure that one's professional obligations are faithfully discharged. In the classroom, at least, it's easier—and safer—*not* to delegate.

CLASSROOM LESSONS
ON EQUALITY OF OPPORTUNITY

In Chapter 1 I observed that people in schools see the goal of equal opportunity as "each child reading to the best of his or her ability at that stage of development." I also noted that educators see individualized instruction as essential to the achievement of this goal. The foregoing discussion of the contexts and conduct of reading instruction, however, suggests that the modal classroom severely constrains the specific means teachers will use to meet individual needs. Both the pursuit of routine and the pursuit of control limit the teacher's ability to provide truly individualized instruction. What follows is a closer look at the dimensions of opportunity in the mobilization of bias in the classroom and its impact on economically disadvantaged students.

Assessing Needs

In proposing a theoretical framework for opportunity in Chapter 1, I suggested that the three dimensions of opportunity—needs assessment, materials provision, and educational interactions—affect one another. These reciprocal effects are important in evaluating how teachers assess educational needs, because the provision of materials and the structures of interaction promote narrow definitions of reading needs. As we saw earlier, test results are interpreted in light of each child's response to the teacher's pursuit of routine and control. Observational assessment is based on how well a child masters the behavioral "forms" required to demonstrate cognitive achievement; these forms represent a narrow interpretation of "appropriate" social and cognitive development. In fact, teachers' perspectives paralleled many of the principles Laurel Tanner (1978) describes in her three-stage developmental model of discipline. Stage I, the Basic Disciplinary Stage, requires that children be able to listen, follow directions, ask questions when they don't understand something, share materials and resources with others, and respond to training that maintains order (pp. 29–30). As we saw earlier, the routines teachers pursue in all the social contexts of instruction require precisely these capabilities; teachers apparently share

Tanner's assumption that children who do not exhibit these behaviors are "in a state of arrested development and their life options will be few indeed" (p. 29). Moreover, teachers also concur that such children will be unable to progress to Stage II, the Constructive Stage (characterized by peer reciprocity, cooperation, self-direction, and a sense of justice) or Stage III, the Generative Stage (featuring autonomy, social responsibility, problem conceptualization, and problem solving) (pp. 32–39). These assumptions represent a single model of behavioral development which teachers believe to be universally valid for all children; cognitive development, in this view, reflects these behavioral "stages." No teacher questioned these assumptions; all who discussed observational needs assessment based their judgments on each child's display of "basic" disciplinary capabilities in the social contexts of instruction. The pursuit of routine in the various contexts in which children learn to read thus limits teachers' vision of what children "need" in order to improve their cognitive development.

By the same token, the language teachers use to describe the needs and abilities of their students grows out of the materials the children use and the rate at which they are instructed in their groups. Teachers always referred to their groups in terms of levels: "high" and "low," or "top" and "bottom." This is the same language they used to characterize the texts the children were reading. In other words, the materials children are provided affect the teacher's assessment of their needs. Similarly, teachers refer to high-achieving children as "quick" or "fast," while referring to low achievers as "slow"—and this parallels the pace of the instruction they receive. The nature of group interactions and the materials students use thus affect the assessment of individuals within the group.

What is most remarkable about needs assessment, though, is the way teachers are able to discuss "ability" and "need" as though they were tangible, easily measurable concepts. Despite the unclear technology of needs assessment and their own admission that test results are not always reliable indicators, teachers did not hesitate to use test results to help them decide what materials to provide or how to structure educational interactions:

> The [city-mandated achievement] test is given in November, then machine-scored, and we get results in January or February. Any child who scores below the third stanine is recommended for remediation. When I got the results, I wrote up a list of exactly what each child got wrong, and then I would pull them out for skill teaching—this might mean working on using commas, alphabetizing, or silent consonants. (White Collar Suburb teacher)

> I usually group by ability. The children that come in, we give them a placement test, and we take it from there. At the end of a unit, they're

given a test, and if they do 80 percent or better then they're able to go on to the next level. That's the way I've been grouping them this year. (*Trade City teacher*)

No teacher questioned whether testing was an appropriate means of identifying all students' individual needs. To put the matter in terms of the criteria for assessing opportunity developed in Chapter 1, no teacher claimed that tests were of inadequate quality or that tests were not appropriate to all children. This is not to say that my sample of teachers regarded tests as perfect indicators of reading needs; as we have seen, many teachers stressed the need to supplement assessment by teacher observation. However, the implicit criticism of testing in these cases is general to all children, not specific to some: if testing is an inadequate indicator, it is inadequate for everyone. Part of the mobilization of bias in needs assessment, then, is that teachers' concerns about tests do not discriminate among the different responses many children have to test taking. In the teacher's view, the tests "work" equally well for everyone, and they are limited in the same ways for everyone.

The same may be said of teacher observation as a form of needs assessment. As we have seen, observational assessment grows mainly out of the instructional contexts in which students must demonstrate their abilities. And teachers see observation, like testing, as limited only by the complicated, dynamic social contexts in which it takes place. No teacher questioned the standards against which he or she assessed student behavior; rather, they worried about the lack of time and technology to do the job thoroughly. Thus, although teachers do worry about the quantity and quality of their observations, they do not worry about the problem of appropriateness to the individual.

It is easy to see how the pursuit of routine and the pursuit of control constrain teachers' concerns about needs assessment. The pursuit of routine requires teachers to identify some categories of behavior as disruptive or inattentive—whether or not those behaviors actually hamper learning or indicate a lack of attention. The pursuit of control requires teachers to be in such constant interaction with so many students that they have to limit the things they will notice and respond to. Both these coping strategies force teachers to rely on the same standards to assess everyone, both in testing and in observation. This is an ironic outcome, because *teachers were unanimous in identifying low-income children as those least likely to adapt well to the routines of instruction.* The typical litany included failure to sit still, pay attention, work quietly, follow instructions, and so on. In short, the very behaviors economically disadvantaged students are least likely to exhibit form the basis on which their cognitive needs and achievements are assessed.

The mobilization of bias in the classroom limits individualization in needs assessment in ways which disproportionately penalize low-income children.

Providing Material Resources

Limited individualization is also evident in the material resources teachers provide, the second dimension of opportunity in the classroom. Earlier I observed that the policy-making role teachers play in the classroom is characterized by teacher discretion in the materials they can select for their students. Nevertheless, these same teachers expressed an obligation to use the basal text they were assigned as the foundation of the reading group instruction.

> The things you have to do involve using the series which is acceptable within your town as your base and teach from that. Any materials which have been supplemented by the reading department would be worked into [the basal program]. . . . I don't know offhand if there is, spelled out, "In fourth grade this is what you're supposed to do," other than basically following the basal. (*Blue Collar Suburb teacher*)

Teachers generally expect their basal series to be adequate to the fundamental tasks of teaching reading. No basal can do everything, they would say, but the series is a pretty good start. Only in extraordinary circumstances would they abandon the basal series entirely in favor of other materials. A teacher in Factory City expressed this point of view exceptionally well when I asked her to describe the things she felt she had to do in reading instruction and the things she did by choice:

> I don't really think in terms of "have to do"—I'm given a group of children, and I discover their needs . . . and it's just a matter of meeting those needs. We have a reading series we must use, and it happens to be very adequate, it's very sequential. I don't really feel compelled to do anything. I am supposed to follow the book, but it seems to me that's the appropriate thing to do. I like the series, it's well laid out, and we've worked with it for three years now and I've come to enjoy it.

With respect to the tangible resources they provide, then, teachers are apt to rely on the basal series used in their school; other materials are quite clearly supplementary.

The same conclusion applies to the materials used for seatwork, particularly workbooks. Harris and Sipay (1980, p. 104) suggest that seatwork permits "individualized skills practice . . . in which each child works on the particular reading skills in which he or she needs to improve." However, my sample did not provide much evidence that they used seatwork in this fashion. Only four of my 49 respondents reported variations in the worksheets they provided their students; and of these teachers, two reported that this variation was a matter of the number of worksheets they provided different students, rather than the type of work that the worksheets required:

> I give more time to the lower level group because we have to worry about getting them on grade level. I will do more in the workbook activity with them. I'll give them five examples as opposed to one example. We do the same skill on the board that we do in the workbooks; we'll do more skill sheets. (*Trade City teacher*)

These findings suggest that with respect to the initial provision of tangible resources for reading instruction, teachers tend to focus on making sure that materials are available in sufficient amounts, paying less attention to the criteria of quality and appropriateness. In fact, no teacher expressed concern over the quality of the basal series; and those who expressed concern over appropriateness used the series anyway, relying on supplementary materials to compensate for any problems the children encountered:

> We are not limited to just that [basal] reader, but we are expected to cover what is in that. Some children don't do well with that, so we use phonics-type books in addition to [the basal series]. The only problem is that your time is so limited, not just in finding the materials but to work with the children and then to follow through on it all. (*Trade City teacher*)

> We have a new reading series, which I'm not too pleased with yet; it's Addison-Wesley, and it's basically linguistic. Some sight, but mostly linguistic. Not all children learn that way . . . and I'm finding that about six or seven kids are just dropping out, and [are not] able to keep up with the others at all. So those will probably be the ones I'll have to refer, or they'll have to repeat the grade. (*Trade City teacher*)

These comments also suggest that the criterion of appropriateness is hardest to meet with the low-achieving child. As one teacher put it,

> My basic philosophy is, if a child is going to learn to read, they can read anything. It can be any approach. . . . Children that use the SRA [reading series] have a stronger background in [phonics], but the children that are poor readers are still struggling in SRA. Whether it's a phonetic approach or a stand-on-your-head approach, they're still struggling with it. (*Blue Collar Suburb teacher*)

The response to this problem is somewhat ironic. Teachers have to start out with the assumption that the basal reader is essentially appropriate to everyone. The children most likely to experience difficulty with any reader are the ones in the lower groups. The teacher's sense that the basal must come first, coupled with the fact that it takes the lower groups longer to "cover" the required materials, restricts the time available for the teacher to search for and use "more appropriate" supplementary materials. The criterion of appropriateness, then, is least likely to be met with lower-achieving students.

An even knottier problem is raised by the question of how much individualization can be achieved even when teachers *do* replace their reading materials. Some teachers in my sample were using new textbooks, and their comments implied that a change in materials may not, in fact, be much of a change:

> We have a new reading series this year, which entails a lot of interaction on the teacher's part. I like the books—I think they provide a lot of skill practices before the children read. . . . I think I'm basically doing the same things, it's just that I have changed the order in which I do them. (*Trade City teacher*)

These observations suggest that teachers tend to rely on the same instructional routines even when using different texts or worksheets. Changes in materials do not necessarily produce changes in teaching behaviors. And given the problem of professional uncertainty and the paradox of collective instruction, it's not hard to see why. Deciding which materials are "right" for a child is difficult enough; deciding which mode of instruction is "right" is even more so. Multiply this problem by 23 or more children—as the paradox of collective instruction requires us to do—and the reasons for the limited effect of changes in materials on individualization are all too clear. The teacher's struggle to maintain order and rationality in a non-rational context explains Fullan's conclusion (1982, p. 154) that "many changes in curriculum materials have not resulted in any real change in how the classroom operates."

Structuring Interactions

This brings us to the third dimension of equal opportunity: the extent to which classroom structures for educational interactions can promote individualization. The foregoing discussion suggests that Goodlad's general observation on this point is warranted:

During the past 15 years in particular, teachers have been exhorted to take account of and provide for student individuality in learning rates and styles. Our data suggest, however, that this is not something often or readily done. Students worked independently at all levels but primarily on identical tasks, rather than on a variety of activities designed to accommodate their differences. . . . On the whole, teachers at all levels apparently did not know how to vary their instructional procedures, did not want to, or had some difficulty doing so. (1984, pp. 105-106)

A closer examination of the different social contexts of reading instruction substantiates Goodlad's view. Whole-class reading instruction, for example, is not intended to accommodate individual differences; it assumes that with respect to a particular skill or knowledge area, the children in the class are *not* different from one another. The social context of seatwork is essentially the same for everyone; while the materials students use may vary slightly, the routines they engage in during seatwork do not.

Ad hoc groups are a somewhat different matter. Ideally they would promote individualization in *both* the materials used and in the newly created group context. However, as we saw earlier, ad hoc groups are temporary, short-lived, and clearly supplementary to ability groups. One might argue that their temporary nature is itself an accommodation to individual differences and dynamics; teachers can disband a group once its members' "needs" have been met. But no teacher discussed ad hoc grouping in those terms; rather, they indicated that ad hoc groups met only for as long as the time available for them would permit, not for as long as was "necessary." Even more to the point, instruction in ad hoc groups paralleled patterns in ability group instruction. In this respect, ad hoc groups can promote individualization only to the degree that ability groups promote it.

A much larger proportion of my sample—30 percent—reported one-on-one contacts between teachers and children as a means of providing individual instruction. Most of these respondents, however, also noted that the classroom context severely constrains opportunities for individual help:

It's difficult to divide up my time among individuals this year because there are a number of social problems. Last year, with the more independent group, I could do that kind of thing. This year, I don't do anything completely individual. (*Blue Collar Suburb teacher*)

Honestly and truly, the reading group is all I have time for. Individual help is something that comes few and far between. If I can hit one kid, or two kids, once a week, for five or ten minutes, I'm lucky. With the size of the classroom, and what we're attempting to do, . . . there just isn't any time. (*Factory City teacher*)

This leaves the reading group as the primary social context within which teachers attend to individual needs. It is mainly in the reading group that teachers must try to provide educational interactions in sufficient amounts, of sufficient quality, and appropriate to each child. And *it is mainly in the reading group that the pursuit of routine and the pursuit of control take their toll on the teacher's ability to address individual differences*. There is a great deal of research evidence to suggest that the basic difference among reading groups is simply the pacing of instruction (Goodlad, 1979; Shannon, 1983). My own sample of teachers provided confirmation of these findings. The first response to the question, "How do you try to meet individual differences among your students?" almost always referred to variations in the pace of instruction for the different "ability" groups—even when the students varied along dimensions other than the rate of learning:

> I have three distinct groups, one very, very bright; it's the type where you just have to explain something once and they pick it up. Auditorally, visually, they're just exceptional. My middle group is pretty good visually; auditorally they still have a problem. Then I have a low group that's very, very slow; they have a lot of trouble with their blending, word attack skills, short vowels. With the top group, it's just a breeze. They're not even blending words anymore, they're so proficient at it; they're just reading them out of the textbook, and I ask them comprehension questions, and they just sail through. The second group is getting to that point; I'm not spending that much time on blending. But the third group is extremely slow; they just need so much help with those word attack skills and comprehension—they're just very weak in all those areas. (*Factory City teacher*)

Some (although not all) teachers also indicated that they respond to differences between the reading groups by spending additional time with their lower groups:

> I try to take the low group every day, the Dinosaurs group, which is the beginning book in first grade. I definitely take that group every day, and I definitely take the next group. My highest group, my middle second grade group, they're not all that far behind, so I'll try and get them in every day, but they can pretty much handle it if I miss a day. (*Trade City teacher*)

Taken together, then, these observations suggest that the sorting of children into ability groups as a way of responding to individual differences can promote at best some variation in the amount of interaction children engage in with their teacher, and in the pacing of the instruction that they receive. To put this in terms of the criteria for assessing opportunity, the social context of ability groups promotes interaction in sufficient amounts, but only with respect to the amount of time teachers give to different children. There was no indication that teachers worry about meeting Criterion 2, the quality of interaction, except with respect to the disruption of routines; the quality of the routines themselves was not called into question. And with respect to Criterion 3, interaction appropriate to the child, teachers concerned themselves only with the pacing of instruction. Attention to other kinds of differences (visual vs. auditory learning, for example) is provided outside the reading group context.

This is not to say that there are no other differences in what goes on in different reading groups. While exploratory in nature, the recent studies by Eder and Felmlee (1981, 1983, 1984) suggest that there may be very real differences among groups with respect to Criterion 2, the quality of interaction among group members and the teacher. These studies suggest that instruction in lower groups is more likely to be interrupted by teachers' responses to inattentive or disruptive behavior; that teachers are less likely to reprimand students in lower groups for violating others' oral reading turns; that student interactions in lower groups produce more inattentive and disruptive behavior than students might be likely to display on their own; and that students in lower groups are more negatively affected by outside interruptions than are students in higher groups. However, these differences are unintended consequences of ability grouping; teachers do not consciously seek to produce these patterns, nor are they intended to address differences among children. Although Criterion 2 may *need* attention in reading groups, it does not *receive* attention.

The practice of sorting children into ability groups suggests several important issues. First, the restrictions on how teachers attend to individual differences through ability grouping are clearly a result of the pursuit of routine and control. The pursuit of control narrows the means teachers use to meet Criterion 1; these means all revolve around the amount of time students spend with their teachers. Some teachers try to meet Criterion 1 by varying their time with children according to "need"; others do so by giving everyone roughly equal time. But in either case, the focus is strictly on teacher-child interactions. Indeed, one of the fundamental purposes of reading groups is to give children an opportunity to interact more easily on an individual basis with their teachers, not with one another. As we saw earlier, too much interaction with other children is usually seen as an indicator of poor skills, even though teachers recognize potential academic benefits:

I like to have children help each other. It's excellent when the peers work together. . . . [But] in my class there's a lot of behavior problems. They are so busy trying to communicate with other children, they don't have time to concentrate on what they are supposed to be learning. (*Trade City teacher*)

Just as the pursuit of control limits the means teachers use to meet Criterion 1, so routinization limits the means they use to meet Criterion 3. By trying to follow similar routines in all reading groups (even while acknowledging that different children will respond to these routines differently), teachers rule out options that would allow them to vary aspects of instruction other than pacing. In fact, by giving more time to behavior management in lower groups (Eder, 1981), teachers acknowledge the poor fit between typical instructional routines and the children assigned to these groups. The routines they try so hard to enforce apparently fail to meet Criterion 3, requiring instruction "appropriate to the child," and yet their response is to work even harder at enforcing them. This conclusion puts the research of Durkin (1978–79) and Shannon (1983) in a new light. Durkin's findings suggest that teachers do not instruct in comprehension—that is, instead of explaining to children *how* to develop or improve comprehension skills, they act as " 'mentioners,' assignment givers and checkers, and interrogators" (p. 523). Likewise, Shannon argues that teachers believe instruction consists of the application of commercial reading materials and that the instructional routines they use in applying these materials prevent them from reflecting on whether what they are doing in fact constitutes instruction. If Durkin and Shannon are right—and my argument so far certainly suggests that in this respect they are—then this is an important sense in which classrooms fail to provide equality of opportunity for children in lower reading groups. Children in higher groups often manage to figure out for themselves how to acquire and develop skills necessary for reading; even if they don't receive explicit instruction, they nevertheless manage to "pick it up" on their own (and some teachers' distribution of instructional time bears witness to this). Children in lower reading groups do not manage to figure these things out for themselves; what they need, according to Durkin and Shannon, is more instruction, not more mentioning, assigning, checking, and interrogating. What reading routines do is to promote the latter rather than the former—which is to say that routines can make the instruction in lower reading groups more inappropriate (Criterion 3) even as teachers struggle to provide it in greater amounts (Criterion 2).

Another important issue raised by ability grouping is that it not only limits teachers' attention to differences *between* groups, it also limits attention to individual differences *within* groups; and this is likely to be even more true for low groups than for higher groups. This is ironic because one of the presumed advantages of grouping is that it affords teachers more opportunities to establish close relationships with their students and to assess their needs more accurately. Several of my respondents, however, suggested that the very process of grouping requires some denial of individual differences. As we saw earlier, teachers occasionally put some of their students into groups that, strictly speaking, are not quite appropriate to those students' needs, in order to get a manageable number of groups; in some cases teachers even design their instruction to promote a workable distribution of skills. Teachers insist on organizing classrooms into the same basic pattern of three or four reading groups, irrespective of the actual range of differences among their students:

> In my room I deal with three reading levels, . . . 11, 13, and 15. So I have a variance in abilities. From one another, there must be a thousand differences. (*Trade City teacher*)

> We have everything from kids who can't read to kids who are reading everything in sight. . . . I have four reading groups right now. (*White Collar Suburb teacher*)

> In my class there are more similarities than differences, because I have more of a readiness group. They came with a very weak language development. Most of them did not know their beginning sounds, so I had to start with a real basic program of phonics, just learning their beginning sounds. . . . I try to get three even size groups in, only because it frees my time to walk around the room and see what they're doing. (*Factory City teacher*)

These observations suggest that the routines associated with reading group instruction force teachers to resolve the paradox of collective instruction ("teach everyone but meet individual needs") in favor of treating students similarly rather than in favor of treating them differently. Teachers confronted with a wide range of skills and styles (leaving aside for the moment the nature of these differences) confront a difficult educational problem. Earlier in this chapter, I quoted from a teacher who began the school year with seven reading groups and who solved her problem by teaching skills that would permit her to reduce the number of reading groups to three. If she had maintained her classroom organization according to initial ability differences, she would have failed to deliver instruction to everyone. Thus, her educational problem was complicated by management considerations; ultimately, her solution to the problem was managerial in nature. She taught the children the skills they would need to function in a reduced number of reading groups, because it was only in that context that she could manage to deliver reading instruction to everyone. The paradox of collective instruction was "resolved" for this teacher by narrowing the parameters within which she had to individualize. This mitigated the management complications, but may have compromised instructional effectiveness. The persistence of the three reading group arrangement can depress or distort teachers' reflections on individual needs. Teachers are forced to *label* six to nine children as similar to one another—whether or not they actually are—and as different from everyone else—whether or not they actually are. If this labeling process does not easily produce three distinct groupings, teachers may take steps that actually *create* the appropriate range of differences. The need to teach everyone produces three roughly equal-sized groups regardless of whether or not that pattern is appropriate; and teachers treat students in the groups as similar to one another in an effort to achieve that classroom organization.

The process of grouping in and of itself thus limits teachers' ability to attend to a variety of individual differences among their students. Teachers provided further evidence that the *results* of grouping also constrain their attention to individual differences, particularly within the lower reading groups:

> With the low group, you start them out just about the same, because they all need just about the same skills. As they go along, I might give one child a slightly different worksheet. With the top group, I have more latitude; I give them independent assignments, book reports, things like that. (*Blue Collar Suburb teacher*)

> With my lower group, I have to keep reinforcing the skills. The skills that the upper groups have are going beyond; my top group is working on similes and metaphors and things of this sort. [But] I would say with my lower groups I work on reading skills a great deal more. [With] my upper groups, I work on appreciation a lot, enjoyment of reading, getting good feelings from it, and broadening ourselves. My highest group is off doing more individualized things like research projects, writing reports, and sharing with each other. So there's a tremendous amount of broadening. (*Factory City teacher*)

Not all teachers claimed to provide more diversity in the group learning experiences of high achievers than of low achievers, as these teachers claimed to do; however, no teacher claimed to provide greater within-group diversity for low achievers than for high achievers. Many did discuss attempts to individualize *outside* the reading group context, but as we have seen, these attempts are supplementary, secondary, and often sporadic, despite teachers' best intentions. The need to "get the groups in first," felt most strongly for the lower groups, uses up most of the available time and leaves the low achievers with the fewest opportunities to pursue self-selected and/or individually tailored reading activities.

The complications of power and influence in classrooms reinforce the distribution of opportunities suggested in this analysis. Homogeneous ability grouping keeps low-achieving students whose behaviors fit poorly with reading group routines in close proximity with one another; low-achieving students are thus most likely to be influenced by the behavior of other low-achieving students, producing poorer quality interactions (Criterion 3) in lower groups than in higher ones. Teachers must work harder in those groups to enforce their behavioral norms and gain consent to their academic plans for these students; in spending more of their own power resources on lower-achieving children, teachers deny these children opportunity to develop the capacity to create their *own* educational plans—that is, to exercise power over their own education. "Brighter" children, taught at a faster pace in reading groups that often occupy a smaller portion of their time, have more time available for self-directed or cooperative reading activities; and the capacity to plan one's own education, like other capacities, is strengthened with practice. Teachers assume that "slower" children are less capable of "handling" such opportunities. Lacking the opportunity, it is no wonder they also lack the skills. In the end, their lack of planning skills prevents these children from gaining a sense of educational empowerment.

In short, the classroom mobilization of bias favors the following practices: Assess children against the same standards by following the same procedures; use the same materials and supplement them as time, imagination, and energy permit; treat teacher-child interactions as central to every child's learning; vary pacing, but rely on essentially the same instructional routines for everyone. These practices hurt the teacher's ability to respond to *every* child's individual needs, but the penalities are more severe for low-income students, who are disproportionately assigned to low-achieving reading groups.

THE MOBILIZATION OF BIAS
AND THE PARALYSIS OF INNOVATION

The profession of elementary education hardly suffers from a shortage of reform proposals; scholars have advocated a variety of changes intended to improve equality of opportunity at the classroom level. My findings on the mobilization of bias in the classroom suggest an important conclusion about the future of classroom innovation: There are a number of ways classrooms *could* change to accommodate better the educational needs of economically deprived children, but the coping strategies teachers use in response to the paradox of collective instruction, the problem of professional uncertainty, and the complexities of power and influence make significant teacher-initiated changes unlikely.

With respect to assessing individual need, the two reforms most commonly advocated involve devising tests more appropriate to children of different economic and ethnic backgrounds[5] and improving teachers' approaches to observing and reflecting on children's classroom behaviors (Davy, 1983). Both proposals assume that strengthening assessment in terms of Criterion 3—appropriateness for each child—would substantially equalize educational opportunities. However, while "more appropriate" testing may indeed be desirable, even if difficult to achieve, it would have limited impact on teachers' assessment practices because teachers use test results in conjunction with observation; for new tests to make a difference in assessment, observation practices would have to change too. This is particularly apparent in view of the fact that more teachers referred to their observational information than to their test information when asked to describe how they assessed their students.

This leaves us with the option of improving teachers' ability not only to observe classroom behaviors but to reflect appropriately on what they see. The problem teachers face in this dimension of opportunity is that the instructional routines against which children's needs are assessed do not permit them to display a very wide range of capabilities, either cognitive or social. Advantaged children generally master the "forms" of instruction better than economically disadvantaged children do; as a result, economically advantaged children look less educationally needy. Furthermore, the problem of professional uncertainty makes it very likely that the pursuit of these routines—and the model of social and cognitive development they promote—will continue to characterize life in classrooms during reading instruction. The maintenance of instructional contexts that facilitate familiar routines supersedes the call to diversify assessment; the incentive to protect what little stability the classroom offers outweighs the incentive to improve diagnosis. One can hardly blame teachers for not wanting to tackle the task of diversifying assessment in their own world when the technical experts have been less than successful in theirs.

Prospects for change in the second dimension of equal opportunity, the provision of material resources, are similarly constrained. Most proposals intended to enhance individualization in the materials children use to learn to read focus on the criterion of "appropriateness to the child." However, the debate over the meaning of "appropriateness" in testing extends to the analysis of reading materials.[6] Given a lack of agreement in the scholarly community over what constitutes "appropriate" material for poor and minority children, it is no surprise that teachers rely so heavily on basal readers. The debate exacerbates the professional uncertainty they already face in the classroom and promotes what Shannon (1983) calls the "reification" of instruction—reducing instruction to the application of commercial reading materials. This problem would not go away even if teachers were to find and use materials that everyone agreed were "more appropriate." Teachers would adopt such material and try to use it for everyone, rather than using it to diversify material opportunities for different students. The forces that produce a mobilization of bias which narrows the selection of reading materials thus paralyze the incentive to innovate in this dimension of opportunity.

This brings us to the third dimension of equality of opportunity, the structuring of educational interactions. Once again, a number of reform proposals address Criterion 3, the appropriateness of interactions. Some scholars, for example, call for the dismantling of homogeneous ability groups. The most persuasive of these is Jeannie Oakes (1985), who studied the effects of tracking in 297 secondary school classrooms. She found that "students in different groups were exposed to dramatically different qualities of knowledge" (p. 192); that "high track students had more time to learn and more exposure to what seemed to be effective teaching behaviors than did other groups" (p. 193); and that "the brightest and highest achieving students appear to do well regardless of the configuration of groups they learn with" (p. 194). Her research also casts substantial doubt on the educational assumptions guiding homogeneous grouping. Alternative forms of classroom organization, in this view, would promote closer attention to individual needs and would enhance teachers' ability to provide educational interactions appropriate to each child.

However, the findings of this chapter suggest that the modal classroom, left to its own devices, is not likely to achieve organizational or instructional reform; moreover, it is not entirely clear that even if reorganization were implemented, opportunity would be equalized to any significant degree. Abandoning homogeneous ability groups requires a degree of innovativeness that classrooms are not likely to stimulate or accommodate. After all, the paradox of collective instruction is one of the classroom dilemmas that ability groups help to resolve, while the routines pursued in these groups help teachers to cope with the problem of professional uncertainty. As suggested earlier, departures from these routines in alternative modes of organization or interaction, such as one-on-one or ad hoc group instruction, are brief and temporary, and in many cases the routines pervading these alternatives are not very different from the routines pervading reading groups. Innovations tend to be add-ons, rather than replacements or substitutes for business as usual. The reason for this pattern is clear: innovation heightens uncertainty. The incentive to innovate is paralyzed by the inevitable disruption and ambiguity new practices promote. Of the many teachers I interviewed, only one indicated that she had once abandoned ability grouping for an entire school year, and only because her students that year were not able to master the routines of "independent" seatwork when they were not in their reading groups. The following year she went back to her normal grouping practices. Having once learned how to deliver reading instruction to classrooms divided into ability groups, teachers are likely to maintain that organizational pattern, because they know how to manage their resources of time and energy in the three-group setting. The teachers who aim their instruction at getting children into the "right" number of groups illustrate the energy teachers will invest in avoiding the uncertainties of innovation. The problem here is not pernicious or dull-witted teachers; the problem is the inherently uncertain and paradoxical nature of the professional tasks teachers confront.

The classroom mobilization of bias thus shapes schooling for the poor both now and in the future. The analysis offered in this chapter demonstrates that all three dimensions of opportunity in the classroom are significantly affected on a daily basis by the teacher's pursuit of control and routine, which serve as coping strategies necessitated by the paradox of collective instruction, the problem of professional uncertainty, and the complexities of classroom power and influence. These classroom dynamics and teachers' responses to them severely limit the means teachers use to pay attention to individual differences in assessment, the provision of resources, and the structuring of interactions. The classroom mobilization of bias poses greater difficulties for economically disadvantaged children, who are more likely to be assigned to lower reading groups in classrooms at all levels and in all school districts, and it restricts the likelihood of teacher-initiated innovations which might equalize opportunities.

While teachers might not describe the limitations and constraints of the classroom context in quite the same ways that I have portrayed them, most would readily agree that classroom opportunities are, in fact, limited and constrained. Based on many years of intensive conversation and extensive work with classroom teachers, Sarason observes:

> Faced with numbers and diversity of children *and* the pressure to adhere to a time schedule presents the teacher not with a difficult task but an impossible one. I say impossible because I have never met a teacher who was not aware of and disturbed by the fact that he or she had not the time to give to some children in the class the kind of help they needed—and the need for help, it should be emphasized, is frequently not due to any basic intellectual defect. (1982, p. 187)

Teachers are acutely aware of the inherent constraints in the social contexts of instruction, and it is for precisely this reason that most school systems supplement classroom instruction with extra help from "outside." Many low-income and minority children receive additional instruction from Title I/Chapter 1 teachers and district reading consultants, and the following chapter explores the contributions reading specialists can—and cannot—make to the provision of educational opportunity.

3

More of the Same
Reading Specialists
and the Mobilization of Bias

I had one little boy who came in one day and just didn't feel like working on his reading. He protested, "Why do I have to come to reading
anyway?" So I thought it would be good to have a little talk and I
asked him, "Why do you think you have to come here?" He began to
look sheepish and said he didn't think he should tell me. But finally he
said, "My teacher's in poor health." I sort of hid my smile and asked
why he thought that, and he said, "She keeps telling me she has to
save all her strength for me!" (*White Collar Suburb reading consultant*)

Although this youngster's diagnosis of his teacher's health may have
been off the mark, he was right about one thing: Special services in reading
instruction help teachers more often than they help children. Although
reading specialists are supposed to expand the opportunities available to
children learning to read, especially in the tutorial instruction they provide
low achievers, their services actually replicate and reinforce the classroom
mobilization of bias. A careful examination of the terms on which they give
assistance to classroom teachers and instruction to low-achieving children
shows that Title I/Chapter 1 teachers and district reading consultants
usually provide "more of the same" in the learning opportunities available in
and out of the classroom.

While not the whole story, this analysis can go a long way toward
explaining why evaluation studies have not demonstrated conclusively that
the services funded by Title I/Chapter 1 programs are responsible for
improving the achievement of low-income children.[1] The story here is much
like the story told in Chapter 2. The failure of special reading services to
expand children's opportunities is due, not to inadequate teaching, bad
intentions, or lack of funding, but to the social dynamics surrounding
special instruction and its relationship to the classroom.

NEITHER FISH NOR FOWL:
WHAT SPECIALISTS DO AND HOW THEY DO IT

In the four school districts I investigated, there were two major kinds of reading specialists. *Reading consultants*, paid from school district budgets, were responsible for three kinds of tasks: administering the mechanics of the reading program, monitoring and assisting the teachers, and working with individual children.[2] Consultants periodically gave the standardized reading tests that assess children's progress and kept track of results as the program required. Many made the initial decisions about placement in the reading groups at the beginning of the school year, which teachers then adjusted as they saw fit. Consultants were also responsible for distributing textbooks, worksheets, educational games, and so forth, both on a routine basis and when teachers asked for extra materials. Children experiencing difficulty in their reading groups would often go to the consultant for additional testing and diagnosis.

My sample of consultants also served as experts-in-residence. Many prepared or coordinated school-wide workshops, as well as suggesting new materials or activities for particular teachers to incorporate in their reading lessons. When new programs were initiated, the reading consultants often bore the brunt of implementation, monitoring the use of new materials, responding to complaints, and making necessary adjustments. Finally, reading consultants were asked to help classroom teachers in overcoming any trouble they might have had in specific aspects of reading instruction. If a teacher had difficulty explaining vowel sounds, for example, a consultant might do a demonstration lesson on vowels in the teacher's classroom, or suggest alternative materials or approaches.

Depending on the number of schools they served, consultants also worked directly with children who needed special help in reading. Typically this required them to tutor a number of low-achieving students outside the classroom three or four times a week, a practice colloquially known as the "pull-out" approach. Some consultants worked with "gifted" children on occasion, but far more often they gave their attention to "slow" learners. The districts I sampled had different rules for selection, but they usually included some combination of teacher recommendation, consultant diagnosis, and test results. The nature of a consultant's remedial services depended on the classroom reading program and on the combined preferences of the classroom teacher, the consultant, the principal, and the district reading supervisor. Due to budget reductions, many school districts had to cut back the size of their consultant staffs; when there were fewer consultants to allocate to the same number of schools, it was this aspect of their jobs— working with children—which was the first to be dropped.

The second major kind of reading specialist is the *Title I/Chapter 1 teacher*, paid from federal funds and subject to Title I/Chapter 1 rules.[3] Each school with a Title I program had one or more Title I teachers assigned exclusively to that school, with most working on an hourly wage, part-time basis. As in most programs nationwide, the Title I teachers I interviewed concentrated their efforts in reading instruction (J. Anderson, 1983), providing remedial services primarily on a small-group, "pull-out" basis.[4] In one of the four districts, however, Title I teachers were being asked to shift into the classroom for remedial instruction and teacher assistance, in order to spread the benefits of Title I services more widely without diluting their impact on the population of target children.[5] As federal funds decrease and the pool of Title I/Chapter 1 teachers shrinks, this practice is likely to become more common (Gaffney & Schember, 1982, p. xii). The other districts were also increasing the time Title I teachers were spending in the classrooms, and all four of the districts emphasized the coordination of special services with the classroom program of instruction.

Many Title I teachers provided administrative and "expert" services to the teachers in addition to the tutorial help they gave to low-achieving readers. In fact, in several schools the Title I teacher was referred to as the "reading consultant." A Title I teacher in Trade City explained:

> According to the rules, . . . I'm supposed to make myself available to help children who need special reading help. That's supposed to be it. But it's much more than that, because I sit in on all meetings, I help form in-school policy. I keep an inventory of all the reading materials. . . . I supply the teachers with what they need, and I do the [textbook] orders.

Another Title I teacher, working in Factory City, painted a similar picture:

> I am in charge of inventory, passing out all the materials to the teachers, and then collecting it. . . . When they test, . . . I have helped the teachers correct the tests to interpret the scores. . . . I look at it as if I have two separate functions. One is working with the children, try-ing to bring them up to grade level, and my second function is working with the teachers, making sure that their reading program is working along in the classroom.

The particular distribution of a Title I teacher's responsibilities depended on the school he or she was in, rather than on the federal legislation or the federal, state, or local administrative rules establishing guidelines for their activities. In contrast to reading consultants, Title I teachers did appear to spend a larger proportion of their time working with children. But on the whole, the activities of the Title I teachers in my sample did not look very different from the activities of the district reading consultants; differences between them seemed to be more a matter of degree than of kind.

This mixture of responsibilities for both kinds of reading specialists poses interesting problems in their working relationships with classroom teachers. Fullan's review of the limited research available on district consultants (1982, pp. 181–82) emphasizes the multiple and somewhat conflicting roles specialists assume with respect to classroom teachers. As administrators, their job is primarily to help the teachers; as "experts" and tutors, they are supposed to help students. But the very fact that special tutorial help is necessary attests to the inability of the classroom teacher to meet the needs of all students so that each is reading "to the best of his or her ability." Add to this the advice and counsel specialists are expected to give teachers, and the result is a "service" that is easily interpreted as a threat. Offering support and criticism at the same time is no easy task; as one White Collar Suburb consultant put it, "I'm neither fish nor fowl." Understanding how specialists manage to provide this kind of supportive criticism is one key to understanding their contributions to the classroom mobilization of bias.

Both classroom teachers and specialists pointed to the potential threats posed by the provision of special services for reading. Classroom teachers gave evidence indirectly, primarily by confiding that they were "not threatened" by help from the school reading specialist. These assurances were not elicited by any direct questions from me about whether or not they felt threatened. A few examples will illustrate this observation. One teacher in Factory City recounted the following story:

> Last year we lost a teacher and we reorganized, and I ended up with a split grade. I kept my original group of 13 slow first graders, and I ended up with an additional 12 very bright second graders. I had never taught second grade, to top it all off, and I got these kids in September. So I just didn't know what to do. The principal was very good about it; he brought in materials, he sent the reading teacher to help me . . . and it worked out beautifully. I didn't feel threatened, I think because I was so glad to get the help because I didn't know what in God's name I was doing. I'm not insecure about my job; I feel I'm a good teacher and I do a good job, and I feel the principal knows that as well.

Another teacher, describing the general working relationship between the classroom teachers and the Title I reading teacher in her school, noted, "There's no hostility; there's friendliness, understanding, and a willingness to help back and forth. We actually help each other." And still another teacher, whose reading consultant was shared among several schools, assessed her working relationship with the consultant as follows: "I have always felt that I could go to her at any time, that she was there to be helpful, not to criticize. I have never felt criticism from her in any way." In these examples, the classroom teachers denied a proposition which I never advanced: that classroom teachers usually feel threatened by the help offered by a reading specialist. To be sure, their unsolicited denials do not constitute proof that specialists pose a threat to their classroom colleagues. But these remarks do suggest that classroom teachers see specialists as a potential challenge, and they believe that tensions would develop unless staff members actively work together to avert them.

Specialists seemed all too aware of the hostility their "help" can provoke. Their response was to approach classroom teachers with caution and a measure of deference. The need to earn the trust of classroom teachers was by far the most frequently articulated theme in reading specialists' descriptions of their working relationships with classroom teachers. A reading consultant from Trade City said it best:

> They have to trust me. They have to first realize that I am not there to criticize. I'm there to help. The minute I lose their confidence, I'll never be able to do anything for them. I am there only as a teacher, helping them; I am not there as a supervisor or a "snoopervisor."

The consultants and Title I teachers I interviewed resolved the dilemmas of supportive criticism by downplaying their supervisory functions and treating classroom teachers as peers. A consultant in White Collar Suburb was quite direct on this point:

> I try to be a help rather than a supervisor. None of [the consultants] in the district really want supervisory authority. We get a lot more mileage out of being peers with the teachers than out of being authorities.

Three of the 15 specialists interviewed made a point of mentioning (without being asked) that their salaries are no higher than those of classroom teachers, as if to emphasize their status as teachers' peers.

Comments like these suggest that an "ideology of supportiveness" guides the relationship between reading specialists and classroom teachers. A Title I teacher from Trade City summarized this ideology most clearly:

> When you come into this program, your mentality has to be changed, because you don't make the decisions like you do in the classroom; you support the decisions that another teacher has made. . . . You can't

be dogmatic if you're in a tutorial situation, because the kids aren't really yours, you're just there to help.

Further evidence of the "ideology of supportiveness" is furnished in the way reading specialists emphasize the centrality of the classroom experience for a child's progress in reading. When asked, "What do you think your job is with respect to reading?" most specialists replied in terms of the classroom. The clearest example came from a Title I teacher in Blue Collar Suburb:

> [My job is] to help the kids to function better in the classroom. We're getting the children, and they're falling farther and farther behind in their reading, and it makes it more difficult for them to function in the classroom. Well, obviously it's not just in the classroom; you want them to function well in life. But right now their world is bordered by the classroom. . . . So I think that's our main objective.

Another Title I teacher in Trade City put it more succinctly: "I am a tutor, basically. . . . I support the teachers in the skills that they are trying to get over in the classroom."

As a result of the ideology of supportiveness, the specialist's ultimate goal of expanding opportunities for children is subordinated to the goal of helping teachers. Put in terms of the features of classroom life discussed earlier, reading specialists are used in two capacities: to mitigate the problem of professional uncertainty, by providing administrative assistance and professional advice to teachers; and to help resolve the paradox of collective instruction by providing more "individualized" instruction to students. In the following discussion I will argue that specialists' efforts to help teachers reduce uncertainty limit both their ability to influence teachers' classroom behaviors and their choices in providing instruction directly to students. The ideology of supportiveness dominates the power and influence relationships between specialists and classroom teachers, so that the services specialists provide are unlikely to expand opportunity inside or outside the classroom.

READING SPECIALISTS
AND THE PROBLEM OF PROFESSIONAL UNCERTAINTY

Both classroom teachers and reading specialists were asked to describe the contributions specialists make to the school reading program, and to discuss their working relationships with one another. Their responses suggested that the assistance of reading specialists involves both advantages and disadvantages for classroom teachers, depending on the impact of their services on the professional uncertainty that characterizes classroom reading instruction. Most importantly, the interviews suggested that, because of the "ideology of supportiveness," the perspectives and behaviors of classroom teachers significantly influence the perceptions and behaviors of reading specialists.

How Special Services Help Classroom Teachers

A number of classroom teachers mentioned several specific benefits of the reading specialist's activities. For the most part, their remarks did not claim significant improvement in the reading abilities of their students; rather, they focused on the specialist's support for the teacher's role in the classroom. First, they remarked on the benefits of the administrative tasks reading specialists perform. A fourth-grade teacher in Trade City commented:

> [The Title I teacher] sets up our reading groups in the beginning of the year . . . so I don't have to do it, and that's very good. . . . I enjoy re-linquishing that responsibility to her.

Other teachers mentioned the advantages of having a reading specialist who reviews, coordinates, and distributes reading materials on a routine basis; as one respondent in White Collar Suburb put it, "She's really a resource person."

A second advantage of the specialist's job, according to classroom teachers, was the availability of professional expertise in reading. Reading specialists are expected to be more familiar with the series in use in the district, and with supplementary materials as well; they are also supposed to be more expert in the use of diagnostic techniques, providing suggestions for teachers who are perplexed about how to meet individual children's needs. Both Title I teachers and reading consultants were often expected to be well-versed in how to teach particular skills in reading and to be able to explain "appropriate" methods of instruction to teachers who needed assistance in that area:

> If I had a question about a particular child, how [I could] help this child better, I would tell [the Title I teacher] about this child, and she would give me suggestions about different things I could use, different books, workbooks, or techniques. (*Factory City teacher*)

First-year teachers, or teachers teaching a new age group for the first time, may also rely heavily on the aid of Title I/Chapter 1 or consultant staff, as did this teacher in Trade City:

I used to be a kindergarten teacher, and when I took over first grade, [the Title I teacher] was very helpful to me in showing me different methods of teaching with the reading program—I had never done it. She's instructive, when you ask her.

Notice this teacher's conclusion: ". . . when you ask her." In teachers' accounts of specific instances when they had been helped by a specialist's expertise, it was almost always the classroom teacher who had initiated the interaction. Rarely did a teacher praise a specialist who simply dropped in to the classroom to observe and then offered advice or new materials. In those cases where a teacher did indicate appreciation for specialist-initiated help, the teacher had usually issued a general invitation to the specialist in the past. As one teacher said:

[The Title I teacher] constantly brings me materials to help the children. If she sees something new, she knows I always like anything innovative, so she's always bringing me things.

A third facet of the specialist's job which classroom teachers viewed as advantageous to them was the time specialists spent working with low-achieving children on an individual or small-group basis. Teachers usually referred to such remedial time as "reinforcement" of what they were doing in the classroom. In her description of the Title I teacher's remedial activities, a Trade City teacher explained:

[The Title I teacher] reinforces skills that I am working on with those particular children. . . . She works with them individually one-to-one [and] she can make clarifications, whereas in a group situation, I'm not always able to do it.

Not only does this tutorial time presumably enhance the experience of "educationally deprived" children, it also affects the experience of the rest of the students. A few classroom teachers pointed out that, when the Title I students leave the room for remediation, "it gives [the teacher] a chance to work with smaller groups of children in [his or her] own classroom; they can get a little bit more individual attention."

All three of the benefits of special reading services cited by classroom teachers help to reduce the professional uncertainty they experience in trying to meet children's needs. Specialists' administrative services help to mitigate the difficult allocative decisions classroom teachers face as they distribute limited resources in crowded, busy, and unpredictable classrooms. Of those resources, teachers believe their time and energy to be particularly important, and the administrative activities of reading specialists help to conserve both and reduce conflict. Although research does not conclusively demonstrate that an increase or decrease in the administrative responsibilities of classroom teachers directly affects the amount or quality of time teachers spend in instruction (Levin, 1984), nonetheless, when teachers are relieved of administrative tasks, there are simply fewer choices they have to make about how to allocate time. In the words of one teacher whose school was planning to cut back its Title I staff, "It's just going to put more on us when she goes this year."

Similarly, the educational "expertise" provided by both consultants and teachers is readily understood in the context of uncertainty reduction. Classroom teachers can call on the judgments of professional experts who are presumed to know more than most teachers about the process of reading and the resources available to enhance student learning. The lack of a technical culture and the ambiguity of the social contexts of instruction are not so keenly felt when there are experts available. Interestingly, although consultants do have additional training in reading, it is not at all clear whether Title I/Chapter 1 teachers are also more "expert" in reading than classroom teachers.[6] Nevertheless, that Title I teachers are *treated* as experts was evident in the observations of a Trade City teacher:

> [The Title I teacher can] give us the kind of documentation that we need when we go into, let's say, a Planning and Placement Team meeting. It's one thing for the classroom teacher to say, "I feel the child is reading at this level or that level," but when it comes from the [Title I teacher] who has also done formal testing with the child, I think that it substantiates the teacher's position to a greater degree.

Specialists, too, commented on the way their expertise can mitigate uncertainty. They are typically asked, as one Title I teacher observed, "whether the kids are really producing what is expected of them, if [they are] capable of doing it. If a [particular child] is not capable of doing it, [they ask if he] should be recommended for testing, so he could be placed where he can function." A teacher may ask a specialist to evaluate the teacher's own assessments and instructional activities as well. A Trade City reading consultant assisting in the introduction of the district's new reading series said that the question teachers most frequently ask her is "if they are doing what they are supposed to be doing. That seems to be their main concern. It seems to be a year when we're searching, making sure what we're all doing, especially with the new reading program." A Title I teacher in Blue Collar Suburb said that the teachers mainly wanted to know:

> . . . how they're doing compared to other schools. . . . Are they moving fast enough, or are they moving too quickly? Even though emphasis

has been put on teacher judgment, no matter what the tests say, when the teachers feel [that perhaps] the child should be up or should be lowered, they're still hesitant in moving the child up or regrouping.

Finally, the desire to reduce uncertainty explains why teachers only appreciate the "expert" suggestions they have asked for. Unsolicited information serves to increase, rather than decrease, ambiguity; it widens the range of options, raising questions instead of answering them. A specialist's advice thus tends to be offered—and appreciated—on a "by invitation only" basis.

The tutorial function of reading specialists also reduces uncertainty in classroom reading instruction. When "problem children" are removed, the teacher is left with a group that is smaller in size and is meeting with some success in the classroom program. This has a double effect: it reduces classroom crowding and eases allocative pressures; and it reduces the range of individual differences the teacher must try to meet. In short, the classroom program "works" for the children who remain after the remedial children have left, requiring less guesswork for teachers trying to meet the needs of their students. When the remedial children return, they have usually been tutored in the skills they needed to improve in order to work better within the program of classroom instruction. When the tutoring is "successful," the classroom program then "works better" for the remedial children too, reducing yet again the uncertainties teachers face in trying to meet their needs.

How Special Services Bother Classroom Teachers

Just as the advantages teachers see in special reading services can be interpreted in light of the desire to reduce professional uncertainty, so, too, can the disadvantages they cite. The relationship between classroom teachers and reading specialists is not without its difficulties, although only about 20% of the classroom teachers interviewed offered specific criticisms.[7] Eight teachers indicated that there was seldom enough time available for consultation and coordination with the school specialist. Surprisingly, these teachers were distributed among all four districts, which varied widely in the availability of special services in different schools. A teacher in Blue Collar Suburb noted:

I have found in this school that time and space is very difficult. If there's a question I want to ask [a Title I teacher], or that she wants to ask me, we have to make the time; but as far as any informal communication or discussion, there isn't any, because we just don't see one another.

And a teacher in White Collar Suburb, where each school had its own consultant, commented:

> I just can't take the time during the day to go see [the reading consultant], and she doesn't come in before nine. If she could get here at eight-fifteen or something, that would help.

Teachers dislike limitations on their contacts with specialists because it prevents specialists from "coordinating" remedial instruction with what the teachers are doing in the classroom. A retired first-grade teacher in Trade City put it this way:

> Sometimes [the consultants] seem to be working entirely on their own, so you feel you don't know what they're doing and they don't know what you're doing. So there is a big conflict. I don't believe there's any time allotted in the school schedule for that—if you do talk it's usually before school or after school or your lunch hour.

And predictably, the highest praise went to specialists who consult carefully with classroom teachers, determining what skills the teachers were emphasizing in the classroom, and pinpointing the areas in which the teachers believed the children needed the most assistance. Classroom teachers blamed the failure to coordinate either on the insensitivity of the specialists or on the overloaded "system" which restricted opportunities for consultation.

Teachers also complained about the impact of tutorial services on classroom schedules. While admitting that this was a minor issue in the provision of services, eleven teachers mentioned the complications of allowing different children to leave the classroom for different reasons at different times of day:

> The classroom teachers have to do a lot of bending for the Title I teachers, for example, in the time the kids have to leave the rooms. Now, I know they have to have a schedule, but the kids leave during science, or social studies, or whatever. I do realize that they go off for a purpose, but I must admit I grudge the time a little.

At the heart of these problems is the potential threat they pose to stable classroom instructional routines. The successful reading specialist, according to classroom teachers, is the one who enables the children he or she tutors to function better in the classroom, particularly in the reading groups to which they have been assigned. Specialists who fail to coordinate with classroom teachers concerning the skills they teach or the schedule they adopt heighten the professional uncertainties with which teachers must cope. In the words of Ann Lieberman (1982, pp. 256–57), "People who are sent in to aid the teacher . . . may often be seen as hinderers, not because teachers do not need help with their work, but because the complexity is now increased and the control disturbed."

The ideology of supportiveness is evident in specialists' responses to classroom teachers on these issues. In approaching the teachers about releasing the children for tutorial services, specialists acknowledge the difficulties their activities pose for the classroom schedule. As one Title I teacher observed,

> I think it's always difficult because you're taking the children out of the classroom, and there's no good time to take them out. They're missing something. Very often it's penmanship, social studies, science, something. And I think we all have mixed feelings about that. These kids can't afford to miss any classroom time, but yet we're taking them out.

Specialists also recognize their own removal from the classroom situation, preferring to respond rather than to initiate:

> I feel that I would rather be approached than to go in and make suggestions. Because how do I know what someone else's situation is? I'm in my room taking care of my groups, so naturally I don't know what's going on in some other room. . . . So if they come to me and ask for suggestions, I give them. But I wait for [the teachers].

One reading consultant said that she relies on the principal to let teachers know that her job is to help and support them in their classroom efforts, hoping that this would promote the kind of coordination the teachers are looking for:

> The tone that the principal sets helps, in introducing [me] and saying many of the things that I could help [the teachers] with; then they know, and there shouldn't be any problems, because the principal has set the tone, how I will be there to help the teachers. I think that's a key.

Several respondents did provide some legal justification for the ideology of supportiveness, particularly with respect to "coordinating" Title I services. For one thing, federal regulations pertaining to Title I/Chapter 1 encourage "the coordination of Title I instructional services with services provided under other programs, including the regular instructional program provided by the LEA" (Advanced Technology, 1983, pp. 5–6). Title I teachers and supervisors also pointed to the requirement that services funded by Title I "supplement, not supplant" the instruction in the regular classroom setting. What is remarkable is that neither of these guidelines must necessarily be interpreted to have anything to do with teaching behaviors. A careful reading of the relevant documents suggests that the first rule—"coordinate"—pertains to district-level curriculum decisions, while the second—"supplement"—pertains to funding arrangements (Gaffney & Schember, 1982). Yet both guidelines have become ensconced in Title I/ Chapter 1 teaching tradition. Specialists appeared to believe that if they provided services that differed from those in the classroom, they would be "supplanting" the classroom program, instead of supplementing it; furthermore, they seemed to think that different kinds of instruction could not be "coordinated" with one another. Their version of "coordination" was, in fact, replication. In the end, the street-level operationalization of these administrative guidelines demonstrates the propensity for reading specialists to help their classroom counterparts avoid professional uncertainty. By taking their cues from the classroom, reading specialists define the "special needs of educationally deprived children" in terms of the needs of their classroom teachers.

READING SPECIALISTS
AND THE COMPLICATIONS OF POWER AND INFLUENCE

The ideology of supportiveness adopted by reading consultants and Title I teachers is an important feature of their power and influence relationship with classroom teachers. It affects the available resources, the way each party uses these resources, and the context in which they conduct their relationship. And it ultimately affects the contributions specialists can and cannot make toward expanding equality of opportunity in public schools.

Resources

While both teachers and reading specialists have access to a number of power and influence resources, teachers have the upper hand. On the face of it, we might expect specialists to have two important resources in their access to information and their control over material goods. Even if they lack sophisticated knowledge of instructional theories, diagnostic techniques, and the like, reading specialists still have information about the resources available in their schools (tests, texts, dittos, and the like), and they exercise some discretion concerning which teachers receive which kinds of resources. On the other hand, the information specialists have loses some of its potential influence because it is not sufficiently connected with the rewards of teaching. Despite the emphasis specialists and principals place on the "help" specialists can give classroom teachers, there is no guarantee that "expert" advice or "better" texts will bring results. The inclusion of specialists has not changed the structure of incentives that teachers face; the rewards of teaching remain tied to the classroom experience. For this reason, teachers rarely find their working relationships with specialists intrinsically rewarding; a specialist's help is only rewarding if it is productive in the context of the teacher-child relationship. Professional uncertainty means that specialists cannot guarantee that their information or material resources will deliver in the classroom context, so they are in no position to make either promises or threats; the "help" they offer may turn out to be no help at all, or even worse, to be a hindrance. The problem of professional uncertainty thus impinges on the world of the reading specialist as much as on the world of the classroom teacher, diluting the resources specialists might use in exercising influence over classroom teachers.

More important, the ideology of supportiveness means that specialists will only provide information and material resources that coincide with the teacher's agenda for classroom instruction. One might think that the specialist's roles as administrator, tutor, and "expert" would make the specialist the primary planner for low-achieving children. But this is not the case. *The ideology of supportiveness subordinates the specialist's plans to those of the classroom teacher.* Specialists are encouraged to make their plans for students or teachers only after they have apprised themselves of the teacher's plans. The pressure to "coordinate" with the classroom program makes teachers the primary planners; specialists rely on teachers to tell them when their help is wanted, what kind of help is needed, and which students should be the targets of their help. The specialist's need to earn the trust of classroom teachers, and his or her reluctance to approach teachers without an invitation, gives teachers a measure of power that specialists lack.

This is not to say that specialists lack influence, however. The information and material resources they provide can alter in small ways what the teacher does; and the lack of time to "coordinate" does provide a modicum of autonomy for specialists in delivering services directly to children. Certainly the influence of a particular specialist will depend in part on his or her style as well as on the context of the school. My sample of specialists also varied in their compliance with administrative rules and guidelines. But these individual variations do not significantly affect the power and influence resources available to teachers and reading consultants. Although specialists do have access to information and control over material resources, professional uncertainty and the ideology of supportiveness place the primary power to plan in the hands of classroom teachers.

Strategies

With this distribution of resources, it is not surprising that classroom teachers and reading specialists rely on persuasion, bargaining, and negotiation in the exercise of influence. They can neither threaten to apply sanctions nor promise to bestow rewards. Instead, specialists must persuade teachers to accept whatever help they are able to give, either by appealing to common values or goals, or by showing a teacher how she may be interfering with her own goals. Furthermore, specialists have to establish their own credibility by a "track record" of suggestions that really work. As one consultant said, "If the criticisms I make are helpful, they will be better received." A Title I teacher in Blue Collar Suburb told me how she was planning to strengthen her credibility with the classroom teachers in her school:

> We've been having a problem with teachers misunderstanding Title I this year. . . . Maybe in the past they have had bad experiences with Title I and what their children were doing there—I don't know the reason, but we're going to try to have a welcome, an open house for the teachers, and tell them our philosophy about things.

These attempts to build credibility are consistent with what we saw earlier in the specialist's attempts to earn the trust of the teachers. Trust and credibility go hand and hand; both are essential to good bargaining and persuasion.

Specialists are anxious to maintain the flexibility that persuasion and negotiation require. Another Blue Collar Suburb Title I teacher explained how the Title I staff in her school coped with the need to deliver services to eligible children without infringing on the classroom teacher's prerogatives:

> There are a few [teachers] that really aren't overjoyed that the kids leave them [for Title I], and they may not recommend children as readily as others. But we are trying to do something about that now. We just started forming a committee to work up a curriculum for Title I, and it will state our guidelines, our objectives, and so on. . . . Hopefully it will be flexible enough—I hope it doesn't become too specific, no "We have to do it this way" kind of thing, just rather the guidelines.

Others, in accord with the "peer" relationship they try to establish with teachers, work to demonstrate reciprocity—a key feature of negotiation. Said one Title I teacher in Trade City:

Sometimes I'll pick up ideas from [the classroom teachers]. I'm the first one to say, "Hey, what a great idea, I can use that."

A Title I teacher in Factory City showed how reading specialists use their access to information and teachers use their ability to plan in striking bargains that suit them both:

This year one teacher wanted to put her whole classroom on one level, on grade level. . . . And we compromised. I had placement-tested all her children, and they had come out on levels 12 and 13, and she had tried to place them in 15, which was much too high. And some of the other teachers knew she had a slow class, so they were giving her flak too. So we compromised—we said to her, "Okay, if you want to put them all on one level, let's lower it and put them on a 13." And she accepted it, and that's what we're doing.

And a reading consultant illustrated how she relies on persuasion when she is unable to accommodate teachers' plans for their students:

[The teachers] would come and say, "I want you to take Johnny Jones," and I would say, "Well, I have 20 children, that's all I can work with in the afternoon in four periods." "Why can't you take him?" Well, I try to explain things in detail—sometimes I resent doing that, because if I say I cannot take them, that I would put them on a waiting list, I think [the teachers] should accept that. . . . But most people eventually accept it, and if they don't understand it, I will share what my thinking is and why I can't do what they would like to see done.

When reading specialists are successful in exercising influence over teachers, they rely on bargaining and persuasion, and always with a view to the teacher's classroom agenda and structure of incentives.

Contexts

The prevalence of persuasion and negotiation between teachers and reading specialists makes sense not only in terms of the resources at their disposal, but also in terms of the environment within which they conduct their relationship. Of the four contextual features shaping power and influence as identified in Chapter 1, the most important to a clear picture of the teacher-specialist relationship is teacher autonomy. The literature analyzing the social realities of teaching devotes considerable attention to the consequences of isolation in the teaching profession, not the least of which is autonomy in educational decision making (Goodlad, 1984; Lieberman & Miller, 1979). The classroom door is almost always closed when teachers are busy delivering instructional services. Even when reading specialists are urged to move into classrooms, they tread lightly once they are there, knowing that they are on the teacher's turf. And there is very little a specialist can do if a teacher chooses not to take advantage of the specialist's services. A Title I teacher assigned to two schools in Blue Collar Suburb reported:

> At my other school, certain teachers have been doing things certain ways, and I don't know whether I should say they don't care, [or] they prefer doing what they've been doing. But their one backup is that their achievement test scores have been extremely high, so they say, "We must be doing something right, so why change?"

And a reading consultant confided:

> Sometimes personalities are opposite; I'm thinking of one particular person whom I do not have any rapport with whatsoever, so I stay away completely. I do not go near there. . . . It doesn't have anything to do with reading, or teaching, or anything professional. We just don't mix.

The autonomy characterizing the teacher's tasks helps to explain why specialists emphasize a peer relationship with their classroom colleagues, despite their "expertise" and quasi-administrative responsibilities (Lortie, 1975, p. 195).

It is in light of this autonomy that the other contextual features of power and influence must be understood. For example, teacher autonomy means that reading specialists are somewhat more dependent on classroom teachers' discretionary choices than teachers are on the discretionary choices of specialists. While specialists do perform services that teachers value (testing students, assisting with grouping, providing materials, and working with low achievers), these services are things teachers *could* do themselves if they had to (and many now do). Teachers can still get their rewards from students even if specialists take on fewer of these tasks or don't do them well. However, specialists' rewards are tied to the cooperation of teachers as well as to the cooperation of students. Teachers who do not ask for their help, who fail to recommend students for remedial services, or who actively refuse assistance, deprive specialists of success in at least one area of their professional responsibilities. This diminishes the influence specialists might otherwise be able to exercise over the school reading program; specialists need teachers' consent before they can have much effect, and not all teachers are willing to give it.

All of this is not to say that coordination and cooperation are in and of themselves bad practices. What is problematic here is not the process, but the results. If anything, by increasing coordination and putting specialists to work in classrooms, schools may be producing exactly the opposite effect from what they intended. Rather than permitting specialists to exert more systematic influence over teachers, "coordination" helps teachers to exert more power over specialists. It permits the teacher to do a better job of informing the specialist of her plans for the children having difficulty, and puts the teacher in a better position to obtain the specialist's consent and cooperation with her efforts. Specialists can still use their access to information and their command of material resources to persuade, bargain, and negotiate with teachers; but teachers are the primary planners, and the specialist's ideology of supportiveness protects the essential autonomy of the teacher's planning and implementation. With the teacher's consent, specialists can indeed provide "help"; the question is whether the help they give teachers can also help students, and it is to that question we now turn.

READING SPECIALISTS
AND THE CLASSROOM MOBILIZATION OF BIAS

In Chapter 2 I argued that the paradox of collective instruction requires teachers to treat everyone alike while still "individualizing" instruction to "meet children's needs." One assumption behind Title I/Chapter 1 is that disadvantaged students have "special educational needs" requiring "special services" (National Institute of Education, 1977, p. 17). As a result, Title I/ Chapter 1 teachers providing instruction to students are expected to use "individualized" techniques as a way of meeting such needs (NIE, p. 28). Similarly, reading consultants providing remedial instruction for low-achieving children are supposed to be "more expert at both diagnosis and individualized instruction than most classroom teachers are" (Harris & Sipay, 1980, p. 333). Both kinds of specialists are also expected to encourage teachers to try new materials or instructional methods that improve their ability to meet the needs of disadvantaged students in the classroom as well. Interview results provided several instances in which special reading services did indeed fulfill these expectations. Since specialists often function simply as different people providing reading instruction, there is a good possibility that a particular Title I/Chapter 1 teacher or reading consultant may happen to work better with a particular child than does that child's classroom teacher. While progress in these cases may not be predictable or consistent, almost every specialist could recount cases where a child who simply was "not getting it" with the classroom teacher, suddenly "got it" during remedial instruction. Similarly, several teachers mentioned instances where they tried a new approach, or modified an old one, in response to a specialist's suggestions.

Nevertheless, it is also clear from these interviews that the provision of special services in reading does not go very far toward expanding the variety of means schools will use to address individual needs. Instead, *specialists support the mobilization of bias already operative in classroom structures.* In providing advice or administrative assistance, the ideology of supportiveness leads specialists to reinforce teachers' classroom practices. While specialists may recommend that particular children be shifted into new groups, or that the teacher provide supplementary materials for particular lessons, the basic patterns of classroom instruction remain unchanged both in substance and significance. This is especially true when classroom teachers ask for advice and assistance; they naturally make requests which will not threaten to any great degree the stability of decision making achieved within the uncertain context of classroom life. And since most reading specialists started out as former classroom teachers, they are alert to what Doyle and Ponder (1977) have aptly termed "the practicality ethic" guiding teachers' responses to suggestions. Part of that ethic requires teachers to ascertain how congruent a proposed change would be with the way classroom activities are normally conducted (p. 8); presumably, the more a specialist's recommendation represents a departure from routine, the less likely it is that the classroom teacher actually will implement it. By mutal consent, the reading specialist and the classroom teacher keep the field of individualizing alternatives for the classroom teacher relatively restricted. Thus, the power and influence relationship between reading specialists and classroom teachers, grounded as it is in the ideology of supportiveness, tends to encourage teachers to do more of what they were already doing.

Perhaps even more to the point, in their tutorial activities, consultants and Title I/Chapter 1 teachers *themselves* often do what classroom teachers are already doing. As discussed above, the way specialists spend their time with children depends largely on the classroom teachers' articulated preferences. One teacher's praise for a Title I teacher in her school tells the story:

> I have five kids in my low group, and four of them work with the Title I teacher. She comes in, asks me what I'm working on with them, and tries to work on what I'm working on with them. She stays really close to where I am; she asks me if I think there are specific skills I want them to work on, and although she uses different techniques and books, she stays with me.

That this pattern is typical is suggested by the nationwide District Practices Study (Advanced Technology, 1983, pp. 5–30):

> Principals, Title I instructors, and regular classroom teachers in our sample were asked to describe similarities and differences between regular and Title I instruction. A number of respondents said that the same skills and sequence of skills were provided in both. Title I instruction was said to be more individualized and used a slower, more basic approach.

Notice the claim in this 1983 study that Title I/Chapter 1 is more "individualized." This was a theme in the comments of school people in my sample as well. However, no one provided very specific evidence to support their belief in the increased individualization offered by remedial help. Many specialists reported using "different materials" or "different approaches" from those used in a child's classroom, but they did not explain just *how* their materials or approaches were different. Nationwide data on this point are not much more helpful. The recent Study of the Sustaining Effects of Compensatory Education (Carter, 1984, p. 12) reports that, in comparison to the regular classroom setting, compensatory instruction involved "smaller instructional groups, higher staff-to-student ratios, more student on-task behavior, less teacher time in behavioral management, a more harmonious classroom atmosphere, fewer negative comments by teachers, and a higher quality of cognitive monitoring, on-task monitoring, and organization of activities." Title I/Chapter 1 students were exposed to "different methods and practices," "more elementary or basic reading material," and "a much higher use of audio-visual equipment" than were regular classroom students. These results suggest that there may be some differences in the *amount* of instruction Title I/Chapter 1 students receive (e.g., a more harmonious atmosphere with more monitoring) but there is no indication of how different the instruction really is in its quality or appropriateness. We don't know how much smaller Title I/Chapter 1 groups are, how much more time participating students spend on-task, or how much improvement results from "activities" that are better "organized." The information concerning the appropriateness of tutorial services is even less specific; using "different methods," "more basic materials," and "more audio-visual equipment" may or may not constitute more appropriate instruction.

The lack of clarity on this issue was most apparent in my interviews with district officials. Before I began these interviews, I did a preliminary analysis of the data provided by teachers and reading specialists, and the results suggested essentially what I have been arguing in this chapter: that reading specialists provide children with more of the kinds of services they already receive in the classroom. I summarized these findings during my interviews with district-level officials and asked them to respond to my conclusion. Here are several examples of what I was told:

I'm not sure that what we try to do is give them more of what they get in the classroom. [Interviewer: Can you explain what different things are provided?] In terms of remedial [instruction]? I don't know whether I can or not. Other than to say that our remedial staff are working more closely this year with the regular classroom teacher than ever before. . . . The instruction in reading lab is almost directly keyed to the instruction in the classroom. Not to say that we use the same materials, but we cover the same concepts. . . . So if a youngster's having difficulty with comprehension, he's going to have comprehension when he goes to the reading lab. Before, the reading lab had their own program set up, of skills that a youngster needs, but it did not necessarily coincide with what that classroom teacher was doing. Now there's direct correlation. (*Factory City Curriculum Supervisor*)

A major thrust [in Title I] has been to do away with the pull-out program so that the reading teacher will work directly in the classroom, so there'll be that communication which is not taking place now. . . . By having the reading teacher zero in on skills that the kids need in a classroom, I think that will be very helpful. [Interviewer: Do Title I teachers or reading consultants provide anything very different from what is happening in the classroom?] They use the same materials, usually. They use a variety of other materials. [Interviewer: Why is that the way they approach it?] Because you don't want to give the child something he or she associates failure with. [But if they're using similar materials—] It's not similar. They're using different materials, they're using booklets, kits, that they're not usually exposed to. It may be the same skill, but it may be a different bit of material, that the child has not been exposed to. (*Trade City Reading Supervisor*)

[Interviewer: One problem I've noticed is that in the effort to coordinate Title I services with the classroom, it often seemed that Title I just gave the child more of what they got in the classroom.] No, no. They may have been giving more of what the kids got in the classroom but on a different basis. For instance, there may be a certain skill that the classroom does give, but they're not getting it. So Title I will try to reinforce this, to give it so the child will get it. . . . They try to keep close to what the classroom is doing; we cannot, as Title I, supplant the regular classroom work. [Interviewer: Why is that?] We cannot say, "Because he's getting Title I, he's not getting reading in the classroom." He must, at the same time, get reading in the classroom. (*Blue Collar Suburb Director of Elementary Education*)

[Our Title I people and the reading consultants] work very closely with the classroom teacher, but [they] may be using different materials or different approaches to help bridge a gap with the children. [Interviewer: How are they different?] They may be doing very much the same thing, but they may be using a different approach. The classroom teacher has to concern herself with 25 children whereas the [specialist] takes the children out in small groups. (*Trade City Assistant Superintendent of Curriculum*)

At no level of the school system was I able to gather data substantiating the ability of special services in reading to provide academically needy children with learning experiences that were significantly and systematically different from what they had received in the classroom. There was almost no evidence that specialists use means of individualization other than those that classroom teachers are already using. The preceding analysis of the power and influence relationships between teachers and specialists explains why.

This pattern of service replication persisted in all three dimensions of equal opportunity. Reading specialists, for example, assess children's needs in exactly the same ways as do classroom teachers. During the interviews, consultants and Title I teachers were asked several questions identical to those asked of classroom teachers, such as, "How do the children you work with differ from one another in reading?" and "How do you identify the different reading needs they have?" Their responses were startlingly similar to those of classroom teachers, as the following samples of specialists' observations suggest:

You can tell [where students are] by how well they express themselves, if they know more than one meaning for a word, if they can stay with a task, and how well organized they are.

Any age group will see different levels of maturity, different paces of learning, etc. Children come with different experiences. Some come with vast traveling experiences, which a greater socioeconomic background can make possible. Child care experiences can vary too. There are also differences in the way a child will learn how to read. Some respond to a visual, "sight-and-see" method. Others really prefer the linguistic approach.

I think some children just get it quickly; they don't need a lot from me; they move faster. Then there are those children who just plug along and they need all kinds of reinforcement. There are some children I can just move along the program, the way the program goes; and there are others I have to take out.

The standards for assessment portrayed here, like the standards used by teachers in the classroom, depend as much on how well students conform to the behavioral routines demanded by classroom instruction, as they do on more "cognitive" skills and abilities supposedly tapped by standardized testing.

As for the provision of material resources, it is unclear which opportunity criteria are met by the "different books" specialists claim to use. On the one hand, some specialists indicated that they try to pay attention to children's "learning styles" in the materials they use, thus addressing Criterion 3 (appropriateness to the child):

> Our reading system is very heavy in phonetic analysis, and you do have kids who for one reason or another have not picked up on that. I work with sight words as well as the other, because some children just learn better by a sight word approach.

However, as we saw in Chapter 2, many classroom teachers do the same thing as this Title I teacher—provide supplementary materials for children who do not work well with the classroom-based series. Furthermore, as this same Title I teacher went on to observe:

> We try and follow pretty much the program the school system is using. We are just a supplementary service to the teacher; that's something we emphasize, we do not take over the reading.

The ideology of supportiveness reading specialists adopt thus prevents them from "going too far" in providing substantially different materials to the students they work with. The specialist's attention to the distinctive needs of one set of clients—the children—is subordinated to the attention he or she must pay to the other set of clients—the teachers.

There is also some question as to how "different" alternative materials really are. One Title I teacher noted:

> What I am here to do is to give supportive services to the children with the work they are encountering upstairs in the classroom. So we're doing the same type of skills. We're not using the same materials that the classroom teacher would use. We use a lot of manipulative materials, different workbooks, but it's basically still either paperwork, boardwork, and some manipulative [work].

As discussed earlier, teachers and specialists alike emphasized that the supplementary materials used during tutorial sessions "covered" the skills and concepts children were working on in the classroom. This might assure an adequate quantity of instructional materials for each child on any given skill, thus improving the school's ability to meet Criterion 1 (materials in sufficient amounts). For children whose "needs" can be met simply with more "reinforcement" (i.e., repetition) of a particular skill, this approach is appropriate; it will indeed expand the opportunities available to these children. But for children whose needs differ from those of their classmates—and it is important to remember that Title I/Chapter 1 legislation assumes that the educational needs of poor children *are* different—simply providing more materials covering the same skills may not expand their opportunities at all. Some children need "more of the same"; many do not. Furthermore, even in this respect, specialists may not be expanding opportunities very much, since as we saw in Chapter 2, many teachers routinely provide additional materials in the classroom to "reinforce" the skills individual children may be "deficient" in. In short, it is difficult to see systematic differences in the kinds of materials reading specialists provide needy students; the evidence I have presented does not support the claim that specialists substantially expand the school's ability to meet individual needs through the provision of material resources.

The case for "more of the same" is even stronger in assessing specialists' contributions to the third dimension of equal opportunity, structuring educational interactions. Here we find that *remedial instruction virtually reproduces the patterns that characterize the social contexts of classroom reading instruction.* For one thing, specialists providing tutorial services face the same kinds of professional uncertainties that classroom teachers face. A Title I teacher in Factory City illustrates the point:

> The students who fall into our program sometimes regress. . . . And it's kind of frustrating in that sense. Sometimes a large percentage of them—they seem to learn a skill, you'd be willing to swear they have mastered it for life, and then all of a sudden you retest in a certain situation under different circumstances, and they don't seem to know the skill.

His sentiments were echoed by a fourth-grade classroom teacher in Blue Collar Suburb:

> The thing that is sometimes frustrating is that when the . . . achievement tests are given in the spring, in the past I've found children that I thought really had come along, and yet the scoring doesn't show that. I'm not a big believer in that kind of testing anyway, and yet it sometimes is frustrating; I think, I've really worked, they've gotten the extra help [from reading specialists], and yet there's only two or three months' growth perhaps from the year before.

It is not surprising that the behaviors of reading specialists in the face of professional uncertainty would parallel those of classroom teachers confronting the same problem. Even when they use "different techniques and books," reading specialists typically use them in a context of group instruction very like that of classroom ability groups. This will become even more true as Title I/Chapter 1 programs and district funds are cut and the number of students per specialist increases (J. Anderson, 1983).

Even more telling, reading specialists face the same paradox of collective instruction faced by classroom teachers. Tutorial sessions seldom afford the luxury of one-on-one interaction; more often than not, specialists must resort to group instruction in order to meet the demand that all eligible children receive services. Reflecting on their tasks in group instruction, the remarks of the following reading specialists are strangely reminiscent of the perspective of classroom teachers:

> I have fifth grade readers, and I find big differences in their level. Some are reading at a third grade level, some a little higher. There's a range. Some of their weaknesses might be in different basic skills.

> I do third and fourth grade reading. . . . Basically, even though they all may score roughly in the same group, their skills are very different. Some may have good attack skills, but don't know how to apply them. Some have poor skills, and also poor comprehension.

> We group [our remedial students]. . . . We have a sheet that we send to the teacher—we have discussed it and we set it up—as to what skills they are working on that particular week. He or she sends us those skills and that's what we focus on. So the skills you're working on varies from group to group, or even from individual to individual, because you [will] find within a group there's a youngster that can't deal with that skill.

Given the same social dynamics that teachers confront in the classroom, and constrained by the ideology of supportiveness in setting instructional agendas for students, it is not in the least surprising that reading specialists usually provide "more of the same" in their instruction of low achieving students. In particular, given "more of the same," it is not surprising that Title I/Chapter 1 students have not caught up with their noncompensatory peers. The common wisdom says that special services in reading help to resolve the paradox of collective instruction, simply by existing; extra services are intended to compensate for the inability of classroom teachers to respond to each child's needs on an individual basis. But the common wisdom is wrong. Special services perpetuate the paradox.

Liberal hearts may well bleed. If the foregoing analysis is right, the more than $3 billion spent on Title I/Chapter 1 grants to LEAs in 1984 could be viewed as a colossal waste of federal money, state time, and local talent. Unfortunately, the observations and interpretations I have offered admit of no easy or obvious policy recommendations. Federal compensatory education funds are now institutionalized in the budgets of 90% of all local school districts; they pay the salaries of approximately 170,000 full-time educators; and they provide services to over 4.8 million low-achieving children. Few legislators would be willing to run the political risk of recommending that poor children (in their districts) receive fewer services or that teachers (in their districts) lose their jobs. And few educators would volunteer for the job of telling classroom teachers that there will no longer be a place to send their lowest achieving students for extra help. Simply abolishing Title I/Chapter 1 is neither politically nor administratively feasible. School districts are equally loath to give up the few reading consultants they can still afford. However tenuous the connection between "extra help" for teachers and systematic improvements in student achievement, both consultants and Title I/Chapter 1 staff help teachers cope more successfully with the problem of professional uncertainty and the paradox of collective instruction.

Many contemporary critics who express concern for the continued low reading achievement of economically deprived students have begun to look elsewhere in the school for a place to pin their hopes. They have stopped looking at technical expertise and have started looking at leadership. A growing community of scholars argues that the best way to insure that both reading specialists and classroom teachers meet the needs of all students is to install principals who provide instructional leadership to the entire school. They contend that the activities of classroom and specialized teachers will only be successful in the context of "effective schools" led by "effective principals." This effectiveness, it is said, guarantees good results for rich and poor students alike. The following chapter extends the analysis of schooling for the poor into the office of the school principal.

4

The Power of Suggestion?

Elementary School Principals, Effectiveness, and Equality

I think it's the age of accountability—you have to know what's going on. . . . I feel accountable both ways, to the kids and the teachers, and of course I'm accountable to my superiors, but they don't threaten me or anything. It's not that type of accountability. (*Blue Collar Suburb teacher*)

Like reading specialists, elementary school principals have multiple responsibilities and clienteles in their relationship to the school reading program. As this Blue Collar Suburb principal pointed out, they are expected to make sure the school fulfills its mission in ways which keep students, teachers, parents, and district officials reasonably satisfied with the school and the principal's contributions to it. Unfortunately, the demands of these different clienteles often conflict, especially when it comes to low reading scores, and school administrators find it difficult to keep everyone happy while at the same time keeping the school "on track" in its essential purposes. Complicating this problem is the fact that the principal's most important clients—the classroom teachers—operate with a large measure of autonomy and discretion, giving them ample resources to resist any administrative encroachments on their territory.

Some reformers contend that the tension between principal accountability and teacher autonomy can be successfully resolved by an "effective principal. The rhetoric of reform in the effective schools literature suggests that school performance improves under the leadership of an effective administrator who is knowledgeable about instruction, articulate about the school's goals, aware of "what's going on," and efficient in soliciting and following up on feedback. "Effective" principals, according to this literature, stand in contrast to "typical" principals, who are too overwhelmed by the dailiness and pettiness of "business-as-usual" to be able to spend much time providing instructional leadership.[1] My own sample of principals varied greatly in the extent to which they followed the precepts of the "effective principal" model. However, despite their differences, these principals confronted a common two-fold enterprise in leading and administering their schools. On the one hand, principals are required to be *classroom supporters*, making sure that teachers have what they need to keep their classroom programs functioning "at the appropriate level." At the same time, they are also required to be *classroom problem solvers*, addressing any short-term or long-term weaknesses in the classroom experience. My interview data suggest that, in fulfilling these responsibilities, principals' accountability to classroom teachers usually supercedes their accountability to their other clients, primarily because of the autonomy with which teachers do their jobs. As a result, principals treat the classroom mobilization of bias as a given in their leadership of the reading program, so that neither "effective" nor "typical" school administrators significantly expand the range of opportunities available to low-income children learning to read.

PRINCIPALS AS CLASSROOM SUPPORTERS

Typical and effective principals alike have as a major part of their role the responsibility to "keep everything going." This involves such tasks as making sure materials are available, maintaining staff morale, assuring quality instruction, and the like. Put in terms of the paradoxes and problems of classroom life described in Chapter 2, principals support teachers in the patterns of behavior they rely on to help resolve the paradox of collective instruction, the problem of professional uncertainty, and the complications of power and influence. Ironically, this is not because they are acting like remote administrators who don't understand the constraints and paradoxes teachers face, but rather because they understand the teacher's context all too well.

Knowing What's Going On

A prerequisite to the principal's ability to maintain satisfactory classroom experiences is that he or she must know what is going on in each classroom. Whether or not principals know very much about reading instruction, their interest and presence in the classroom matter to the classroom teacher as signs of support. Teacher interviews indicated that, even when principals vary widely in their knowledge about materials and instruction—a variable that is supposed to distinguish "typical" from "effective" principals (Hoffman & Rutherford, 1984; Leithwood & Montgomery, 1982)—they still exhibit a similar level of concern about keeping in touch with the classroom. A Factory City teacher, whose principal had received a grant to institute a dual-series approach to reading at his school, reported:

> Our principal . . . is not the type who just sits in his office all day. He knows where you're at and how you teach and where your kids are at all times. He really cares. . . . He'll come in the room, and I won't even see him at my desk, and a day or two later I'll see a note regarding my lesson plans.

A Blue Collar Suburb teacher whose principal was also very knowledgeable, having earned an advanced degree in reading instruction, similarly observed:

> [Our principal] is always in and out, and if you have a question or a problem he's always happy to help you. I've found him very helpful and willing to participate in anything I ask him to.

On the other hand, a Factory City teacher, whose principal knew very little about the reading series they were using, still reported that her principal was interested in and aware of what was happening at the classroom level:

> She is a wonderful principal, wherein she comes in [and] she usually knows exactly what each teacher is doing. . . . She always asks me, "Your kids are doing great; is there anything else I can do?"

When teachers expressed appreciation for the principal's "visibility" and "awareness," they were more likely to emphasize the personal support the principal could thereby provide, rather than any technical information about materials or instruction the principal might supply. This pattern was evident in the responses of teachers working with both "effective" and "typical" principals. A second teacher from the Blue Collar Suburb school whose principal had specialized in reading instruction, indicated that the helpful information the principal provided was important not only for professional reasons but for personal ones as well:

> Our principal is very good at constructive criticism—he offers concrete suggestions. I remember telling him once that the kids just didn't seem to be tuning in, and he said, "Try this—write the main objectives on the board and follow through." That happened a long time ago, but I remember it. . . . He's really interested in us as people. "If you ever have a problem, come and talk to me." He really means it; whenever you say anything, immediately he'll invite you into his office and close the door.

Likewise, a Trade City teacher whose principal was unable to provide informed assistance still commented on the supportive attitudes he displayed in his classroom visits:

> [Our principal] is extremely conscientious. I know many places where people say, "I never see the principal" or "He doesn't show up" or "They don't observe." But he's very good. You'll see him, not only when you expect to, but he'll come in just to observe the bulletin boards, or to say "good morning." So you know that he's aware of what you're doing. It's just having someone know that you're here, and that you're doing a good job. You want somebody every so often to pat you on the back . . . [to] come in once in a while and say, "I appreciate what you're doing." It's like anything else—you have to have some confidence.

This kind of nontechnical "involvement" affords principals the chance to be classroom supporters, even when they lack expertise about how to assess needs, what materials are available, or how to conduct instruction. In particular, principals who "know what's going on," even in a very general way, can support teachers in their pursuit of routine and control. Several teachers, for example, indicated that the principal's display of interest in the children supported the search for control through intimacy, by reinforcing the children's perception that their teachers cared for them:

> I've been very impressed with [our principal's] relationship with the children. . . . Despite being the only principal in such a large building, he knows every family, he knows every child: "Oh, you're looking nice today, is that a new jacket?" "How is so-and-so in your family?" He definitely shows that school is a caring place to the children. (*Blue Collar Suburb teacher*)

> [Our principal] makes a habit of coming in each day, in the morning and the afternoon, to see how the children are working and how they're performing, and how they're progressing. It's good because the children know that I care, that the principal cares, that we care a lot how they're doing. (*Factory City teacher*)

Principals who are "visible" and "aware" can also support teachers in their attempts to establish a commanding role in the classroom. Teachers tended to notice the absence of this kind of support more than its presence.

> [If] we had a behavior problem and would send the child down to the office, [the child] would come back five minutes later. There was no fol-

low-through on the administrative level—a little slap on the wrist and that was it. (*Trade City teacher*)

For their part, when principals described the benefits of knowing what's going on, they too focused less on the technical help they were able to give teachers than on the insights their awareness could provide about the demands teachers face in the classroom. Thus, both effective and typical principals used their knowledge of "what's going on" to support teachers' attempts to cope with life in the classroom. One Trade City principal who appeared not to have the kind of knowledge about instruction that "effective" principals are supposed to have, nevertheless visited classrooms frequently and assisted teachers by giving help to individual children (attending to the paradox of collective instruction) and by supporting the teacher's pursuit of control.

I would say that I get into every classroom every day at least once, sometimes even twice a day. . . . If I go around and I find some of the children really don't understand, it's awfully easy to sit down and give them some help. Because . . . [there is] no way [a teacher] can get to 25 youngsters. . . . Any teacher who can control a group can teach. . . . [Because of] your mere presence in the classroom, because [the children] know that you're coming and you're checking, they will do better.

The Factory City principal who had received a grant to institute a dual-series approach to reading at his school also used frequent classroom observation to support the teacher's coping strategies, in this case the pursuit of routine. He assisted teachers trying to solve problems with individual children who were "not getting it," while at the same time attempting to maintain uniform routines for the class as a whole.

I'm in there at least twice a day. . . . I pick up some things that a teacher doesn't see, because they're closeted with these kids, things like vision problems. . . . [The teachers] are so busy handling all their groups and getting everything done, sometimes they work it through with the group but they don't get a chance to look at the individual.

In short, both "typical" and "effective" principals tried to maintain an awareness of "what's going on" in the classrooms for which they were accountable. And whether their technical understanding of reading instruction was superficial or sophisticated, they used their knowledge to support teachers in the pursuit of routine and control.

Supplying Materials

Of the three dimensions of equal opportunity, the one that receives the most attention from the principal is the provision of tangible educational resources—texts, workbooks, worksheets, dittos, even classroom furnishings. More teachers (nearly half) commented on the helpfulness of the principal in procuring materials than on any other behavior. The only district in which praise for the principal's work as a supplier of resources was noticeably absent was White Collar Suburb, in which each school's reading consultant assumed that responsibility. But in every other district, teachers whose principals varied in their "effectiveness" noted the principal's supportiveness in procurement and tied that support to the principal's understanding of the classroom situation teachers confront:

> The principal wouldn't hesitate to get any material I needed. If I needed books or cassettes and we didn't have them, he finds out where to get them. I think he views himself as an expediter, and that makes our own job a lot easier; we already have so much to attend to. (*Blue Collar Suburb teacher*)

A concern with materials also shows up in the principal's relationship with the school reading specialist, as one Title I teacher noted:

> We talk about [the reading program] almost daily. [The principal] will say such things as "How are things going? Does everybody have all the materials they need? What do you see that we'll be needing before the end of this year? Who needs help? How can we help that person? Are all the books in? What's lacking?"

Even more to the point, no matter how "typical" or "effective" a principal was in his or her knowledge about reading materials, he or she relied primarily on the teachers' preferences in procuring supplies. A Trade City teacher whose principal was a former high school administrator, and was barely acquainted at all with the school's reading series, noted:

> [The principal] can be helpful. For instance, I mentioned to him yesterday that I was waiting for a teacher's manual in our language program, which our overburdened reading teacher has tried to get for me, and he said, "Why don't you just call the publisher directly?" I will probably do that sometime today. He will be very direct about that.

Another Trade City teacher whose principal was knowledgeable about reading and relatively active in visiting classrooms, supplying materials, and so forth, stated:

> As far as materials and things like that, he has been super. . . . We'd been working on long and short vowels, [and] he went to the teachers' store and got ditto books and things like that, just for extra materials to have. Or he's very good about asking, "What do you need?" or "If there's anything you need, come to me." He goes out and he gets what we need.

That principals make their accountability to teachers a priority in this dimension of opportunity is perhaps most evident in the words of one principal: "What we try to do is to get the materials the teachers need on the level they need it."

A few principals regularly supplied teachers with materials that supplemented the classroom basal series.

> I run off samples of materials . . . and give them [to the teacher]. If a teacher is having difficulty with a concept, it is up to me to be the resource person . . . and hunt for supplementary materials . . . that would work with the youngster. (*Factory City principal*)

However, teachers were much more likely to comment on the responsiveness of the principal to the teacher's articulated preferences than on the principal's initiative in supplying materials the teacher had not requested. The main difference between "effective" and "typical" principals in procuring materials seems to be that a principal displaying "effective" patterns will ask teachers more frequently and specifically what they need, while a "typical" principal will wait for teachers to come with requests. In both patterns, however, teachers' preferences dominate the principal's procurement activities, and the principal's willingness to act as a supplier is based on a shared understanding of the pressures teachers face. The findings described in Chapter 3 are thus repeated here: The principal's provision of tangible resources is likely to maintain classroom patterns of opportunity in the reading materials children use. Teachers are unlikely to ask for materials that disrupt the stability of classroom patterns, and principals are unlikely to insist that a teacher make use of any materials the principal supplies on his or her own initiative. The sample texts or workbooks principals may distribute are generally regarded as suggestions; only one teacher took her principal's provision of supplementary resources as a directive, and none of the other teachers interviewed in that school followed suit. In short, principals displaying "effective" behaviors, as well as those who are more "typical," help to maintain the classroom mobilization of bias in the kinds of materials teachers use.

Supporting Instructional Routines

A similar theme is played in different principals' responses to classroom instruction; principals are likely to reinforce instructional routines just as they reinforce teachers' usage of materials. Principals' attempts to support classroom instructional strengths involve several kinds of administrative activities: providing assistance with grouping, promoting innovation, and encouraging interaction about instruction. They do all these things with a view to teachers' preferences.

Principals' descriptions of their concerns in grouping students focused less on the needs of students than on the workability of classroom organization for the teachers. A Factory City principal whose detailed knowledge about the school reading program and clear focus on achievement scores seemed to reflect a commitment to effectiveness (Leithwood & Montgomery, 1982) described her approach to grouping children for reading instruction as follows:

> It starts with the organization, getting the children into the proper groups, and . . . giving the teachers a load that can be handled easily— grouping the children so there aren't four or five reading groups. . . . Also [I try] to work in the children who need help so that when the remedial reading teacher . . . takes children . . . the classroom teacher doesn't feel there's a lot of interruptions.

In contrast, the following two Trade City principals were much less knowledgeable about reading and had fewer opportunities to visit classrooms; yet their concerns about grouping were equally dominated by their awareness of the classroom teacher's predicament:

> In September we try to organize by reading levels. . . . We place [students] initially in their homerooms by reading levels, if possible . . . [and] we try to keep each teacher limited to three reading groups . . . so that there isn't that much movement in the hallways by 8:50.

> We have not been as lucky this year as we have in the past, where a teacher will have three to five reading groups in the morning. Three to me is ideal; four is okay; when you're going beyond that, then you're taking up an awful lot of time. . . . We took in thirty-six minority kids from an inner city school [and] a problem arose. The discrepancy in the reading levels by the minority kids was too great . . . and we ended up having five, six, seven groups. With the aid of the reading consul-

tant we were able to move around and get them down to about five groups, which isn't ideal but not too bad.

These comments are all the more telling because neither principal displayed many behaviors associated with "effectiveness." The first served two elementary schools and was hardly ever in classrooms; the second was the former high school administrator who knew very little about the specifics of the reading program in his school. Despite their intellectual distance from the classroom, however, both principals saw grouping as a way to help teachers cope with the day-to-day demands of classroom life. In fact, with respect to educational interactions, principals must confront the same paradox of collective instruction that teachers confront. Like the teachers described in Chapter 2 who occasionally keyed their instruction to getting children divided into a manageable number of groups, principals often assume that managerial solutions can "fix" educational problems. And the solutions principals espouse are predicated on teacher preferences for routine and control.

A second way in which principals support the strengths of classroom interactions is by promoting innovations intended to improve instruction. Indeed, one of the hallmarks of "effective" principals is that they "establish norms for risk-taking among staff, [stressing] continuous change in programs in the direction of better serving student needs" (Leithwood & Montgomery, 1982, p. 321). However, although the principals in my sample did vary in the degree to which they promoted classroom-level innovation, all of them generally let the teachers decide which specific instructional risks they wanted to take.

> I know I have a lot of latitude in what I do. I know I can share something new that I might try, and [the principal] will always like the ideas. He takes time to look over samples of what I've done, and he'll come into the room to see how it's working. (*Blue Collar Suburb teacher*)

> If I have a new idea and I want to try something, he's right on the spot trying to get it for me. (*Factory City teacher*)

In the few cases where the principal initiated a particular innovation, it had to do with the materials teachers were using rather than the instructional routines that dictated how the materials were used:

> Our previous principal . . . came to me on trying a pilot study. I think he might have been a little bit distressed about test results and the like, and in order to improve them . . . he came to me with the [new] materials and asked me to look them over. (*Trade City teacher*)

The Factory City principal who, with the help of a state grant, had instituted a new reading program at his school, was also concerned with material rather than instructional innovation. His case is a telling one, because he had developed the grant proposal in response to teacher dissatisfactions:

> The reason I made the changes is because the teachers complained to me. . . . Some of the better teachers came to me, once they got to know me after awhile, dropping hints, telling me about the number of non-readers they had in the upper grades.

Thus, in encouraging teachers to innovate, or in proposing innovations themselves, principals take teacher preferences very seriously indeed. They are unlikely to advocate innovations that would dramatically alter classroom instructional routines.

Principals can also support classroom strengths by facilitating the implementation of innovations imposed from outside the school, which again are very likely to be in material resources rather than instructional patterns. Once again, the pattern here shows principals helping teachers to maintain existing instructional routines. At the time of the interviews, Trade City had just begun to implement a new reading series. Two principals permitted teachers to delay implementing the new series if they wanted to.

> I have to admit that there are some teachers who are *still* staying with the original series. Some teachers were able to convince the reading consultant [to let them] stay with [the old series] for another year or two because they've gotten it down so well and it has proven so successful. For other teachers, it isn't for them. . . .

> We didn't have enough money to start [the new series] all the way, so what we're trying to do is start it in kindergarten and grades 4 and 5, and next year we'll either drop down or move up. . . . Now, we discussed it with the teachers—any time we have any kind of new approach we discuss it with the teachers, the reading people, and everyone involved, and [the district administrators] let you do pretty much what you want—but the teachers decided, okay, if we have some money, let's start top and bottom and we'll meet in the middle, rather than the beginning to the end.

No principal described an instance in which he or she simply forced a teacher to use a series against the teacher's will. Even if the teacher capitulated to the principal's preferences, it was only after the principal had explained his or her position and persuaded the teacher to go along.

The reason for the principal's caution in suggesting that teachers alter any feature of classroom life is clear. Changing a reading series represents a threat to stable classroom routines, at least as far as the teachers are concerned. To a large extent, a child's tasks in the classroom are the same whatever the textbook (Fullan, 1982, p. 154), but a new text may change the teacher's assessment and materials routines, and temporarily increase the number of decisions a teacher must make about which supplementary materials will work well with the new series, how much time to spend in different reading groups, etc. Some textbook series emphasize meaning and comprehension skills, while others emphasize phonetic and decoding skills; a change from one to the other will alter the teacher's definition of what constitutes a reading "need" and how to meet it (Chall, 1967). Some series provide more seatwork than others, and a reading consultant in Trade City described the consequences of this kind of change:

> There is not as much seatwork with the new program compared to the old program, because [with the new program] you do the workbook with the child. You begin with the workbook. So you're doing it almost the reverse of what we're used to. This takes a lot of practice. . . . So the teacher has to provide on her own for individual differences. They're finding it's a lot of work; they must make their own [seatwork exercises].

Although, as we saw in Chapter 2, a change in materials rarely produces sweeping changes in instructional routines, even simple adjustments in instruction necessitated by new materials disturb classroom stability and increase uncertainty. Thus, principals seeking to maintain the strengths of classroom experiences by helping teachers adjust to innovations rely on individual teachers to articulate limits on the amount of uncertainty they feel capable of handling.

A final way principals can support classroom strengths is by encouraging interaction about reading instruction. "Effective" principals, it is said, encourage "cross-fertilization of ideas" (Hoffman & Rutherford, 1984; Leithwood & Montgomery, 1982). Of particular interest here is the way principals try to "facilitate" good relationships between the school's reading specialist and classroom teachers. Some principals were much more "effective" in providing opportunities for contact than others were; however, these same principals were quite clear in describing the consultant or Title I teacher as a "help" to the classroom teacher. A case in point is the working relationship that developed among an informed and active Trade City principal, the classroom teachers, and the two reading specialists assigned to his school. The principal observed:

> From what I have been seeing, I would say [the relationship between the classroom teachers and the Title I teacher] is a very good one, be-

cause our particular [Title I] teacher has been here a number of years and she's well respected among the faculty. . . . The [Title I] teacher is not there as a threatening figure or authority, but merely to go in to help the classroom teacher to succeed in helping the child learn. . . . I don't think the classroom teachers feel threatened by it.

Even though this principal had told me earlier that he often selected specific teachers to receive additional support from both the Title I teacher and the reading consultant, neither specialist was very heavy-handed in her dealings with the teachers. The Title I teacher assigned to this school was cited in Chapter 3, but her remarks bear repeating here:

[My relationship with the teachers] goes well, because I feel that I would rather be approached than go in and make suggestions. Because how do I know what someone else's situation is? I'm in my room taking care of my groups, so naturally I don't know what's going on in some other room. . . . So if [the teachers] come to me and ask for suggestions, I give them. But I wait for them.

Although this principal appeared to be "effective" in explicitly encouraging instruction-related interaction between the teachers and the reading specialists, both the specialists saw themselves as subordinate to the teachers; neither was likely to disrupt classroom instructional routines with the "help" they provided.

This pattern was repeated at the Factory City school whose principal displayed more "effective" behavior patterns than any other principal in my sample. This was the principal who visited classrooms once or twice daily and who had applied for and received a grant to introduce a new reading program at his school; all the teachers interviewed noted that he had high expectations for his faculty, and he was quite aggressive in sending the Title I teacher to support specific classroom reading programs. By his own account, he emphasized interaction with others about instruction:

These teachers and I have been together for quite a few years now, so we know [each other] pretty well. . . . They all seem pretty receptive to suggestions. We just did a lot of planning and Saturday workshops. We even did a workshop this summer, and we had 100% attendance. I think everybody looks for direction anyway, and they're very receptive to positive criticism and suggestions on how to improve things.

This principal attributed his own success as an instructional leader at least in part to the willingness of the teachers at his school to let him lead. His grant proposal grew out of teachers' preferences, and the planning sessions and workshops he described worked because the teachers wanted them to. The principal had surely earned credibility with the teachers as an instructional leader, but that credibility was complemented by the teachers' support for his leadership. Although his decisions appeared to be based on the anticipated reactions of his staff members, rather than on his outright solicitation of their wants and needs, nevertheless their preferences about instruction still figured in his methods of supporting classroom strengths.

This principal, like the Trade City principal described earlier, also used the Title I teacher to support specific activities in specific classrooms. Yet the classroom teachers at this school still described the Title I teacher's assistance as guided by their preferences:

> [Our Title I teacher] has been more than cooperative; she's been very cooperative with the Holt. She takes some of the frustration away. [Interviewer: Has she ever done a demonstration lesson?] No, probably because I have never asked. . . . Reading I kind of like to work around myself. [The Title I teacher] has never made any specific suggestions, other than [to] show us how to do Holt, or [to] demonstrate some reading games.

And the principal's description of the Title I teacher's responsibilities was also framed in terms of service to the teachers:

> The reading teacher here is very good; she's well-organized. She's really doing a lot more; she's really working in the capacity of a reading consultant, even though she's just a reading teacher. But that's because I give her that kind of responsibility. . . . She takes care of getting books, materials, supplies, all that now. She and the teachers [also] do the grouping each year.

The principal's support for strengths in the classroom experience thus reinforces the instructional patterns already in place. Principals do not make independent judgments selecting specific program patterns for support—even when their behaviors appear to exemplify effective instructional leadership. Instead, principals rely on teachers to recognize their own strengths and to ask for support accordingly, whether explicitly or implicitly. Even when they are active in implementing innovations or promoting interaction about instruction, principals keep teachers at the center of classroom decision making.

PRINCIPALS AS CLASSROOM PROBLEM SOLVERS

That principals structure their support of classroom strengths around teacher preferences is perhaps not very surprising. That they do the same in solving classroom problems, is. Here, too, the point of departure for the principal's activities is the experience of the classroom teacher—her or his perceptions, preferences, and patterns of behavior. Consequently, principals who try to address weaknesses in the reading program generally do not alter the instructional routines teachers use to cope with the demands of life in classrooms.

How Principals Find Out About Problems

My sample of principals had three main internal sources of information about problems in the reading program: test scores, classroom observation, and direct communication with teachers. Of these sources, the last clearly predominated; the second was largely shaped by teacher preference; and the first was rarely used to root out specific problems requiring changes in classroom routines.

Principals vary in how much attention they pay to test results. "Effective" principals use testing for "continuous monitoring of student progress in the [reading] program" (Hoffman & Rutherford, 1984, p. 88), and some principals in my sample did just that. However, test results were rarely used to raise questions about particular classroom practices. Only one teacher recounted an instance where a principal used test scores to indicate a need for change in the classroom instruction her students were receiving:

> You know that [the principal] is looking for a certain amount of performance, a certain amount of achievement. When your test results come back, say 50% of your kids failed one thing, he might indicate "What happened here?" with a question mark.

A few other teachers also commented on their principal's attention to classroom-level test results, but not for the purposes of altering classroom practices. Rather, test scores were used to indicate the need for supplementary services outside the classroom:

> We've gone over the test results and talked about the children, and [have] also [been] doing referrals for different ones, [determining] what programs would be open to them.

The most common pattern of all was for principals to pay attention to test results in a general, school-wide way, rather than on a class-by-class basis:

> [Our principal] has expressed an interest in really trying to raise the children's scores on the standardized tests which they will be taking. . . . So they had the scores for each school and they were able to pin-

point which skills [were in need of improvement], and there were a number of skills that the children did very poorly in—alphabetizing, dictionary skills.

Test results, then, are not likely to be used as sources of specific information about classroom-level problems in reading instruction.

A second possible source of information is classroom observation for the purpose of teacher evaluation. In many districts, formal evaluations are increasingly preceded by a conference in which the principal and the teacher negotiate what the principal will look for; in these cases, the teacher provides guidance to the principal by specifying what problems the principal should pay attention to. A Blue Collar Suburb teacher observed:

> We have Action Plans that are agreed on between the principal and the teacher. Whatever you feel weak in or want suggestions on, that's what he'll evaluate. I would sit down and write out an action plan, on the goals I want to reach, and he'll give concrete suggestions about how to reach them.

Another Blue Collar Suburb teacher described at length how her pre-evaluation conference helped her to persuade the principal to support a goal she had established for her lowest group:

> We have to have objectives [for classroom observations]. Mine at that particular time was to take my slowest group, which was an extremely slow group in reading, and to bring them along at the end of the year . . . to be reading at a 2–1 level. I went to my principal [with] my objectives, we sat down, and we talked about it. He said, "Jill, I think you're very foolish. . . . Do you feel that a hundred percent of [the children in that group] should reach that 2–1 [level]?" I said, "Yes, I do." He said, "Why not take eighty percent?" I said, "No, I want a hundred." Well, during that whole year [the principal] would come in and observe and sit in the group, watching constantly. In between we'd have other conferences to see how [the group] was going. Then at the end of the year, [we had] a final testing program for these children, [and] I had reached my goal. [The principal] was super.

Interestingly, the principals were more likely than the teachers to mention formal teacher evaluation; these two teachers were the only ones who described "official" observations to me. The principals were the ones who told me how the process was supposed to work:

> We usually don't make [classroom] visits on a hit-or-miss basis. Of course, any principal should feel free to drop in at any time. But for

teacher evaluations, we mutually agree—that is, the teacher and my-self—on what I am coming to see. If it involves a reading lesson, the teacher will tell me what she is planning to do, and which children she hopes will respond in particular ways. (*White Collar Suburb principal*)

When principals approach evaluation in this way, they seem to be following the precepts of the "effective principal" approach, by establishing clear goals, identifying the problems that stand in the way of these goals, and then solving the problems they have identified (Leithwood & Montgomery, 1982). But in applying this model to formal teacher evaluation, my sample of principals transferred to their teachers the responsibility of establishing goals, identifying problems, and proposing solutions.

The third source of information about problems with the reading program was the most widely referred to by principals and teachers in all four districts, and that is direct communication with the teachers themselves. Teachers in all twelve schools—even teachers who were relatively hostile toward administrators—told me that if they were to tell their principals that they were having a problem with reading, the principal would do something about it.

[Our principal's] expertise does not fall in the primary [grade] level. But if I tell him that I'm having a particular problem, that I would like this child tested or I need some background information, he's very cooperative in that sense. He will try to search out the source of some help to me. (*Trade City teacher*)

I really don't even feel like discussing the principal. . . . They're so bogged down with all their rules and regulations, lack of personnel, lack of funds, I don't know where to go anymore. . . . If there were a problem, they would, I'm sure, do something to help. But you'd have to go to them if there were a problem. (*Trade City teacher*)

The principals' comments were also peppered with examples of teacher-specified problems:

I try to meet with the teachers informally every morning when they come in; I always make sure I say hello to them, and "How are you?" And I always ask the twenty-four dollar question, "Do you have any problems?" And they realize that I'm talking about not only social [and] behavioral problems, but academic as well. And if they do have a problem, they will tell me. For example, we had some teachers come up and tell me that certain books were not really accomplishing what they were intended to do. So we sat down, we had a meeting, we discussed it, we found an alternative, and that's how we go about it. (*Trade City principal*)

[The teachers and I] talk about things like "Do you think the material's too hard? Do you think it's not structured enough? Do you want me to call in the curriculum assistant to help you with your program?" Things like that. (*Factory City principal*)

The Factory City principal cited above was one of the most frequently praised for visiting classrooms; the Trade City principal paid close attention to test scores in setting his goals. Even "effective" principals like these relied on teachers to identify their own problems. This source of information did not appear to be related to the availability of other sources of information. Principals do not turn to teacher communication because they lack information; they do so because they are committed to taking teacher preferences seriously.

The Kinds of Problems Principals Identify

Given the principal's reliance on teacher practices and preferences described above, it is not surprising that principals are most likely to identify problems that can be resolved within existing classroom routines. For example, no principal mentioned test results as a warrant for significant changes in classroom routines; test scores are seen as diagnostic tools aiding teachers in the application of classroom routines. Some principals referred to test scores as a means of deciding which materials are appropriate for which children:

The testing is the important thing with teachers; it's very diagnostic, so that they could pinpoint where the difficulty is for youngsters, and they have materials to use with them.

Others use tests to check on whether children are in the proper groups:

I keep track of all the reading scores. They can be reduced to one notebook, and I can see, because the testing from Holt is criterion-referenced, you're not looking for 100 percent; and if I see a child is making 100 percent on every one of the Holt [tests], then possibly he needs to have a different text so he can be regrouped and go faster.

In both these cases the classroom problem is interpreted as a matter of grouping or materials. Based on these interpretations, the principal takes action in ways that leave the basic classroom experiences of the teacher unchanged. Admittedly, a school or district may completely replace its reading series on the basis of vociferous complaints about low test scores. But even in the face of those more dramatic changes, as I have already suggested, principals take steps to help teachers avoid increased uncertainty, ultimately reinforcing teachers' preferences and practices.

Principals' descriptions of formal and informal classroom observations also suggest that they tend to spot problems which can be resolved within the existing behavioral routines of the classroom. To begin with, principals define and identify children's "needs" much as teachers do—even when they vary in their expertise about reading instruction. A less-than-expert principal from Trade City observed:

> If I watch a reading group, and I see kids' minds wandering or someone talking, to me that's not a successful reading group. (*Trade City principal*)

A more knowledgeable Factory City principal stated:

> [I try to determine] whether [the children] have been taught mastery; are the children very secure in what they're saying or are they struggling? . . . Are they comfortable with the vocabulary [and] . . . transferring into it when they answer the questions?

The usual approach is to interpret any problems as problems in grouping or in the choice of materials, as the same principal went on to say:

> If I see a child is continually struggling, there are two reasons for struggling. Either he needs more help than we're giving him, or the pacing is too fast and he needs to be regrouped. Sometimes he can stay with his group if we supplement it with remedial reading.

Similarly, a principal from White Collar Suburb commented:

> If I just pop in to observe the children [and] they're having a lot of trouble answering questions, I ask if the children and the material are properly matched. Or if they are answering too easily—I want the material to be challenging but not frustrating.

All of these examples typify the principal's practice of spotting problems which can be corrected within the context of the teacher's normal classroom routines. Problems which cannot be solved in that way—for example, the persistent failure of many economically disadvantaged children to make significant progress in homogeneous ability groups—are reinterpreted as problems which *can* be solved—the unsuitability of the material or the pacing of its presentation.

Since principals treat teachers as the most important source of information about classroom difficulties, it is not in the least surprising that they do not identify problems which would indicate a need for substantial classroom change. As we saw in Chapter 2, the teacher's incentive to preserve stability in classrooms overwhelms the incentive to probe deeply for the source of classroom difficulties. Teachers pursue routines to solve problems; they don't see the routines as potentially problematic in themselves. When they report reading program difficulties to their principals, they are most likely to report relatively minor difficulties with the materials they are using or with the grouping arrangements they are working with; so quite naturally, these are the problems that take up the principal's time. In short, all three sources of information about problems focus the principal's attention on problems that can be solved within the context of present classroom routines.

How Principals Solve Problems

The first observation to make here is that some principals simply *don't*. Twenty-five percent of my sample of teachers made no reference at all to the principal's activities as a classroom problem solver, and a few specifically said their principals avoided a problem-solving approach, even if they were active in other ways.

> [Our principal] is very involved. [But] he would not voice any concerns unless a parent had voiced them to him. If there aren't any waves, he's not going to make them. (*White Collar Suburb teacher*)

> People here are just sort of left on their own, and if there's no problems, if there's no parental complaints, the classrooms are quiet, then fine, everything is great. As long as test scores in reading and math are fairly acceptable, there's no problem. (*Blue Collar Suburb teacher*)

> [Principals] really don't like to have the boat rocked; they really don't want to hear about those problems. Although they'll never admit it. They'll always say, "I'm here to help," but . . . I see the teachers who are new, and would run to the office for help—[the principals] didn't like it, you're bothering them, you're going into their world. (*Factory City teacher*)

When principals *do* take a problem-solving approach, they often begin by trying to understand the scope and nature of the problem. And most principals do that by trying to see things from the teacher's point of view. Empathy is a useful resource in the repertoire of techniques principals can use to solve problems in the classroom, and it is a resource both "typical" and "effective" principals can rely on. A Trade City principal whose behavior patterns were generally "typical" described how he initiated his attempts to address weaknesses in the classroom:

> The principal's got to be aware that the teacher's job is a very, very difficult one, a very frustrating one, a very tiring one. So our approach with the teacher has got to be a positive approach, even if the teacher is doing something that is not right educationally for the kids. . . . So what I try to do first of all is to try to understand the teacher's plight . . . [when] we sit down with the teacher [and] discuss a certain child. . . . And 99% of the time the teacher will appreciate this approach.

A Blue Collar Suburb principal whose behavior patterns were more generally "effective" similarly observed:

> I think my first year I came on a little bit strong [with suggestions] and put people on the defensive. I had a supervisor who said, "Don't back them into a corner because then they'll spring." So you really have to look for a positive side, and you'll find it most places. There's far more good going on, and you work on that first, and then say, "Have you ever tried this?"

Another Trade City principal, who tended to display many more "effective" behavior patterns than the previous one did, was similarly empathetic with teachers:

> If I see something in the classroom I don't like, I never like to judge anything until I know exactly what is going on. Because sometimes, you could see something and misinterpret what you see; you could hear something and misinterpret what you're hearing. So if I see something that might arouse my curiosity as to what is actually going on, then I will sit down with the teacher and ask for an explanation—"What were you trying to accomplish? I didn't quite understand."

With this shared understanding of the pressures teachers confront, principals can then choose from several options for action. None of these options requires the principal to *order* a teacher to do anything; all assume that primary responsibility for what goes on in the classroom rests with the teacher. Principals thus defer to the teacher's legitimate authority as classroom policy maker. The first and most popular option is for the principal to make suggestions or recommendations about alternatives the teacher could try. Many teachers discussed advice their principals had given them to help solve a classroom problem:

The principal will suggest on her own certain things that the teacher might use; in the plan book she might write particular notes as far as . . . what a teacher may do in a particular reading group. . . . For instance, you can see my reading vocabulary words [on the board]—quite a bit of that is from the principal, as far as how she feels I could incorporate vocabulary in the daily reading. (*Factory City teacher*)

[Our principal] will leave suggestions in your mailbox, and she has a bulletin board downstairs with all kinds of ideas that you could pick up. And she comes in, she listens to the reading group, and if we ask her to join in or give suggestions, she's very good. (*Factory City teacher*)

While praising principals who provided helpful advice on request, teachers criticized those who issued directives and infringed too extensively on their autonomy:

The biggest problem I've ever had with a principal is a principal worrying about "what downtown will think." . . . There are principals who will say, "You have to teach spelling for thirty minutes every day," and they will check your lesson plan and come in and spot check that you are doing this. But the way I work, if something has gone wrong in the morning, or something has gone right and I want to keep going on it, spelling can be another day. . . . Days just are not the same. But some principals just won't take that into account. . . .

[I used to work with] a principal who was strictly structured, and you could not present any new ideas. He had his own ideas about the way things should be done. . . . And I was honest with him when I made my move [to another school]; I knew that here I would have that freedom.

Interestingly enough, the teachers in these examples were referring to principals other than the ones they were currently working with; it may be that teachers sort themselves out in their decisions about where to work in order to avoid principals who regularly threaten the teachers' classroom routines. In any case, remarks like these were rare. For the most part, teachers assessed their principals' problem-solving behavior as follows:

I guess they feel, as long as you're following the program, doing your job, the children should improve their scores. But they don't actually come into the room and tell you what to do.

Thus, whether a principal volunteers helpful suggestions or not, he or she usually gives tacit consent to the structure of opportunities for learning to read that teachers are already providing.

Of course, classroom problems may persist in spite of a principal's suggestions. A teacher may indicate a willingness to "cooperate" and fail to do so; or the suggestion may not work. In such cases, if the principal decides to pursue the matter, he or she can turn to a negotiated solution. One principal described a bargain he had struck with a teacher who was unwilling to adopt the district's new reading series:

> My very first year as a principal, there was a teacher who was almost ready to retire. And she did *not* accept the change in texts that had taken place about three years before. . . . We kind of worked out a compromise where she was willing to [use the new series] with the two top groups, but the lower groups she still felt would benefit from the older series. So it was a little bit of give and take on our parts.

Another principal described at length a successful attempt at persuasion:

> A couple of years ago, we had a kindergarten teacher here who'd never taught before. . . . This gal thought she'd be a far better teacher if she put these workbooks into [the kids'] hands the first day, not realizing that the child can't even hold a pencil properly, his muscles wouldn't even be able to handle the type of thing that she was doing. It was necessary for me to sit down and talk with her about this; but she was convinced the children could do this. She was willing to go along with me, but I could see that she did not accept it fully. Although I've taught every grade, first through seventh—I think I know pretty much the gamut—I think the kindergarten teacher thought, "This guy doesn't know what he's talking about, he's never worked with kids that small." So we have a principal in town, a lady principal who taught kindergarten for about fifteen years, and I said, "Let's try bringing her in and see." So she sat down and pointed out [to the teacher] many of the things I had said, and I think [the teacher] was able to accept it more from her than from me.

In their direct problem-solving contacts with teachers, then, principals rarely behave in ways which transgress on the teacher's essential autonomy in classroom decision making. And even those suggestions which they do make are offered cautiously, so that the basic patterns the teacher has already established in the classroom are not violated.

Principals also attempt to solve classroom problems indirectly by delegating them to reading specialists. Here, too, they help to maintain the classroom teacher's autonomy by emphasizing the ideology of supportiveness. All but one of the principals referred to the reading teacher as a person who provides "help" to the classroom teacher. A principal from Factory City commented:

> [The reading lab teachers] work with children . . . using materials which coincide with Holt but are not Holt. . . . I think the teachers know that [the reading specialists] are here to help them.

Similarly, a Trade City principal reported:

> [The reading teacher] sets up the reading groups and the organization. . . . When a child is newly registered in the school, the reading teacher would take the child [and] do an assessment, so that the child could be placed right away. It saves wear and tear on the teacher and also hastens the placement of the child.

Many principals also stressed the need for specialists to coordinate their activities with those of the classroom teacher:

> I think in some instances people thought [the reading specialists] did their own little bag of tricks, that they really didn't know too much that was going on in the classroom. There is a closer tie into Holt now than there has been, and I think this is what the classroom teachers were looking for. (*Factory City principal*)

Specialists' accounts of principals' behavior confirmed these findings. Several specialists, as we have seen, mentioned that the principal eased their entrance into the school system by describing them as "helpers" during conversations with other faculty members. Other specialists said that principals are primarily helpful in upholding specific decisions the specialists had made.

> They support my recommendations, usually, and they back me. . . . In one case where I tested a child, he said to me "Are you sure about this?" Because it happened to be a political thing. And I said, "Yes." So he said, "We'll go with it." And we did go with it, and we rolled with the punches. He backed me in some things where it would have been easier to go the other way. (*Trade City reading consultant*)

At first glance, it might appear that principals who support reading specialists in this way fail to conform to the pattern I have been describing; backing up the reading specialist may not preserve the autonomy of the classroom teacher. However, it is significant to note that the specialist *needs* the backing of the principal in order to do his or her job. Because teachers' practices and classroom routines are consistently regarded as the foundation on which most other educational decisions are built, specialists need principals to countenance their encroachments on the classroom teacher's domain. The principal's support for specialists is an acknowledgement of, rather than a threat to, teacher autonomy.

In short, when principals take action on problems they have not avoided or explained away, they rely on two strategies. They may choose direct intervention, usually by making suggestions; or they may choose indirect intervention through the reading specialist. Whatever strategy they use, the kinds of weaknesses they address and the way they address them do not seriously challenge teachers' decisions about classroom routines in anything other than superficial matters. This is so because principals depend on teacher preferences and practices in both identifying problems and defining solutions.

PRINCIPALS, TEACHERS,
AND POWER IN THE SCHOOL

This analysis of the principal's impact on the classroom reading program has obvious implications for the distribution of power and influence in the school. Like reading specialists, principals can certainly influence what goes on in classrooms by their offers of information and resources and their skill in bargaining and persuasion. However, teacher autonomy often thwarts a principal's attempts to exercise power, because the power to plan remains primarily with the classroom teacher. This is somewhat ironic in view of teachers' very real feelings of powerlessness vis-à-vis "the system," because the findings of this chapter, together with those of the preceding two chapters, suggest that *teachers are more likely than anyone else in the school to exercise power—not just inside the classroom but outside as well.* Their plans, their practices, and their policies in reading instruction set the agenda for most of the work done both in their own classrooms and in tutorial and administrative settings. Specialists and principals take their cues from teachers, defining and resolving problems in terms of the teacher's experience and thus consenting to and often supporting the teacher's plans. But teachers, unaware of the power and influence they exercise over others in the school, are unable to marshall their own resources and bring them to bear jointly on the problems they confront on a daily basis. The result is that the school reading program operates in a kind of power vacuum, not from the absence of a will to power but from the absence of consciousness. No one in the school is in a good position to use their power to address systematic patterns of failure in the classroom. This power vacuum is evident in all three dimensions of influence outlined in Chapter 1—resources, strategies, and contexts.

Resources

Of the various resources principals can draw upon to influence the school's reading program, the two most important—and the most likely to vary with principal "effectiveness"—are their access to information and their ability to plan. Principals clearly differ in the amount of information they have about reading programs, not only about the ones in use in their own schools, but about alternative programs as well. And my school-level interviews suggest a connection between variations in information and variations in influence. Principals who are not knowledgeable about reading lack the credibility they need to enter the teacher's domain. But principals who *are* knowledgeable about reading instruction are in a position to offer credible advice to teachers; the teacher's perception that a principal has expertise can function in the same way as the perception of a specialist's expertise. Knowledgeability about reading involves *both* knowledge of the materials *and* knowledge of "what is going on" in classrooms. Principals who are in the classroom a lot but lack technical knowledge of the skills and content matter of the reading series, and principals who are quite knowledgeable about programmatic matters but who are not in classrooms very often, cannot have as much influence as a principal who is knowledgeable about both the materials and the educational contexts of reading instruction.

The ability to plan is another power resource that varies among principals. Of course the ability to plan will be affected by the size of the school, the extent of the principal's administrative responsibilities, and the amount of staff support the principal can draw upon. Principals who spend their time "putting out fires," as one put it, lack the time and reflection necessary, not only for planning, but for following through with plans. Principals who do plan, like principals who demonstrate their knowledge, increase their credibility. And teachers feel the effects of a principal's plan; they may not always like it, but they are usually aware of it:

> [Our principal] wants his staff to push, push, push, especially to get the students to grade level. So we are under pressure that way. One pressure . . . is "Where are you every two weeks?" And sometimes you could be almost on the same story! The pressure can be good and bad. He's very much aware of what's going on in reading, [and] it keeps you on your toes.

Principals who plan, who communicate their plans to teachers, and who monitor teacher behavior accordingly, are principals with an important power resource.

However, interviews with principals and teachers alike demonstrate that in their planning, communication, and monitoring, principals still defer to the teacher's classroom experience. The principal's plan is almost always based on the plan the teacher has already put into effect. Even when the principal's plan involves changing materials or reading groups, the teacher's classroom instructional patterns remain essentially the same. Moreover, merely setting a goal need not require specific changes in behavior. One of the districts I sampled required schools to establish their own achievement goals and to evaluate their own progress by writing "Instructional Plans for Improvement." However, no principal or teacher interviewed in that district mentioned any behavioral changes attributable to the use of an IPI; teachers' classroom plans still dominated their instructional agendas.

Teachers are not unaware of the power their autonomy gives them over what goes on in the classroom. During 28 of my interviews with teachers, there was sufficient time for me to ask them, "Who has the most influence over reading in your classroom?" A few teachers (nine in all) pointed to someone other than themselves:

In this school, it's the reading specialist and the learning center coordinator. She is in charge of resources, and she is the one that brought in the new series.

I would say the [Title I] teacher and the principal. If you have a good principal, he'll have a meeting with the teachers and get their feelings about what they would like or not like, and bring it downtown.

I'd say the parent, because it's the parents who give the child the initial enthusiasm for reading. If the parents don't care about reading at home, it's got to carry over to the child.

I would say the powers-that-be downtown. We're just pawns: they tell us what to do, and we're pretty much locked in to doing it. Even if we didn't like the series, we'd still have to use it.

But the remainder of teachers who were asked this question (nearly 70%) maintained that they were the most significant policy makers for the reading program in their classroom. When asked who has the most influence over reading, these teachers responded:

I think the teacher [has the most influence], because no matter what type of program you have, the way the teacher presents it has a lot to do with what happens. The program itself doesn't teach reading, *you* teach it—it's the way *you* present it.

I might sound pompous, but I think I am [the most influential]! Basically I have to decide what should be used and what should be left out.

While these teachers were aware of the power they exercised inside the classroom, they did not seem to realize that the impact of their day-to-day choices extended far beyond the classroom walls. For their part, principals recognized how important it was to help sustain teachers and how difficult it was to remedy deficiencies in the classroom experience, but they did not explicitly treat this as a limitation on their power, only on their "effectiveness." Neither principals nor teachers are left in a position that permits them to exercise their ability to plan very consciously—teachers because they feel constrained by factors outside the classroom and do not recognize the extent to which they, in turn, influence those factors, and principals because they blame themselves for not having planning resources that the school is simply not set up to give them. This "power vacuum," as we shall see shortly, limits all educators' ability to plan for systematic improvement.

Strategies

Teacher autonomy also limits principals' ability to manipulate rewards and sanctions; as a result, principals generally must rely on persuasion, bargaining, and negotiation to influence teacher decision making. We have already seen examples of these strategies illustrated above. The district officials I interviewed confirmed this finding in their own descriptions of principal behavior. During these interviews I asked the following question: "In many of the schools I visited, principals spent a lot of time paying attention to problems connected with the reading program. I noticed that most of them did not actively seek out problems to solve—they waited for teachers to tell them what troubles they were facing and what they wanted principals to do for them. What is your perception of what is going on? What can principals do to effect change in the classroom?" One respondent, a Director of Elementary Education, concurred with my observation that under normal circumstances principals can do very little in the way of threatening to apply, much less actually applying, sanctions:

[A principal can] get in there and observe; find out what [the teacher is] doing; suggest changes in methods; bring in anybody else that he feels is necessary in order to change. To find out if maybe he's seeing the wrong things, he can call me in, I can look at it, maybe I feel the same way, maybe I don't. There's nothing else you can do! Unless [the principal] follows [the teacher] along, and writes down, "Teacher is still not taking suggestions, refuses to do this." And the whole process has to be documented, that he has offered suggestions, and that the teacher has refused to take suggestions. Then we can bring the process to recommending that the contract not be renewed. But it's a very, very difficult thing, because you have to show that [the suggestion] you're giving [the teacher] could have helped, or may have helped, and she would not take it.

An official in a different district painted a similar picture:

When I was a principal at John Smith School, [if] I felt a teacher could have done better in kindergarten or first grade, I would bring her in and say, "Look, I don't think you have the tools necessary for third grade. I am encouraging you to take this first grade." Thank God I never had a situation where they said, "Well, I'm not leaving third grade!" You're saying to me, "Why didn't you phase her fanny right out of there?" Well, it takes too much time. Priorities—I didn't have the time to jot her [actions] down every day. Persuasion—put that individual where she or he can best function.

District officials also provided illustrations of how principals use their resources to try to persuade teachers to improve instruction. First, they have to establish their credibility:

If the principal has made himself or herself a competent individual in the general area of reading—you don't have to be an expert on it—but if you know what the key signs are to a good reading program and you don't see them happening, then you sit down and have a very serious conversation, and you map out a program of improvement for the individual and say, "Now you've done it your way for a period of time, and it's not working. Now, these are the things that I've seen aren't working, and these are the things that I want you to do that *will* work, and therefore that's the way we're going to go." . . . You do a lot of analysis of the kids and of the program and of that individual's approach to teaching. I'm convinced that when adults work together, one of them "sells" the other a concept, or an idea, or a motivation. (*White Collar Suburb superintendent*)

In this official's remarks, the resource that permits a principal to insist that a teacher cooperate with the principal's plan is the latter's knowledgeability about reading, which provides the tools necessary to analyze "the kids, the program, and the individual's approach to teaching." Another official recalled how he tried to establish empathy with teachers—another key feature of bargaining—during his days as a school principal:

I don't think [a principal] can just start from scratch and say, "This is what I want you to do." I think that, as a building principal, as any leader, you have to build a rapport, right from the opening day of school. I used to tell my teachers that I would be as supportive of their efforts as I could be, and if they ever felt that they had made an error in judgment that could cause them or myself some consequences, please inform me. Because it's easier for me to take the heat. . . . With that kind of premise, that kind of basis, when you go to the teachers and you offer suggestions about how they can improve techniques or strategies, I've found that most teachers are receptive.

Finally, officials provided further illustrations of bargaining and negotiation between principals and teachers. A Director of Developmental Programs constructed a hypothetical scenario in which a principal and teacher established achievement goals for her classroom, with the principal's success resting on his knowledge of the reading program.

When I sit down for my year evaluation, I [might] tell Mrs. Jones that she can give me more than five months' [growth in student achievement]. She can say to me, "Jorge, I would have given you more, but remember, you gave me 28 kids, and I wound up with two new ones by April." "Okay, I can buy that, Mrs. Jones; let's see what I can do next year. Next year, I'm going to try to give you [only] 28 [students], and I'm going to try not to put more kids in your classroom, and I'm going to see if you can grow up to twelve months, which is what your colleague did up on the third floor." I think there are ways, if you have a handle on testing and curriculm. If you don't have a handle on the educational growth of your building, then forget it.

Another discussed the process by which teachers and principals establish what the principal will look for during formal classroom observation:

If [the teacher is] not meeting [her] goals and objectives, [the principal] is supposed to sit with the teacher and ask, "What's the problem?" And if [the teacher is] facing a situation that would prevent [her] from reaching [her goals], that [she] had not anticipated—[then the principal would say,] "Rewrite it, see how this goal looks—can you reach this now?"

To summarize, what district officials told me about the strategies principals can use to influence what goes on in classrooms was entirely consistent with reports from teachers, reading specialists, and the principals themselves. Principals use information and the ability to plan as resources for persuading or bargaining with teachers. Neither persuasion nor negotiation is likely to result in substantial change in the classroom—unless the teacher wants it to.

Contexts

The limitations on principals' power and influence are not due solely to their inability to manipulate rewards and sanctions. Persuasion and bargaining are not inherently less potent than coercion as a means of exercising power, as Nyberg (1981) rightly observes. Thus, the task is to understand why principals—"effective" and "typical" alike—are constrained in their attempts to exercise instructional leadership by bargaining with and persuading classroom teachers. For this we must look to the context of teacher-principal transactions.

The first important feature of this context is the nature of the dependency relationship between teachers and principals. Since teachers' professional rewards are rooted in the classroom and the relationships they are able to establish with students, teachers need not depend on their principals very much for anything other than the provision of resources to continue the classroom program. But principals' rewards are rooted largely in good relationships with successful teachers. The result, as Cohen and Murnane (1985, pp. 25–26) argue, is a skewed dependency relationship:

> Principals depend on teachers more than teachers depend on them. Teachers, after all, work in their own self-contained classrooms, and they often can get along decently even if their principal is a boob. A good principal can help teachers, of course, but good principals are not required for teachers to do their jobs. Principals, by contrast, need teachers who do good work if their school is to run well—and if the principal is to be seen as doing a good job. A pack of poor teachers can probably do more to wreck a principal's working life, and perhaps his reputation, than poor principals can do to damage teachers' work and reputations.

This skewed dependency relationship gives principals—even "effective" ones—a powerful incentive to let well enough alone. At the same time, it robs teachers of the incentive to initiate serious professional give-and-take with their principals over the dilemmas they confront in their classroom. Teachers have little to gain by revealing the confusion and frustration of life in classrooms to the administrators charged with monitoring and evaluating them. Instead, they are inclined to tell principals what workbooks they need, which children need Title I/Chapter 1 services, and when to send the reading teacher with supplementary materials.

Reinforcing this pattern is a second contextual feature: teacher autonomy. Despite the potential threat to their careers posed by "a pack of poor teachers," principals are discouraged from active intervention in the classroom by school norms and structures that preserve teacher autonomy. Once again, the incentives are to let well enough alone, and this incentive is a powerful one for both parties. That teachers prefer to operate with the classroom door closed was a frequent theme in my interviews:

> Our principal comes across as a down-to-earth person. He never approaches a teacher with an "I am the principal, you're just a teacher" attitude. He never reminds you of that, and he treats you like a peer. That makes it nice to work for him. . . . It makes me feel comfortable as a teacher; I know I have a lot of latitude in what I do.

The teacher's preference for autonomy, like most of the patterns displayed in these interviews, can be traced to forces in the classroom context. "Interfering" principals point to—and can increase—the uncertainty of the teacher's job; but principals who keep their distance demonstrate faith in the teacher as a professional who knows what to do and how to do it (Lieberman & Miller, 1978).

> I know of a principal in another school who personally goes in and gives the metropolitan tests to the kids. . . . And he tells his teachers that "By May you shall meet [this goal] . . . " or "By May this kid shall be here . . . ." Our principal doesn't come right out and say, "This is where the kid is going to be," or how much progress he has to make. He doesn't personally come in here and test the kids to see if I really taught them. He trusts us.

As we have seen, principals in turn justify their reluctance to interfere by pointing to the dynamics of the social contexts of instruction. They recognize the changing, unpredictable nature of the classroom, the variations in teachers' instructional styles, and the complex ways in which teacher-child interactions shape the learning that goes on, and they argue that they are not in a good position to assess what is happening or why at any given moment, much less to insist on specific changes. Thus, by recognizing and supporting teacher autonomy, *principals consent to present classroom arrangements*, either by not intervening at all, or by intervening in nondisruptive ways. And if, as Nyberg argues (1981, p. 544), "the central task in the exercise of power is eliciting from others consent to one's plan," then teacher autonomy gives teachers an important, if unconscious, measure of power in the school—regardless of how "effective" a principal's leadership may be.

The prevalence of teacher autonomy limits the impact of a last contextual feature—proximity—on the teacher-principal power relationship. The literature on effective principals suggests that principals can exercise influence over teacher behavior when they visit classrooms regularly, hold frequent staff meetings, and generally increase their proximity with classroom teachers (Brookover et al., 1979; Hoffman & Rutherford, 1984). However, the argument above implies that the power of the teacher who plans in a context of autonomy will outweigh the influence of the principal who cultivates proximity. Proximity may decrease the teacher's sense of *isolation* without affecting at all his or her professional *autonomy* (Corwin, 1974); indeed, several teachers expressed appreciation for their principals in precisely those terms. This interpretation would explain why "effective" principals are nevertheless constrained in their ability to effect significant change in the classroom. Telling a principal to "get in there and observe" will increase a principal's proximity to teachers but may not do much to increase his or her power. At best, proximity to teachers may give principals more data to create and justify educational plans; but it is also likely to increase the influence of "present arrangements" on the principal's thinking. Proximity thus may operate as a two-way street. It can enhance the principal's credibility as an instructional leader, but it can also give teachers more opportunity to secure the principal's empathy for their experiences and consent to their plans, even when teachers do not recognize that this is the result.

AUTONOMY, ACCOUNTABILITY, AND EQUAL OPPORTUNITY

The message of the preceding pages should be clear. Elementary school principals, even "effective" ones, are not likely to expand the range of opportunities to learn to read available in public schools. Most of their efforts help to reinforce the mobilization of bias reflected in classroom reading instruction and the supplementary services provided by reading specialists. Principals believe that the "individualization" necessary to equality of opportunity is essentially achieved by within-class ability groups and remedial reading instruction outside the class, and they see their responsibility to provide materials "on the right level" and to help specialists "coordinate" with teachers as the best way to carry out their accountability to children. No principal, however, discussed the difficulty of assessing what the "right" materials or the "right" group for each child might be. Nor did they explain why a child's reading needs are necessarily diagnosed according to "levels." What this language demonstrates is that principals accept classroom reading routines as a point of departure for everything else that happens to a child in the classroom. Indeed, principals treat classroom routines as a way of defining solutions, rather than as a way of defining problems. Thus, instead of trying to determine whether children are learning to read, they determine whether teachers are using the manuals properly. Instead of suggesting alternative methods of classroom organization for children who persistently struggle in a setting of three reading groups, they send the reading specialist to help the teacher shift the children from three old groups to three new groups. The main difference between "effective" and "typical" principals seems to be that effective principals are simply more aggressive in doing these things. Effective principals can enable students to take better advantage of the opportunity resources which are already in place, but they will not promote the creation of new kinds of opportunities which threaten the teacher's pursuit of routine and control. These principals may use test scores to establish goals, suggest new materials for teachers to try in the classroom, or regroup students to achieve "more appropriate" pacing; but none of these activities is very different from things teachers can do themselves within existing classroom arrangements. A principal's effectiveness is thus no guarantee of improved equality of opportunity.

Nor is it a guarantee of school change. Teacher autonomy all too readily becomes a warrant for noninterference in classroom practices. Even when principals do intervene, effective and typical principals alike rely on teacher experiences in assessing what is going on in classrooms, supporting the strengths of the classroom experience, and identifying and resolving problems. The complexities of power and influence evident in teacher-principal transactions suggests that *principals are likely to interpret students' needs in terms of the needs of their teachers.* Children who fail are, with the help of effective principals, given extra books that work with existing classroom routines; they are put into new reading groups and exposed to essentially similar instruction; they are sent to Title I/Chapter 1 teachers who reinforce the skills they need to work better in their groups. When principals do try to implement new programs, the bargains they strike and the persuasive devices they use are constrained by their own dependence on teacher cooperation and the persistence of teacher autonomy. For their part, unaware of their own power over principals, and caught up in the struggle to cope with the paradoxes and uncertainties of classroom instruction, teachers are unlikely to risk increasing their difficulties by innovating on their own. Thus, in the business-as-usual school—even the one headed by an effective principal—the "loose coupling" characterizing the chain of command is far more likely to promote stability than change (Weick, 1976, p. 6).

The failure of elementary school classrooms to provide equality in any of the three dimensions of opportunity cannot be addressed by instructional leaders who design their own educational plans in deference to the plans of the teacher. Teacher autonomy systematically mitigates principals' attempts to address the weaknesses of the classroom experience, particularly for children who do not meet with sustained success in the classroom reading program. It is in this sense that principals' accountability to children for the outcomes of educational decision making in their schools is ultimately subordinated to their accountability to classroom teachers. "Effectiveness" cannot compensate for the power vacuum that all principals confront in seeking to expand the range of opportunity in the classroom.

5

Conflict, Compassion, and Cooptation

The Home-School Connection

The National Commission on Excellence in Education (1983) concluded its report with an admonition to American parents of school-age children: "As surely as you are your children's most important teachers, your children's ideas about education and its significance begin with you. ... Moreover, you bear a responsibility to participate actively in your child's education." The virtues of parent participation, however, are rather different from what this conventional wisdom suggests. Parent involvement in schooling is far more important for the support it offers the school's mobilization of bias than it is for improving the achievement of disadvantaged students. It induces parents to consent to the ways schools define educational interactions. And it helps teachers to solicit information and assistance that support the structure of opportunities already available in the classroom. As a result, the kind of "parent participation" schools encourage is not likely to produce either the excellence demanded in public rhetoric or the equality intended in public policy. It *is* likely to help maintain the mobilization of bias in reading instruction.

PUZZLES ABOUT PARENTS:
A LOOK AT THE RESEARCH

Since the mid-1970s, a growing literature has explored the complex, complicated, and often conflict-ridden relationship between schools and parents. While Coleman (1966) sparked a good deal of controversy about the relative effects of home and school on children's school achievement, it was several years before scholars began to see the *interactions* between home and school as important in their own right. The findings of the past decade of research suggest a degree of consensus on a number of issues, not all of which are completely consistent with one another:

1. Parent involvement matters for any kind of school program success and for any individual child's school achievement, especially in reading.

On this point, the consensus extends beyond the research community into the ranks of practitioners, policy makers, and parents themselves. The common wisdom suggests that schools work better when parents are actively "involved" in their children's education, both at home and in the school building. While the specific academic consequences of parent involvement are not easily or consistently demonstrated, its general importance is accepted without question. Virtually every PTA meeting, parent-teacher conference, open house, and "know your school night" presumes that parent participation enhances education. The call for parent "input" characterizes compensatory education regulations (Stonehill & Anderson, 1982), "effective school" rhetoric (Hoffman & Rutherford, 1984), teacher and principal in-service programs, and research on individual learning (Durkin, 1984). Fullan (1982, p. 193) states simply that "emerging from [the] research [on parent and community involvement] in schools is a message which is remarkable in its consistency: the closer the parent is to the education of the child, the greater the impact on child development and educational achievement." When educators talk about parents, both publicly and privately, they concur with Fullan's conclusion.

2. Teachers hold strong and usually negative views about the attitudes of low-income parents toward schooling and the school.

Lightfoot (1978) argues that the teacher's view of parents is rooted in a potent combination of myths, assumptions, preconceptions, and isolation:

> Without actually knowing parents, without actually hearing their point of view, teachers and principals have developed strong negative images of them. . . . One of the predominant myths about black parents and poor parents who live in the depressed areas around inner-city schools is that they do not care about the education of their children, are passive and unresponsive to attempts by teachers and administrators to get them involved, and are ignorant and naive about the intellectual and social needs of their children (pp. 35–36).

In their detailed case study of four elementary school teachers, Carew and Lightfoot (1979) go on to observe that teachers' beliefs are intense and persistent, even though "with their busy schedules none of the teachers reported visiting students' homes or talking with parents other than on the telephone or at scheduled parent-teacher conferences, occasional meetings and social events in the school" (p. 236). According to this research, the relationship between parents and teachers provides little to counter the negative image teachers hold of parents who are economically disadvantaged.

> 3. Contacts between teachers and parents do not help teachers learn about parents' real attitudes toward schooling, even though they believe parent involvement is so important.

Fullan describes at length the phenomenological and logistical barriers that prevent teachers from learning about the "subjective world of parents" and capitalizing on what parents have to offer (1982, p. 203). Lightfoot (1978) notes the lack of meaningful contacts between teachers and parents, contacts that would give teachers insight into the kinds of educational attitudes that economically disadvantaged parents really hold. The opinions of teachers about extra-school influences seem to be based on a set of preconceptions rather than on a series of authenic encounters. Lightfoot observes (pp. 27–28):

> There are very few opportunities for parents and teachers to come together for meaningful, substantive discussion. In fact, schools organize public, ritualistic occasions that do not allow for real contact, negotiation, or criticism between parents and teachers. Rather, they are institutionalized ways of establishing boundaries between insiders (teachers) and interlopers (parents) under the guise of polite conversation and mature cooperation.

Even worse, on those few occasions when real exchanges between teachers and parents *do* take place, they are more likely to engender frustration and hostility than cooperation and mutal accord:

> Teachers rarely call in praise of a child. Usually when parents are summoned to the school, the teacher is reporting on some trouble their child is having. . . . Parents, on the other hand, rarely call a teacher to praise her. . . . Whether the contact is initiated by teachers or parents, it becomes a highly charged, defensive interaction (Lightfoot, pp. 28–29).

Given these obstacles to meaningful communication, the presumed importance of the family educational context is matched only by teachers' ignorance of it. Teachers evaluate family influences only through the medium of school-bound teacher-parent interactions.

Given these three findings, the fourth is not surprising.

4. The teacher's desire for parent involvement in school programs is at best ambiguous.

On the one hand, teachers do a number of things to encourage parent involvement with their children's education. Report cards, conferences, newsletters, and open houses are a regular part of the school year. On the other hand, teachers are all too aware of the extent to which parent involvement can increase the professional uncertainty they confront in the classrooms. Lortie's observations (1975, p. 189) suggest that teachers are vulnerable both to parent complaints *and* to parent "assistance." Teachers work hard to "build and sustain a social order [in the classroom] with people over whom they have only limited, place-bound authority," and parent interference of any sort threatens the order teachers cultivate with such care. As a result, despite shared interest in the welfare of the individual child—an interest mandated for the teacher by the paradox of collective instruction and the goal of equal opportunity—all parents and teachers find themselves inevitably at odds with one another. Lightfoot (1978, pp. 22–23) sees these conflicts as rooted in the tension between the necessarily collective, universalistic approach teachers must rely on to cope with large groups of children on a daily basis, and the individualized, particularistic lens through which a parent sees her own child. Add to this the negative images of economically disadvantaged parents that teachers carry with them, and it is no surprise that the "natural enmity" between teachers and parents (McPherson, 1972) should be exacerbated in the case of low-income parents. Under these circumstances, as important as teachers believe the "involvement" of parents to be, their desire for it is understandably ambiguous.

This, then, is the picture of the home-school connection painted in recent research, especially with respect to economically disadvantaged families. What is missing from this portrait, however, is the extent to which the ambiguities of the teacher-parent relationship color teachers' perspectives on the entire enterprise of education. With the exception of Lightfoot, most researchers on parent involvement and its consequences fail to recognize the amount of mental and emotional energy teachers invest in evaluating and responding to children's home lives. Again and again, teachers returned to the home-school connection, especially in their remarks about children's language abilities, social skills, emotional needs, and learning styles. Furthermore, teachers talked at greater length about their relationships with parents than did anyone else in the school, and not simply because they were the ones most likely to see parents. Thus, although parents do interact with principals, with reading specialists, and occasionally with district officials and school board members, the home-school connection is best understood in the context of the teacher-parent relationship and the classroom mobilization of bias. My own interviews with teachers support some of the findings reported above, challenge others, and refine still others. They also help to explain some of the puzzles and tensions that characterize teachers' responses to parental involvement in the education of their children.

PARENTS AND TEACHERS: A RELATION AT RISK

Teachers' descriptions of their relationships with parents varied widely in both tone and content, and this variation characterized all four of the districts I visited. On some issues teachers were somewhat divided; on others they spoke with a single voice. Both patterns are important in assessing the parent-teacher relationship and its consequences for the school's provision of opportunity. Several themes emerged in these wide-ranging discussions: (1) teachers vary in their perspectives on parents; (2) opportunities for contact between teachers and parents are sharply constrained; (3) the things teachers and parents talk about help to support the classroom mobilization of bias; and (4) teachers' ambiguous responses to parent involvement limit the kinds of involvement they are likely to cultivate.

Teachers' Perspectives on Parents

The research on teachers and parents described above, particularly that of Lightfoot, suggests that teachers view low-income and minority parents categorically as apathetic, uncaring, and uninterested in educational matters. However, I found not one perspective, but several, characterizing teachers' beliefs about parent attitudes toward schooling. Moreover, the particular perspective any given teacher articulated did not seem to depend on the district where he or she happened to be teaching. These variations matter, not simply because they help to refine the portrait of teacher attitudes in the literature, but because the varied perspectives were *not* accompanied by much variation in the actual transactions between teachers and parents, an argument I will develop below. The immediate task, then, is to describe the different perspectives on parents that I encountered in my interviews with teachers.

Perspective 1: "Parents don't care." An extended excerpt from an interview with a frustrated and angry Trade City teacher provides a compelling example of the overwhelmingly negative perspective on parents that a few teachers articulated.

Most parents really don't care. Their only contacts with the school are bad contacts. The biggest problem is there's no parent involvement at all. I think most teachers would say that, not just the ones here. If parents took the concern of bringing up these kids a long time ago, giving them something before they even walked in the door in kindergarten, kids wouldn't be in a mess. I had a parent who said she didn't like the way I was teaching reading, and her daughter's one of the ones in third grade who is reading at a beginning first grade level. [Teacher reads letter aloud.] "I am writing to ask you to please send homework with Jennifer"—who gets homework every night anyway. "If you can't do that then I will get angry and when I come in to see you I will go to the principal"—spelled wrong—"about your way of teaching. I have helped Jennifer with her homework every day. If you give the words and have them study them before the test they would learn"—spelled wrong— "better. I don't believe school system has changed when I was in school of how to teach. Because I cannot be there as often as other mothers I don't mean I don't care about Jennifer learning. I will prove it by talking to the principal about you and how you teach reading." This is what we're up against. . . . You hate to say it, but in most cases, when you confront [a parent] with something, they look to everybody and everything but themselves.

This kind of perspective, however, was rare. Only three other teachers spoke of parents categorically as "uncaring, unsympathetic, and ignorant of the value of education." Nevertheless, they are an important group because the strength of their reactions to parents makes them more noticeable than their less intense colleagues.

   Perspective 2: "Parents care, but they can't get very involved." The fifteen teachers who took this view saw low-income parents as having the right attitudes toward schooling but lacking the necessary resources to get involved and help their children. One resource parents lack is time:

I have seen a couple of parents; however, you're dealing with the problem of "I don't have a car to come and see you" or "I work, and it is very difficult to take time off from work and come in." So that's very difficult—it's a hard problem to get around. (*Factory City teacher*)

Another resource they lack is information about how to help their children properly:

Because of our reading program, most of this is new to [the parents]. They're not able to help the children because they don't quite understand themselves. . . . When [the parents] see these papers they say, "When we were in school it was 'See Dick, see Jane run.' We never saw anything like this." (*Factory City teacher*)

Most parents really don't remember much about short vowel sounds, long vowel sounds. So that kind of thing, they can't really help their kids with. (*Trade City teacher*)

Most of [the parents] aren't familiar with the [Distar] program; it's kind of a different approach. They write letters differently. The *a* is written like a typewritten *a*; letters are joined together, such as *sh* and *th*; there are lines over [vowels] to differentiate between short and long [sounds]; with the sentences there's no capital letters. . . . This is hard for some of the parents to understand, so basically they're confused a lot of the time as to how to help. (*Factory City teacher*)

Still a third resource some parents lack, especially those who are foreign-born, is the language skill necessary even to communicate with the teacher, much less to follow the teacher's instructions for help at home:

Our parents are lovely parents, very nice. But some of them can't speak any English. They don't know what's going on. They come—they are very interested, they want the child [to be] learning, but they don't know what it is all about. You have to speak in a very simple language—"How is Pietro doing?" "He has to improve"—because I can't explain to her long vowels and short vowels, or consonants. (*Factory City teacher*)

Parents in this school system, most of them don't ask an awful lot of questions. Maybe twenty percent of the parents do not speak English very well, but mostly Italian. With those people, very little communication is possible. Very often one of their older children will come in and almost translate. (*Blue Collar Suburb teacher*)

In this perspective, then, the problem with parents is not their lack of concern, but rather their lack of resources to become effectively involved.

Perspective 3: "Parents care, but their expectations are inappropriate." A third perspective also affirms that parents care, but not about the right things. The problem is not a lack of interest or general support, but rather a misguided or inadequately informed vision of what schools can and should do. Teachers indicated several variations on this theme. In one version, teachers say that parental concerns extend to only a few matters; once their minds have been put at ease on those issues, they tend to trust teachers to handle the more complex and demanding tasks of education. As a White Collar Suburb teacher put it, "Some parents are not interested in frills, but only in basic instruction." Other teachers agreed:

> A large number of parents just accept what you say. . . . There isn't a lot of questioning about the reading programs, not in this area. This is probably one of the most disadvantaged areas in the town. . . . Most of the parents don't even have education much beyond high school, some not even that, so they look to the teacher as the authority. (*Blue Collar Suburb teacher*)

> I find a lot of parents don't really seem to be all that concerned. I guess because they are really not sure what a child should be learning at a particular point in time. They may feel, "Gee, my kid's in second grade, he's reading!" It doesn't matter what level he's reading at, but they just feel, "He can read, that's super, I couldn't read when I was in second grade!" (*Factory City teacher*)

According to this perspective, parents care about their children's education, but so long as teachers meet their basic expectations, the parents remain on the sidelines. Low parental expectations can result from the parents' lack of education or skill development, or from their tendency to simply trust teachers to do their job. In this view, parents inappropriately see home and school as separate spheres, and their lack of involvement results not from lack of interest, but from the unquestioning belief that the teacher knows what she should be doing—and is probably doing it.

A second variation on the theme of misguided expectations is that parents are overly concerned about disciplinary matters, abandoning academic matters to the teacher. A fairly lengthy excerpt from the comments of a Factory City teacher illustrates the point.

> I have a lot of contact with my first grade parents because most of them bring their kids to school. And most of them will say to me, "How's he doing?" I have mostly dealt with foreign-born parents, especially the Portuguese, who have always lived under the dictatorship. Consequently, whatever I say is right. I mean they do not disagree with me at all in the slightest. The school is my department; whatever happens in this room is my department. . . . What the parent is really interested in learning is, is the child behaving in school? Especially for the Portuguese, that's very important. So I will tell them whether or not the child is behaving in school. Then I will go into the difficulties that the child is having.

Teachers see parents' problem here as too narrow a vision of what constitutes "success" in schooling. When parents fail to pay attention to other important dimensions in the enterprise of education, they are unable to provide appropriate support and reinforcement where it is needed. Parents are not apathetic, they are simply misguided.

Still another variation on this third perspective is that parents can demand too much of their children. Such pressure, teachers believe, can hinder a child's development.

> Parents in this area are very concerned with early reading. That's terrific if the child is ready, but it can cause problems if he is not. (*White Collar Suburb teacher*)

> So many times parents are so negative. They forget that they were once here. Every so often I jumble something on the board for the parents and I say, "Would you like to read that?" and they say, "Oh, I don't know what that says." "Understand that your child doesn't either, that at one time you yourself had to learn, and that it's a growth process." [The parents] expect [the children] to know it overnight—well, it's not possible. (*Trade City teacher*)

Taken together, these three variations on Perspective 3 imply that teachers want parents' expectations for children to coincide with those of teachers. Parents whose expectations are too low or misplaced fail to give their children the kind of support and "reinforcement" they need; those whose expectations are too high pressure their children beyond what they are capable of doing. No teacher recounted a situation in which they adjusted their expectations for a child's achievement in response to a parent's academic expectations (although several did discuss adjusting expectations because of other extra-school factors, a topic I will address later). But it is important to note that all of these teachers see the problem with parents not in terms of a failure to care, but in terms of inappropriate, often uninformed, expectations. Teachers want parents who ask informed questions about what their child is doing and why; but they do not want parents to be *too* demanding or to ask about the wrong things.

Perspective 4: "Parents care, and they show it." Fully 25 percent of my sample of teachers expressed a version of the perspective that parents care about and actively support their children's education, either by remarking on parents' general supportiveness or by giving specific examples of activities parents had engaged in to help their children. Furthermore, the teachers who took this approach were distributed among all four school districts. Following are the comments of teachers who indicated that parents as a group actively demonstrate their concern for their children:

The parents are concerned—they want to know how they can help. I have 28 youngsters and 27 parents showed up [for parent-teacher conferences]. In fact, in some instances I had mother *and* father. My parents seem to be very cooperative this year. (*Factory City teacher*)

You have to have that support from parents for dittos and reading assignments you send home, and 90 percent of them will support you. This year I'm also getting a lot of fathers in. I request to see both parents, whether together or separately. Even some fathers whose kids only spend weekends with them are coming in. (*White Collar Suburb teacher*)

Other teachers provided examples of specific things parents had done to help their children.

Last year I had a reading group that was very, very low. They came to me below grade level. I felt that they had been, for whatever reasons, stagnating. They just hadn't been moving along. . . . I contacted the parents and asked for their help and support, because [the students] had a lot of homework. And for the most part I got it. (*Trade City teacher*)

Some parents will work right along with you. One makes the child stay . . . maybe once or twice a week with me. Then [the parent] will find out from me what I've done, and she'll continue it at home; I'll give her material to work with. She's very cooperative that way. (*Factory City teacher*)

These findings are quite surprising in view of the literature arguing that teachers see parents, particularly low-income parents, as people who are neither concerned about nor involved with the business of education.

Perspective 5: "Parents differ." In a final perspective, teachers drew distinctions among different kinds of parents, in terms of both their attitudes and their actions with respect to the school. Some teachers, for example, differentiated between "cooperative" and "uncooperative" parents:

For some children I find that I can use the parents in a cooperative way. For others, I find I am blocked by the parents; they are just not ready to be helpful. (*White Collar Suburb teacher*)

We have some parents that are really interested; they'll check [the children's] homework every night. They want to know what we are doing and how they can help [their children] with it. Then we have other parents who like to come in and tell us how to teach! And then we have some we can't find at all, to get any help from. (*Trade City teacher*)

Other teachers distinguished among parents in terms of the skills they brought to their role in the school.

There isn't a parent in the school that doesn't want their child to learn, that isn't upset when they're not doing well, wants them to learn, wants to help. Some can, some can't. And I use them as best I can, judging on what the parent's abilities are. (*Trade City teacher*)

Teachers who took this perspective tended not to speak about parents in categorical terms. They saw parents as people with different attitudes and skills, even when they come from similar socio-economic or cultural circumstances. This perspective, too, stands in contrast to the claim that teachers tend to make sweeping judgments about parent attitudes toward the school system.

The teachers in my sample, then, did not speak with one voice about parents of the students in their classrooms. Moreover, the differences in the perspectives teachers adopted may not have been caused by real differences in the parents they encountered. It was not uncommon to find teachers who worked in the same school or district holding very different views of parents. For instance, the following comments came from two teachers who worked in the same mixed-neighborhood Trade City school:

In this school it's a vicious circle of environment, all kinds of problems related to each other, a cat chasing its tail. I'm just such a small cog in the whole process. When [the children] go home, if it's not reinforced, everything I do is practically wasted. It just makes it that much longer before they really grasp something. . . . A bit of interest [from the parents] is hard to get.

I know some parents give more encouragement than others. But still, just about every single parent comes in and they want the kid to read. . . . I would suggest [to the parents] that they encourage [the children] to read, read with them if they can, go to the library, or even if they're watching television, ask the kid questions about the show for comprehension. I don't know if they do it. I'm sure some do.

Teachers working at different schools who confront similar circumstances with parents can also vary in their responses. The following two Factory City teachers, who had virtually the same turnout for parent-teacher conferences, painted very different pictures of their relationship with parents.

We don't have that much contact with parents. Last week we just had parent conferences. I have 25 children; I worked very hard on the report cards, I was very prepared for the conferences, and for two days, I had a total of 18 parents that showed up, out of 25. And then out of those 18 that showed up, one man sat here during that whole conference with plugs in his ears, hooked up to one of those big tape deck radios. . . . I try to tell them as much as I can. But their main interest is if their child is doing good in school and if their child is going to pass. And that's all they really want to know.

I send papers home every night. . . . [The parents] are an active part in the reading program. Checking the homework, making sure that it's done—not even necessarily correcting it, just making sure that it's done, and that they set aside a certain time for the children to do it. . . . [Interviewer: Do all parents do this?] No. So you contact them again, to see if they misunderstood, or perhaps there's some reason for it. Basically, you get 85% [cooperation], but there's always some you won't reach for various problems, family reasons, and so forth. Out of 26, I had 18 parents [show for parent conferences].

The first of these teachers appears to subscribe to the view that most (not all) parents care, but do not have high enough expectations; the second sees most parents as caring and involved, noting differences in parent involvement only when specifically questioned. Although they had experienced the same level of participation in parent conferences, these teachers differed in their evaluation of parent concern and cooperation. The same may be said of the two Trade City teachers; they worked at the same school with parents who evidently varied in the level of cooperation they extended to the teacher, but one saw parents as essentially uninterested and uninvolved, while the other saw parents as very concerned and often capable. Thus, the evidence suggests that teacher perspectives varied somewhat independently of the district they worked in, the school they were assigned to, and the attitudes and behaviors of the parents they actually encountered.

This variation in teacher perspectives is significant in two respects. First, it refines the research which suggests that virtually all teachers hold negative views of poor and minority parents. Many teachers do not see parents as categorically unconcerned and uninvolved, and teachers differed substantially from one another in their perceptions and interpretations of parents' relationship to the school. Second, the following pages will show that, despite the variation in teacher attitudes, their actual transactions with parents were remarkably similar. Teachers' descriptions of the home-school connection suggest that *parent-teacher contacts, regardless of the teacher's perception of parents, help to support the classroom mobilization of bias.* The occasions for contact, the topics for discussion, and the methods used for conflict resolution, reinforce the choices schools already make in teaching children to read. Put somewhat differently, parents' transactions with teachers serve as an essentially conservative force; "involvement" is not likely to promote changes in the means schools rely on to provide equality of opportunity.

Occasions for Parent-Teacher Contact

Teachers provided a great deal of information about the circumstances surrounding their actual contacts with parents. These occasions are important to teachers, not because of the attitudes teachers bring to their encounters with parents, but because of the support those encounters can provide for the mobilization of bias in reading instruction. This support derives in part from the ways in which opportunities for contact between teachers and parents are constrained (Fullan, 1982; Lightfoot, 1978). They are constrained in three senses: first, there are few such opportunities; second, face-to-face exchanges between teachers and parents almost always take place in the teacher's domain (the school—usually the teacher's own classroom) rather than in the parent's domain (the home or place of employment); and third, contact is more likely to be initiated by teachers than by parents. As one teacher put it, "We get together [with parents] mostly on a reporting basis, unless there is a problem." These patterns showed up in all four districts and at all grade levels. And they matter because the constraints on teacher-parent contacts prevent parents from effectively challenging the classroom mobilization of bias.

Teachers pointed to several kinds of opportunities for encounters with parents. Regular parent-teacher conferences and report cards predominated, and teachers indicated that both these devices are limited in the actual amount of communication they facilitate. As we have seen, in many lower-income neighborhoods language barriers can hamper both written and verbal reports on a child's progress. Teachers must conduct as many as 25 parent conferences in two or three days; the constraints imposed by the schedule were apparent in the words of one Factory City teacher: "Some of the parents wanted to stay on and on, longer than the ten minutes I had planned; I had my clock and it didn't help." As for report cards, they are as likely to be a source of confusion as information:

> With the new report cards, even if I have an excellent reader on Level 2, Level 2 is not a fourth grade level, so I cannot give that reader an A. Parents do not like this. Because they thought, "Gee, my youngster's doing beautifully in that group." And it's true. But it's not on grade level so I'm forced to give a B. . . . And this is difficult for a parent to understand. (*Factory City teacher*)

Some teachers supplement report cards and conferences with other occasions for communicating with parents. Several, for example, mentioned regular class newsletters.

> I send home letters approximately twice a month, with things that I would like [the parents] to do with their kids at home—not so much "you sit down and do it," but with them doing it together. I send home vocabulary lists to work on, books that we might have used in the classroom that are pretty good. Or if I come across a game that's easy enough for them to do at home I'll ditto it up and send that home. (*Blue Collar Suburb teacher*)

Other teachers rely on the telephone, usually to report a problem:

> I deal with a lot of the problems by calling the parents. . . . If I think there's something wrong, or I think there's something I don't know, I call. I want to know what's going on. And I think they're pretty honest, too. I tell them, "You have to tell me." I've had to deal with kids with alcoholism in the house, child abuse, abuse of the mother; and you have to know, so you can deal with it in your own time. (*White Collar Suburb teacher*)

Still others described group meetings with parents they arranged of their own accord:

> I always have open house in September. I let [the parents] come in and observe what their kids have learned in that month, to see how much progress they have made and what they can do. And they are shocked, they are really awed. And I get about 95 percent participation, and those who cannot come usually call the school or send me a note telling me they cannot come but they'd be happy to come out for a conference with me. (*Factory City teacher*)

Parent-teacher contacts, then, are usually initiated by the teacher, usually take place at school, and usually involve reporting, problem solving, or both. These patterns are important in setting the stage for exchanges of information between parents and teachers that support the classroom mobilization of bias.

What Teachers Tell Parents

Teachers also provided substantial information about the content of their transactions with parents. Despite the variation in teachers' opinions about parent support for schooling, there was a surprising degree of similarity in what teachers and parents talk about when they have opportunities for conversation. Whether they are communicating through classroom newsletters, occasional casual contact with parents, parent-teacher conferences, or open house meetings, teachers provide parents with information that will help them support the reading program that is already in place.

One important agenda item in what teachers tell parents is information about the reading program and the materials the children are using.

> When I started [meeting with parents] I explained . . . [the] new program [and] what we hoped to cover. . . . At the end of each unit . . . we sent home the booklet plus the worksheets and a letter explaining what we have done. We would say to the parents, for example, "This book was stressing the letter M." (*Trade City teacher*)

> In regard to reading, I explain the program to them as best I can. When I see them individually, I try to explain what the homework is, what sounds we're doing now, so they understand what their child should be doing. (*Factory City teacher*)

Teachers want parents to have information about the school reading program, because parents who know what their children are supposed to be doing can help their children work well within the classroom structure of opportunities. Parents who lack this information are less able to support their child's efforts. More important, information about the reading program can prevent challenges to the classroom mobilization of bias. Teachers can use programmatic information to explain away parents' potential questions or criticisms:

> Sometimes you do get a parent who has a question, and then after talking to [them], you just realize that they weren't communicating—probably you were saying the same thing. And we usually agree. Most parents agree that the kids have to have certain things in homework, that they have to do certain things in class. (*Trade City teacher*)

> Parents are elated that their kids are going to be reading, but I have to explain to them that they're not going to have a book to take home and read every day. I have to explain to them that we are teaching sounds, forming sounds, getting sounds formed as words. And they usually respond to that. I say "When they bring their take-homes home, their worksheets home, don't expect them to read 'The dog ran to school.' They're not ready to read like that." . . . They're only kindergartners, 4 and 5; there's no need to pressure them with that. As long as they get their letters and numbers, the colors and the social skills—it's beautiful.

This teacher's information served not so much to enlist parents as equal partners in the enterprise of reading instruction, as to preempt questions or criticisms of the teacher's practices in providing opportunity to read. Parents presumably ended the school year accepting the Distar reading series and its unusual format; accepting the teacher's picture of "appropriate" kindergarten achievement (whether the teacher's picture was more or less demanding than their own); accepting the sorting of children and their learning into grade levels; and accepting the need for a particular set of "social skills" to complement the requisite academic skills of letter, number, and color recognition as part of "reading readiness."

While visiting this teacher's school, I had the opportunity to do a spontaneous interview with the president of the school's Parent Advisory Council.[1] I was struck by the parallels between her comments and those of the teacher just cited:

> The way they make their sounds and everything [in the Distar program] is a lot different than when we were going to school. Then they told you how to sound it out and everything. Now they have all the different words broken down, and they're pronouncing the sounds of the alphabet a lot different than when I was in school. So really [the teachers] are teaching me and I'm teaching [my kids] at the same time. We called A an A; they call it "Ah" when it has this little squiggle. And then with this clapping stuff—to me, I think a child's going to learn to read anyway, once he gets the basics and knows his sounds; you don't need all this here. But that's the way they do it, and [my children] are doing pretty good. I don't mind, I think it's a good reading program; as long as they're getting out of it what they're supposed to be getting out of it, I don't mind. I'm not going to knock any program that I really don't understand, as long as it does what it's supposed to do. It's teaching my children, and I see a lot of improvement. I like progress.

The information the classroom teacher had provided about the school reading program had evidently succeeded in overcoming this parent's doubts about its methods. She was willing to live with some confusion as to the means teachers were using so long as the program achieved the ends it was "supposed to" achieve. Her comments are highly suggestive in the support they provide for my interpretation of the things teachers tell parents. Teachers use information as a persuasive or a preemptive device; information can blunt criticism by enabling parents to accept the school's version of what children should be doing in reading and how they should be doing it. Information sets the agenda and thus limits the arena for potential conflict.

Some teachers supplemented general information about the reading program with more specific suggestions of things parents can do at home to help their children:

> I have been sending home . . . newsletters with a lot of different infor- mation about things that are going on in school, letting [parents] know what kind of things they can do at home [and] how to review papers with [their children]. . . . I send home flash cards with reading words, and I've asked the parents to have a box where the kids can keep all their school-related materials and practice. (*Blue Collar Suburb teacher*)

> I give parents little activities that they can do at home with the chil- dren. . . . I think that enlisting parents in the reading program is a great idea, and I've found it to be very helpful. It helps the parents to learn some ways in which they can help their children. (*Trade City teacher*)

The second teacher's remarks are very revealing. She speaks in terms of "enlisting" parents and helping them to "learn" how to help their children. This language suggests that, in the teacher's view, some kinds of parent assistance are more likely to be helpful than others, and parents who know about the reading program and who follow specific suggestions from the teacher are more likely to give the kind of assistance that supports the classroom reading program. Parent assistance can help produce a better "fit" between the learning that goes on at home and the learning that goes on at school. It is important to note the teacher's assumption that home learning ought to accommodate to the demands of school learning, instead of the other way around.

Although some teachers asked parents to help their children practice specific skills, they were more likely to ask parents simply to encourage general reading. Teachers who displayed very different attitudes toward parent support for schooling were equally likely to ask parents to promote reading at home. A Trade City teacher who appeared to believe that "par- ents don't care" commented:

> Mainly I try to encourage parents to get their children to read. I tell them, even if it's the funnies, the comics in the newspaper, to let them read. If they're sitting at the table, let them read what's on the cereal box.

A Blue Collar Suburb teacher who believed that "parents care but can't get very involved" because of language barriers nevertheless told me:

I encourage the parents to read to their kids. If a child sees their parent reading, as with anything else, they imitate. In class, if I see a good reader, pretty often the parent is also an avid reader. So I do suggest that the parent set aside a period each day where the child can read, even if it's just ten minutes a day. Usually I don't give any homework in reading per se, so the kind of reading that's done at home is for enjoyment, not for specific skills.

This last comment is also revealing. Teachers do not want parents to give their children specific instruction independent of the teacher's guidelines. Parents should either make use of suggestions from the teacher keyed to the demands of the reading program, or they should simply promote general reading. The assumption seems to be that if parents aren't capable of adopting the school's programmatic approach to reading instruction, involving decoding skills, blending skills, and the like, then they cannot—and should not—provide specific instruction at all; they should simply read with their children for general enjoyment and practice. In any case, whether the information parents receive promotes specific skill practice or general reading, it enables them to support the classroom mobilization of bias in reading instruction.

Another kind of information teachers give parents is how their children are performing in the reading program. This information, too, is consistent with the school's mobilization of bias, which sorts children into "levels" that vary primarily in the pace of instruction.

A lot of [the parents] really don't understand the whole reading program itself; you know, they have the language problem, and they really don't understand it. The main thing I try to stress is what level they're on, if the children are reading on level or below level. That they understand, if their child is not up to level. (*Factory City teacher*)

The information may also focus on specific skills the program offers:

With my parent monthly report, I test the children at the end of the month for all the concepts that they have covered, and I have a little box beside each concept. And if they need improvement in that certain concept, I put an X in that box, which means the child is deficient in that area. (*Factory City teacher*)

Both kinds of information are keyed to the reading program being used in the classroom. Children's needs and achievements are communicated to parents in terms of the materials used for classroom reading instruction.

Given the heavy reliance on materials as a means of providing opportunity, and the interaction between the dimensions of needs assessment and material provision, this finding makes sense.

Finally, teachers provide parents with information about their children's behavior in school. Their transactions with parents are intimately tied to the conceptual features of reading instruction discussed in Chapter 2:

> I've had a lot of help from parents when I have problem kids, kids who have difficulty adjusting to the group, following group routines. Parents oftentimes will communicate to me that there are similar problems at home, and I find there's a definite carry-over, it's not just here. This is the child's adjustment problem at this particular point in his life. (*Trade City teacher*)

Teachers provide information to parents about children's behavior in order to solicit their help in re-forming children, making them able—or at least willing—to work with the kinds of routines that classroom reading instruction requires children to master. Behavior-related information also supports the school's mobilization of bias in reading instruction.

Given these patterns in what teachers tell parents, it is not surprising to find that the questions parents ask teachers are framed in terms of meeting children's reading needs. For example, when I asked the teacher who stressed children's reading levels what kinds of concerns parents voice to her, she replied:

> Most of the time they're concerned because [the child] is not reading on level. They wonder why the child is not reading on level.

When I addressed a similar question to the teacher whose monthly reports to parents included information about reading skills the children need to develop, she responded:

> The parents are usually concerned with whatever area their child is deficient in; they want to know how they can help them.

Other teachers also confirmed that when parents ask questions, they take their cues from what teachers tell them:

> I show [parents] the skills the child is working on, and I tell them about the child's anticipated progress. The parents are very interested in that. They really want to know if the child is *normal*. That means that when the child is finished with first grade, he is ready to go on to second grade! (*White Collar Suburb teacher*)

The parent's concern is, "Is my child reading on grade level?" and "Why isn't this [grade] an A when it was last year?" (*Factory City teacher*)

The constraints imposed by the classroom reading program are also evident in parent questions about what they can do to help their children. An incident recounted by a Factory City teacher using the Distar series provides an especially good example:

One [parent] came in and said, "I don't understand what you wanted from Michael. I told him that the word was rat, and he told me that, no, I had to sound it out, but I don't know how to sound it out." So I said, "He's right." Michael was trying to show her [what he does in school], but she, being the parent, wanted it to go faster, like sight words. And I said, "He says, 'ra-a-a-a-t.' Say it faster—'r-a-a-t.' What word? 'Rat.' Then he uses a sentence—'The rat ate the cheese.'" And [the parent] said, "Oh, I see."

Parents' questions and concerns are thus shaped by the means schools use to assess children's needs, the kinds of materials used in the classroom, and the reading group experiences that structure educational interactions—and this was just as true in White Collar Suburb, where parents are presumably more "aware" and "informed," as it was in the other three districts. Teacher cue-giving and parent cue-taking thus support the classroom mobilization of bias.

What Parents Tell Teachers

The kinds of questions teachers ask of parents and the information parents are likely to provide to teachers also support the mobilization of bias in reading instruction. Several teachers described the insights parents could provide about the things their children were interested in or their general feelings about school. However, by far the most prevalent theme in teachers' remarks about the information they receive from parents concerned home circumstances that have a bearing on a child's school performance. Nearly half my sample of teachers mentioned this kind of information; even more significantly, in *every case* the information concerned problems in the child's home life. Following are some typical examples:

Sometimes I learn very interesting things [from the parents]. For example, I had a new girl this fall who was only at Level 1 in her reading, yet she seemed bright enough in other ways. In talking with her parents, I found out that the home had recently been through a divorce, that the older brother had been in a serious accident and was now more or less a vegetable living at home, and that the older sister had moved out. The basis of the divorce turned out to be child molesting on the part of her father. (*White Collar Suburb teacher*)

The home background [of one of my students] is unbelievable. His father married at the tender age of 17. The mother left him. The father went home to his mother. The grandmother, then, has raised this child, who considers her his mother—he calls her mom. But he knows his father is his father and he knows this other man is his grandfather. But his aunts and uncles he calls brothers and sisters—he cannot differentiate at times. This is the confusion that this child has. The grandmother has made all kinds of excuses for the inability of this child to learn, from "It's the father's fault, it's the mother's fault, it's his eyeglasses. . . . " (*Blue Collar Suburb teacher*)

I had one kid who was doing beautifully at the beginning of the year. . . . Then about the beginning of October he started to become totally unsettled and extremely active. . . . And I was becoming concerned, because he was a bright boy but I could see him beginning to fall behind. Finally his mother came to school after one very angry note home, and she explained that there's family problems, her husband left. And right about the time the father left, she said that she had noticed her son was changing, becoming more active and mischievous. I think that was probably his problem. (*Factory City teacher*)

Each of these incidents suggests that when children start to experience problems in school that they had not previously experienced, teachers look outside the school environment for the source of the problem. Moreover, teachers assume that if a child displays the same "negative" behavior at home that he or she displays at school, the home is at fault. No teacher ever suggested that a child's responses to the school environment could "spill over" and affect the child's home behavior; the direction of causality always ran in the other direction.

When I'm talking with a parent I very often will say "Have you noticed anything like this in the child's behavior at home?" For instance, if I am observing that a child has become particularly aggressive, and I'm asking the parent to come in [to] talk about it, and if I'm seeing something that's only transpiring in the classroom, then I have to look first of all at myself. Am I handling that child differently today than maybe I did a month ago? Maybe I'm not giving that child the time that I did, or maybe I'm forgetting to say nice, kind things to that particular child; and I've got to remind myself that maybe that's what's needed. But if the parent starts to tell me, "Well, I'm seeing this at home. . . ." (*Trade City teacher*)

If things were going wrong only in school, then the teacher assumed responsibility for the situation. If the same patterns existed at home as well, then it was the parent's responsibility.

> I had one child last year . . . who was always out of her seat; she was a very small child, so wherever she went she was running. So I was telling her mother about that, and she said, "I know, she's like that at home, too. We have two openings between the kitchen and the dining room, and she just runs around and around all day long and there's nothing I can do about it." So that kind of gives you a clue. If she's not doing anything about it at home, then how am I supposed to get this child to understand things like this at school? (*Blue Collar Suburb teacher*)

It is also instructive to examine what teachers do in response to information from parents about problems in a child's home life. My findings suggest that teachers adapt their own behavior toward the child in ways which will eventually help the child respond more appropriately to school routines. To illustrate this point, I will draw further upon the comments of the three teachers cited above, each of whom worked in a different district. The White Collar Suburb teacher working with the child who had been molested by her father said:

> I recommended further testing for the girl to see if there were emotional problems getting in the way of her learning. In class I try to make sure she understands what she's being asked to do.

The norms for classroom behavior were not changed; rather, the teacher assisted the child in her attempts to abide by them. The response of the Blue Collar Suburb teacher to the student who was living with his father and his grandmother was to increase her emphasis on the classroom norms and routines in her interactions with him.

> Knowing this background, though—knowing that excuses have been made, I've taken every crutch away from this child, every mental crutch that he's ever used. Now he has to stand on his own two feet; he has to be responsible for his actions. He was a discipline problem last year; he is no longer. Adam's whole problem interfered with his learning process last year, and I'll be darned if it's going to this year.

The Factory City teacher made temporary adjustments in her role as commandant for the student whose father had moved out. She was still the arbiter of the behavioral rules but she accommodated them to the special demands posed by the student's needs. Presumably, once the crisis passed, she returned to her usual patterns of interactions.

> I became more understanding. I didn't lose my patience as quickly in the reading group when he wasn't paying attention. I've become more tolerant, and I've also had him do little things in the room to help alleviate any tensions or strong emotional feelings. I wouldn't say I changed my teaching of reading, just the way I handle him in the group.

These incidents, and the teachers' responses to them, illustrate several features of the demands of classroom life described in Chapter 2, and illustrate how the home-school connection supports the mobilization of bias that results from those demands. Children who are unable or unwilling to cope with the norms and routines of reading instruction confront their teachers with complex and painful choices; they bring the dilemmas of the paradox of collective instruction ("teach everyone but meet individual needs") into the forefront of the many instructional decisions teachers must make. Teachers are more likely to look for difficulties in the home than difficulties in the school when confronted with these choices, even in "better off" neighborhoods like White Collar Suburb. When they receive information from parents confirming their suspicion that "something is wrong at home," they turn to the pursuit of routine and control as their major means of problem solving. Adjustments in classroom patterns and expectations are temporary and are intended to help the child move back toward the mainstream of classroom behavior.

It is important, however, to point out that teachers are not merely manipulating children for the sake of an easier school day. Many teachers invest enormous emotional and physical energy in trying to help children cope with very real and very serious difficulties in their young lives. Teachers were as likely to be compassionate as critical of the circumstances many children face. And it is undoubtedly true that many of the children these teachers discussed were happier and possibly learning more as a result of their teachers' sincere efforts to make things easier in the classroom. As one White Collar Suburb teacher put it, "I can't change what's going on at home, but at least I can make it different in here."

But the real question here is, in what sense do teachers make the classroom different? The data above suggest that despite variations in teachers' attitudes toward the problems children can experience at home, they are remarkably similar in their responses to information from parents about these problems. If the routines of reading instruction are changed at all, they are changed only temporarily. Teachers can certainly make the classroom different from a home in crisis, but they do not make the classroom substantially different from the way it was before they learned about their students' problems. Rather, they use the information parents provide about home difficulties to make adjustments that "meet individual needs" in the short run, intending to return to collective norms and behaviors in the long run. Information from parents, then, is used to support the mobilization of bias in teachers' responses to the demands of classroom instruction.

Teacher Restrictions on Parent Involvement

Teachers believe strongly in the importance of parent involvement for the success of the school reading program, both for individual children and for the school as a whole. A closer look at the kinds of "involvement" that teachers espouse, however, reveals ambiguities in their affirmations. Some forms of parental involvement, teachers believe, are "better" than others; not surprisingly, their preference is for a kind of "cooperation" that supports the school's mobilization of bias in reading instruction. As a result, teachers restrict the kinds of parental involvement they encourage.

The teachers in my sample were virtually unanimous in their belief that parent involvement generally enhances education, while the lack of parental "input" and "participation" may spell failure. Several teachers put this belief in rather negative terms:

Sometimes I am questioned by parents, and they say things like, "When was the last time you read with my son?" Many times I have to turn the question around and ask the parent, "When was the last time *you* read with your son?" or "When was the last time your son saw you pick up a book for information or enjoyment?" (*White Collar Suburb teacher*)

I think there are important things parents can do, like reading to kids, even when they're a year old. We have kids [who] come into kindergarten [and] don't know their numbers, don't know the alphabet, don't know colors—which they really should. I have kids in here yet who can't do the alphabet. I have kids in third grade who can't count past a hundred. (*Trade City teacher*)

Other teachers discussed the importance of parent involvement in more positive terms:

If the teacher and the parents have a good rapport, it's very important, and I can just see the difference in my children. As a matter of fact, this year I have been having a difficult time with one child, but the parent has been coming in regularly each week, two or three times; and the child knows that her mother is interested in her education, I'm interested, and it's really working out. (*Trade City teacher*)

These comments suggest that teachers concur with the research literature concerning the general benefits of parent involvement. Parents who display an interest in their children's education and who take appropriate steps to support it are valued as partners in the educational enterprise. Parents who do not get "involved" or who are "uncooperative" are likely to be held at least partly responsible for the low academic achievement of their children. In short, teachers believe that parent involvement and student achievement go hand in hand.

Several teachers were quite specific in describing the kinds of activities that "involved" and "cooperative" parents undertake, and their remarks indicate some of the restrictions within which parents must operate. One form of involvement they described is for parents to follow the advice and recommendations teachers provide on how to help their children at home. Parents can model good habits by being active readers themselves; they can read to their children and listen to them read; they can check to make sure their children are doing their homework; and some can even work with their children on developing specific skills, so long as they use the suggestions and materials supplied by the teacher. Teachers value this kind of "cooperation" because it helps to "reinforce" classroom instruction. When parents promote reading at home, they help to provide a home environment that is more continuous with classroom life. In effect, "cooperative" parents can serve the same function as Title I/Chapter 1 teachers or reading consultants who "coordinate" their instruction with that of the classroom teacher.

A few examples of appreciative comments from teachers about parent involvement in home instruction will illustrate my point.

I've had parents ask me what *they* could do at home to help their kids in reading. I tell them, listen to your child read and go over their work with them—especially because I don't always get a chance to do that. (*Blue Collar Suburb teacher*)

[I tell parents] their job is to make sure that whatever I send home gets done. . . . Whatever is sent home is to reinforce their work in school, so that . . . it's making a stronger foundation. And eight out of ten parents are cooperative. (*Factory City teacher*)

In these examples, "cooperative" parents behave more or less as surrogate teachers (McPherson, 1972, p. 136). They use the same materials, express the same values, and follow the same rules for instruction that teachers do. The more a parent's behavior parallels that of the teacher, the more approval the teacher is likely to express. Parents involved in home instruction are expected to rely heavily on the teacher's guidance in structuring their activities with their children. This is an important form of support for the teacher's pursuit of routine and control. The teacher's attempt to serve as classroom commandant thus extends beyond the walls of the classroom and into the homes of "cooperative" parents.

While parents are expected to act on the information they get from teachers about instruction, teachers are not expected to reciprocate. Home instruction has little influence on the conduct of classroom instruction. Many teachers were asked to describe what they learned from parents that helps them in teaching children to read.[2] Only two teachers, both from Factory City, said they learned about specific things parents do in trying to instruct their children at home, and only one of them incorporated what she learned from parents into her own instruction:

> [Parents] will tell me some things they've helped their child with at home; they say, "If I do this, he does it better," and then I can use that at school. Or maybe their child has a certain fear about something that I wasn't aware of, and then I can pick up on that and go from there.

The other teacher maintained her attempt to act as "commandant" of her students' instruction; she did not claim to make use of parents' suggestions in the classroom, and she exercised a sort of veto power over parent activities at home:

> Some parents make up little things at home, and they say, "What do you think about this?" or "I try to do this with my child." And I try to encourage them to keep going, it's a good idea. Or else they might go a little ahead, and they'll say "Am I going too fast?" And I'll explain to them, "I think that's good," or "I think maybe you should slow down a little, wait awhile."

Teachers might give several reasons to explain why they do not solicit or make use of suggestions from parents concerning methods of instruction. Many would say that most parents, especially low-income parents, are not involved in home instruction and therefore would have no suggestions to offer. However, it is interesting to note that the two teachers who *did* mention learning how parents instruct their children at home taught in Factory City—the district where parents were least likely to exhibit strong command of standard English, to have highly developed reading skills, or to hold high expectations for the teacher's performance.[3] What this suggests is that teachers may be wrong in assuming that low-income parents are uninvolved in home instruction. Not only do my own findings challenge this assumption, so do those of Delores Durkin (1984). Still, teachers who think that parents do not instruct their children at home undoubtedly do not ask parents what they do in home instruction; teachers are therefore unlikely to receive evidence that would undermine their belief.

Teachers might also fail to solicit or capitalize on parent information concerning home instruction because they believe that what parents do at home is not likely to be transferable to the school setting. In one respect, they are right; parental advice can exacerbate the problem of professional uncertainty and the paradox of collective instruction. Parent suggestions (like those of reading specialists) can widen the range of choices teachers face, especially if home instructional practices are inconsistent with the mobilization of bias in the classroom:

> You have to remember that what you give [a child] to do at home is going to be done under the supervision of his parent, and if he does things differently for you than he does at home, sometimes that doesn't work too well. So you do have to be very careful with some children. (*Trade City teacher*)

Home activities which do not mesh with classroom routines can increase the uncertainty of the teachers' tasks. The home becomes still another—and very different—social context of instruction, one which poses special challenges to the teacher trying to "command" it and to coordinate it with the contexts of classroom instruction. Furthermore, in the social context of home instruction, the child is (at least for the moment) the sole learner, and teachers believe parents will expect them to create the same kind of learning environment at school that a child can experience at home. This confronts the teacher with the paradox of collective instruction:

> Usually if a parent is that concerned I will try and work with them. But some parents have the attitude that . . . "I want you to spend all your time with my kid because I want him to learn this, this, and this." But you can't do that. (*Trade City teacher*)

The demands of life in classrooms thus constrain not only what teachers do in classrooms, but also what parents do at home. Teachers affirm "cooperative" parents who "reinforce" what goes on in classrooms; their involvement in home instruction is most likely to enhance the teacher-parent relationship when it parallels the teacher's practices in classroom instruction.

A second form of parent involvement in the schools I sampled was parent work in classrooms. Fullan's review of the research (1982, pp. 196–200) concludes that such involvement produces "positive outcomes . . . regarding student learning, student attitudes, and parent attitudes" (p. 198). He argues, consistent with the theory of school change developed in his book, that "it is intuitively if not theoretically obvious that direct involvement in instruction in relation to their own child's education is one of the surest routes for parents to develop a sense of specific *meaning* vis-à-vis new programs designed to improve learning" (p. 200, emphasis original). However, the results of this form of involvement appear to replicate those of involvement in home instruction: teachers place restrictions on parent work in classrooms that enhance parental support for the mobilization of bias in reading instruction.

My own data on parents in the classroom must be treated with some caution, because few teachers or other school personnel mentioned parent aides. This in and of itself may be revealing, since Title I/Chapter 1 programs frequently include the presence of paid parent aides; and in Trade City and Factory City I observed aides working in many classrooms. But only three teachers even mentioned parents' work in the classroom, and their remarks were made in passing. In order to elicit more information, I asked specific questions of one Trade City teacher about the impact of parent involvement in classroom instruction, and her responses supported my interpretation of Fullan's findings. First, in classroom instruction, like home instruction, parents take their cues on what to do and how to do it from the teacher, in order to provide "reinforcement" for the teacher's activities:

> I have the mother working in the room, and she starts to pick out kids. Like I have certain kids that need reinforcement on words or whatever, and I usually give her a list, and she goes through it with them. She does a lot of busy things, so that I can concentrate on more of the academic things.

This teacher's school had had an ongoing parent aide program for several years, so I asked, "How has having parents in the classroom worked out?" Her response again focused on the provision of "reinforcement":

> I've found [the parents in the classroom] helpful. It depends on the parent you get. I've had years where I've had parents that were like a second teacher; you could give them something to do and they could teach the kids with it. Other years I've had parents that I've used mainly to correct the papers and to kind of field questions so the kids

don't have to keep coming back to [interrupt] the reading group. . . .
It's more reinforcement than anything else.

Most significantly, the teacher pointed to the meaning parents acquire as a
consequence of their classroom work:

I think the parents are very enlightened after they've worked in here—
they can't believe what it's like. A lot of parents say, "The teacher is always picking on my child" or "I don't know why there's so much talking, or why they can't teach, or why there's so much of a discipline
problem." And then when they come in and they work in the classroom—the mother I have now, she was ready to quit! She said, "I
can't believe it! I can't believe how there's no respect, there's no discipline, you have to constantly be on them."

Nothing in this interview, or in any of the other interviews where I knew
the teacher had access to a parent classroom aide, suggested that teachers'
thinking about the three dimensions of opportunity—assessing needs, providing materials, or structuring interactions—was in any way affected by the
presence of parents in the school. Lightfoot (1978, pp. 173–74) claims that
parents who collaborate with teachers in the classroom are able "to help
teachers become more perceptive and responsive to the needs of their
children; . . . to reduce the workload of teachers; . . . [and to] teach some of
the teachers, who were not parents, something about nurturance and moth-
ering." My data provided no support for these conclusions. Of course, I was
not seeking to challenge them during the course of the interviews, and I may
have encountered different perspectives had I probed the parent-as-aide
issue with other teachers. But surely if parents were a salient influence on
classroom routines or teachers' perceptions, teachers would have volunteered a great deal more information about parents than they did. Parents in
the classroom acquired meaning with respect to the teacher's subjective
reality; but teachers apparently did not reciprocate.

This interpretation of the restrictions on parent involvement in classroom instruction was corroborated by the Factory City parent who headed
the Parent Advisory Council at her children's school. The school had a very
strong parent aide program, and this parent had participated in it for several
years. When I asked her about the impact of having parents in the school,
she replied:

Parent involvement [is] exactly what it means, parents coming in, getting involved, knowing the teachers, knowing what the kids are doing
and everything like that. I also learned the different techniques of the
teachers, how they teach, how they drill [the students], how for me to
tutor my child at home if they needed extra help.

This parent had clearly gained important insights into the subjective reality of life in classrooms for teachers. These insights shaped her perceptions of how children should be learning in school, how teachers should be teaching, and what role parents should play. There was nothing in her comments, either in response to this question or elsewhere in the interview, to suggest that teachers gained insight into parents' subjective reality as a consequence of parental presence and "involvement" in the school. Thus, like home instruction, classroom instruction by parents may increase parents' willingness to consent to the school's mobilization of bias in reading instruction.

These findings on parent involvement raise some very important issues. Both forms of involvement described here help parents to become better acquainted with school people and programs, but neither promotes the kind of mutual understanding that Fullan says is essential to a truly collaborative relationship. Parents who act as surrogate teachers at home by following teacher instructions and using teacher-supplied materials, and who adopt the teacher's perspective through participation in classroom instruction, can support teachers in the coping strategies they use in response to the demands of classroom life. Indeed, they make life easier for the teacher. These parents provide reinforcement to individual children who need it, making it easier for them to progress within the confines of collective classroom instruction; and they give teachers an opportunity to affirm their professionalism, enabling them to supply some answers rather than merely struggling with questions. Both the paradox of collective instruction and the problem of professional uncertainty are thus mitigated by this kind of parent cooperation.

This interpretation may explain why it is easier to identify research which associates improved parent, teacher, and student attitudes with increased parent involvement, and not so easy to demonstrate substantially improved student achievement. Parent involvement may increase the *number* of opportunities children have to learn to read, but it is unlikely to change the *kinds* of opportunities schools can provide. The home-school connection helps schools do better at what they are already doing; it won't help them do things very differently.

PARENT INVOLVEMENT
AND THE LIMITS OF INFLUENCE

The transactions that characterize the teacher-parent relationship reveal a great deal about both the possibilities and the limits of parental influence. I say "influence" advisedly; the exercise of power requires planning, and my analysis suggests that in the vast majority of cases, it is teachers and not parents who make educational plans for children and who struggle to gain the consent and cooperation of others in putting these plans into effect. Even the parent who comes to school with an objection or a complaint rarely has an explicit plan to substitute for that of the teacher. Thus, to the extent that parents affect what goes on in schools—especially inside classrooms—they do so through the exercise of influence, not power.

The constraints on parent influence are most readily apparent in the use of information as a resource. As we have seen, the kinds of information teachers and parents exchange support the school's mobilization of bias in reading instruction. The questions and concerns of parents are keyed to the language and assumptions of ongoing classroom routines; the questions and concerns of teachers are likewise rooted in the ways schools habitually assess needs, provide materials, and structure interactions. This exchange of information raises few challenges to what organization theorists would label "standard operating procedures"; parent participation in these information transactions serves primarily to increase their familiarity with and acceptance of school SOP's. Thus, information turns out to be much more important for increasing teachers' power than for increasing parents' influence. Parents learn the assumptions, the language, and the habits associated with schooling, which makes it easier for them to understand, consent to, and cooperate with the teacher's educational plans. The parent interview reported above is perhaps the most powerful testimony to the constraints on parent influence. Parents who entered the subjective world of the teacher were confronted there with the paradox of collective instruction and the dilemmas of professional uncertainty, and they developed a natural sympathy for the teachers' coping strategies. They learned to understand and support the teacher's search for routine and control, to accept the teacher's choices of materials and learning contexts, and even to defend the teacher's behavior over the protests of their children. Information can substantially reduce the likelihood of parental challenge.

This conclusion is strengthened when we add to the analysis a brief look at the kind of information that parents and teachers do *not* regularly exchange. My own interviews, as well as evidence from other researchers, suggest that there are a number of "non-issues" on the teacher-parent agenda. Contrary to the recommendations of Fullan (1982, pp. 208–209), House and Lapan (1978, pp. 129–130), and Lightfoot (1978, p. 172), teachers make little effort to solicit information from parents about positive features of children's home lives—features that may enhance a child's education even if they can't be neatly transferred to the existing school setting. This is particularly true for disadvantaged children; teachers appear even less likely to focus on the functional features of these children's home lives than on those of their more advantaged peers.

A few examples of the kinds of specific information teachers fail to solicit will help to make my point. Some teachers asked low-income parents about their children's interests—cars, games, dinosaurs, etc.; but teachers did *not* solicit information about children's educational values and aspirations. One White Collar Suburb teacher described how knowing about a particular child's aspirations influenced her educational interactions:

> I have a child who has a friend who went off to a private school, and when [the friend] came back home, the refrigerator in [his] kitchen was [covered] with all the papers. And that's what Stevie wants, basically. He wants to prove to the neighborhood kids that he can drape that refrigerator at home with all kinds of papers. So no matter what he does, he wants me to put a happy face up in the corner, which I usually don't do on the papers—but his mother even brought in some stickers last year and said, "Just use them, stick them on his papers and be sure that he gets the papers home so he can use the new magnets, and the papers will go on the refrigerator." So that fills his need of whatever he thinks is important.

This teacher's knowledge of what this child thought was important helped her to adjust the way she rewarded him for good work. In essence, she was able to let the child have some control over the meaning of his work, choosing his own symbols for success. Teachers who regularly solicit information about children's values and aspirations might be able to experiment with different kinds of classroom rewards and incentives, thereby making learning more attractive to everyone in the classroom.

Teachers could also solicit information about how parents or other adult family members have taught their children outside of school. Durkin's research (1984, p. 74) notes that many successful (i.e., grade-level) readers from low-income homes, like their advantaged counterparts, began to read before they started formal schooling; and their preschool "teachers" were not only parents, but older siblings, uncles, aunts, and especially grandmothers (pp. 68–69). Three teachers in my sample—two of them from Trade City—referred to children in their classes who knew how to read before starting school, but none appeared curious about how that learning occurred or what they could do to capitalize on it. It bears recalling that only one teacher in my sample said that she learned anything from parents' descriptions of how they work with their own children. Clearly, overt instruction in reading and reading-related activities is not a phenomenon restricted to middle- and upper-income households; it represents a wealth of information teachers could use to adapt instruction to the individual learning styles of children from all social classes.

A third kind of information teachers might solicit from parents has to do with potentially productive patterns in a child's relationship with adults and with other children outside school. As we have seen, when teachers do get information about how children interact with others, it tends to be cast in terms of problems at home—fear of an authoritarian father, aggression toward siblings, defiance of the mother, and so forth. Yet teachers could also use information of this sort to uncover the strengths children reveal under otherwise dysfunctional circumstances. An example recounted by Carew and Lightfoot suggests how this could be accomplished:

> Mona seems to be burdened down with adult responsibilities. Her few references to home life usually describe chores: "I had to finish the ironing." "I had to do the shopping." These are clearly not fabrications since, from time to time, Mona has come in with burns from an iron on her arm and is sometimes seen trundling heavy grocery bags down Main Street all by herself. (1979, p. 117)

Mona's teacher responded by trying to "do what she can in class to help Mona enjoy a little of her childhood." But there is little discussion of how a situation like this one, unhappy though it is, may nevertheless be turned to educational advantage. Children like Mona show initiative and resourceful-ness; it might make sense to provide them with more opportunities to learn independently or in cooperative groups rather than under the direct supervi-sion of an adult. Likewise, children of parents working outside the home often spend a great deal of their time with older sibs or relatives, and this is usually treated as a problem; however, this may indicate that they would learn well with older children to tutor them. Several teachers mentioned instances where older brothers or sisters translated for non-English-speak-ing parents during parent-teacher conferences; this is another example of a problem that teachers could turn to advantage, by encouraging the sibling's input into the teacher's understanding of students' and parents' "subjective reality." The point here is not to make life in schools perfectly continuous with home life (Cazden, 1982), but rather to solicit and use information from parents in ways that permit teachers to capitalize on extra-school experiences without necessarily replicating them.

This kind of information, were teachers to solicit it, represents poten-tial power for parents. To the extent that parents provide information that helps teachers significantly adapt instruction to the needs of their students, parents can have a share in the creation of meaning and the making of educational plans in the classroom. But for parents to achieve this kind of power, schools must begin to treat the information parents have about their children as significant—even when it does not fit the classroom mobilization of bias. Parents can offer more than the school is designed to accept; the illustrations above are highly suggestive of that. The final question here is why teachers and other school people consistently fail to seek out important information from parents—particularly low-income parents—that would help them do a better job of assessing needs, providing materials, and structuring educational interactions. It is to this question that we now turn.

"EDUCATIONAL DEPRIVATION" AND EQUAL OPPORTUNITY: A GRASSROOTS PERSPECTIVE

Since the early 1960s, social scientists have struggled to explain the persistent failure of low-income and minority children to attain levels of school achievement commensurate with those of their nondisadvantaged, non-minority peers. There is little agreement in the research community on the causes of this achievement gap;[4] but the same cannot be said of those who actually deliver educational services to children. During my interviews with educators, only the district administrators were asked specifically to explain the skewed distribution of achievement scores by socioeconomic status; however, educators at all levels of the school system volunteered explanations of the gap in the context of their other remarks. The practitioners I sampled focused on different ways in which poor children's home lives contribute to poor school performance, but they were nearly unanimous in their view of socioeconomically deprived children as being also culturally—and hence educationally—deprived. Almost without exception, educators at all levels of the school system pointed to the failure of low-income homes to provide "adequate" preparation for schooling and to "reinforce" what teachers were doing once schooling had begun. This "deficit view" prevailed across the variation in my respondents' perspectives on parents described earlier in this chapter.

This finding suggests an interesting possibility. Many scholarly observers contend that the treatment low-income children receive in school grows out of this "deficit view" educators have adopted with respect to student home environments (Baratz & Baratz, 1970). However, my own data suggest that the relationship between attitudes and behavior may run in the opposite direction as well. The belief that low-income children are "educationally deficient" may grow out of the ways schools habitually treat them, clearly an important effect of the mobilization of bias. What we have here is not so much an attitude problem as an ecological problem. The key to understanding—and perhaps altering—educators' attitudes is to understand the patterns of behavior that help to produce them.

Many of my respondents ascribed the lower reading achievement levels of poor children to their limited experiences with reading and reading-related activities prior to their school years. The first quote below is the clearest statement of the deficit view; the teacher does not describe her students' "background" (i.e., preschool experiences) as different, but rather as nonexistent. Her statement was in response to the question, "In what ways do your students differ from one another in their struggle to learn to read?"

What do you mean, how do they differ? They have a wide range of differences. They come with no background, and that's half our battle. A home background, where they have experiences where they're encouraged to read—there's no encouragement for reading, and that's half the battle. (*Trade City teacher*)

Many other teachers expressed similar views:

Well, there's the motivation and attitude, differences in experiences, and the home situation. Are they interested in learning to read? Have they had the opportunity to go to libraries? (*White Collar Suburb teacher*)

A lot of these children come with nothing—they don't have the books, the pencils and paper—all the things that we're offering, and we think that they have, they don't have. These are all the things of childhood, and they don't have a childhood. (*Blue Collar Suburb teacher*)

For these teachers, the problem with low-income homes is that they fail to provide the kind of experiences teachers can build on in the classroom. Many reading specialists and principals concurred, irrespective of the districts they worked in.

We have a lot of children who have families that don't read at home, so they haven't been encouraged to read. And they don't find it fun, because it's hard for them. (*Blue Collar Suburb Title I teacher*)

Children come from diverse backgrounds. Some come from homes that have books, they have magazines for their children. The children are taken places. In general, these children live in a climate or environment which is conducive to learning. In other homes, many of these opportunities are just not present. Some parents don't put as high a value on reading. (*White Collar Suburb principal*)

When respondents were specific in their comments, they usually pointed to language differences between school and low-income home environments.

> When you're dealing with some kids from deprived homes, their needs are far greater. . . . Their language experience is very, very low because most kids from so-called minority homes—their parents don't speak to them the way other parents do. . . . Language experience is one of the biggest prerequisites in learning to read, and these kids just don't have the readiness to read that other kids come with. . . . A kid needs to be able to conceptualize a word. If a kid doesn't know what a sheep is, he's not going to be able to read about it. Some of my kids didn't know what a faucet was—at home their mother would probably just say, "Turn off the water." Or they don't know left-to-right progression, or directions. If you say "put it on the table" or "put it under the table"—they don't know the difference. (*Trade City reading consultant*)

> Each child brings his whole background, his upbringing, his experience with words. Some are richer than others—some families do a lot of communicating. Some read to the children a lot, so that words and books are meaningful. Some children have already been in the library before they come to school. Their whole language development, listening for words and sounds, is important. (*White Collar Suburb teacher*)

> Many of the children in the [Title I] program are Spanish-speaking, or I should say foreign-speaking—I have a child from Vietnam also. I think that's one of the biggest factors, and the sounds are different with different letters. In Spanish, the I is called an E, so when you're spelling a word and you say E, the child will put down an I. There's a big mixup that way. (*Factory City Title I teacher*)

For these respondents, the primary deprivation low-income children experience vis-à-vis their reading is linguistic. Like the more general comments on the lack of background, the problem of language is framed in terms of deficiency rather than difference.

Given this perspective, it is not surprising that educators take a compensatory view of the school's task in educating low-income children. From their perspective, the school's job is to provide poor children with the linguistic, emotional, and social skills their homes have failed to provide them, so they can take better advantage of the opportunities for learning that schools make available.

Moreover, the belief in the need for compensation was held by educators with very different opinions about parental attitudes and behaviors toward schooling. Teachers, specialists, and principals saw children's home lives as deficient even when they also saw parents as caring, concerned, and anxious to help. No educator ever expressed a view that the extra-school lives of children had their own unique educational strengths as well as liabilities. Only one respondent in my sample of school-level educators mentioned the relationship between income and schooling without explicitly casting his remarks in terms of a "deficit" view of the home background:

> I know this sounds terrible, but I try *not* to learn about their home background. Naturally, I know what's happening at home sometimes— they tell me—but I try not to let that affect me. . . . Sometimes we say, "Oh, well, you know, the kid has problems at home" . . . and we use that as an excuse, and so who's losing? The kid. (*Trade City teacher*)

Interestingly, even this teacher affirms a deficit view of poor children's home lives. He assumes that if he *were* to learn about the home environment, the things he would learn would be negative. As a result of this knowledge, he believes, he would lower his expectations rather than adjust his teaching. To avoid this, he chooses not to solicit any information at all about the home— even though the remainder of his interview showed that he believes the parents of his students care deeply about their children's education and are "involved" in providing support and assistance.

While there are many possible contributors to the "deficit view" of the home lives of disadvantaged children, surely one of the most important is the classroom mobilization of bias in reading instruction. This would explain the views of teachers such as the one just described, affirming low-income parents as caring and concerned and yet discounting the possibility that these parents provide their children with skills and strengths that are educationally important, although different from those provided to non-poor children. In particular, the mobilization of bias in the classroom requires teachers to define only certain patterns of language and social behaviors as appropriate "background" for successful classroom reading. Children who come to school familiar with the vocabulary and syntax found in primary grade readers are defined by educators as children with "bigger" vocabularies, "better" grammar, and "richer" language experiences. Yet there is much research to suggest that the nonstandard vocabularies and syntactical structures of poor and minority children are in fact as rich and developed as those of their advantaged counterparts (Baratz & Baratz, 1970; Williamson-Ige, 1984). Surely the school's reliance on basal readers, combined with the constraints on the availability and variety of supplementary materials, urges upon the educator a view of linguistic deficiency rather than difference. Similarly, children who come to school from a preschool, day care, or home environment which has accustomed them to adult supervision, turn-taking, and school-like ways of organizing their belongings, are defined by educators as having "better" or "more sophisticated" social skills, work habits, and organizational patterns. Again, much research suggests that the patterns of work and play interaction, participation structures, and physical organization found in low-income and minority homes are no less functional or sophisticated than those of non-poor homes (Au & Mason, 1981; Baratz & Baratz, 1970; Labov, 1982; Schultz, Florio, & Erickson, 1982). But educators, caught in the school's mobilization of bias, see only the skills children can use in existing classroom routines. As far as they are concerned, alternative skills and competencies might as well not exist, for there is no way for the school as presently arranged to capitalize on them. Moreover, the teacher's fear of increased uncertainty makes the risks of learning about and accommodating to alternative skills too great.

In the end, the compassionate teacher who wants "input" from low-income parents supports the mobilization of bias every bit as strongly as the hostile teacher who believes parents don't care. Both control the definition and meaning of children's attributes in the classroom. Children's vocabularies, their grammar, their level of "maturity," their "independence," their work habits, their play habits, their social skills—all of these are judged against the backdrop of the ways the schools structure learning. And as we have seen, parent involvement, far from changing the meaning teachers ascribe to children's attributes, affirms it. The close connection between power and opportunity is thus of utmost significance in understanding the home-school connection. Parents who consent to the school's governance of meaning ultimately consent to the mobilization of bias in the school's provision of opportunity. Neither conflict nor compassion can prevent this ultimate cooptation.

6

Leading the Horses

District Officials and
the Pursuit of Legitimacy

Teachers may be directed or encouraged by their principal or supervisor to go into a certain setting, or even recommended to take additional courses at one of the surrounding colleges, to be able to gain strength. [Still,] you can lead a horse to water, but you can't make him drink.

With these words, a Trade City assistant superintendent expressed both the possibilities and the limitations of administrative power. School district officials must operate with two sets of assumptions about school bureaucracy, one a Weberian world of plans, programs, specialization, hierarchy, and rationality, and the other a complex Lindblomian network of negotiations, bargains, mutual accommodations, and compromises. In both contexts, administrators confront on a daily basis the issue of their legitimacy as educational leaders. They struggle to acquire both the resources with which to influence subordinates' attitudes and behavior, and the right to exercise those resources. Whether they are drawing up budgets, conducting workshops, visiting schools, or evaluating principals, district officials must attempt to ensure that their decisions "are widely accepted not solely from fear of . . . punishment or coercion but also from a belief that it is morally right and proper to do so" (Dahl, 1984, p. 53). In this chapter I will examine how school district officials try to do this, arguing that their pursuit of legitimacy helps them to support the school's mobilization of bias, and thereby ensures their political survival.

THE ADMINISTRATOR'S AGENDA

What do school administrators want to accomplish? That is a harder question to answer than one might think. Even though most people think of district administrators as "the" educational policy makers, there is surprisingly little information about what they (or others) see as the administrator's primary tasks. In one of the few published discussions of middle-level district administrators and their impact on schooling, Costa and Guditis observe:

> Objective data on the role and importance of districtwide supervisors are largely unavailable. . . . There is no system in effect for collecting data about [the] effectiveness and influence of supervisors. Their roles, expectancies, and job descriptions are often vague. They are expected to play a low-key role and to make others—teachers and administrators—"look good." Thus, they receive little credit for or feedback about their accomplishments. (1984, p. 84)

Similarly, Fullan's extensive review of the research on district officials turned up "little representative information on what [chief] administrators do and think in their total roles" (1982, p. 160); studies of middle-level administrators, who are "directly responsible for program development and improvement," are "almost nonexistent" (p. 162).

Nevertheless, the few surveys which Fullan did uncover suggest that whatever it is that district administrators want to achieve, it isn't likely to include improved instruction, innovation, or in-service training (pp. 160–62). Indeed, for the majority of district administrators the priority seems to be simple survival. Most superintendents' terms only last about three years (p. 162), and they spend most of that time reacting to fiscal or political pressures that place enormous demands on their time and that leave few opportunities for reflection and planning. The tenure of middle-level administrators is similarly precarious. Costa and Guditis report that:

> Supervisors' jobs are constantly in jeopardy at the bargaining table, but they seldom have an advocate during the negotiating process. When claims are made that there are "too many administrators up in the central office," the "excess" supervisory personnel are usually the first to go. (1984, p. 84)

These pressures place district administrators in a position analogous to that of school principals: In order to achieve the goal of survival, they must take care not to disturb the essential inertia of public schooling. My argument here differs somewhat from the usual perspective on district administrators, which suggests that they are so busy worrying about money, enrollments, and paperwork that they hardly ever think about education. Certainly it is true that administrators spend a great deal more time talking with school board members, other district officials, and building-level administrators than they do with teachers and students (Fullan, 1982, p. 161);

and they are much more likely to discuss school finances, labor relations, and state and federal regulations than they are to discuss curriculum, instruction, and achievement. *But this does not mean that administrators lack an educational agenda.* The problem is not that the survival issues crowd out the educational issues; rather, the problem is that the survival issues shape the educational issues, providing a framework within which administrators interpret and respond to the policy choices they must make. The skills and strategies required for survival essentially determine the educational agenda that district officials adopt. That agenda involves preserving the structure of opportunities that the public school presently provides. This is not an agenda that school officials arrive at by default; it is intentional and conscious, designed to protect the policy investments that they and their subordinates have made in the classroom mobilization of bias.

Evidence for this conclusion is apparent in officials' responses to the problem of unequal school outcomes. During interviews, I asked officials to comment on the fact that not all children learn to read successfully in the classroom setting, and that the children less likely to succeed are the economically disadvantaged. They responded with three kinds of claims: (1) present classroom arrangements are the best we can do and should not be changed; (2) extra services outside the classroom can mitigate or even solve the problem; (3) economic disadvantages impose cultural disadvantages schools can't be expected to overcome. All three responses clearly support the school's mobilization of bias; none suggests the need for significant change. The White Collar Suburb Superintendent of Schools provided an example of the first response:

> My experience tells me that for a whole lot of years, with a whole lot of very intelligent and dedicated people, the classroom setting has been in existence, and if it could be improved upon, somebody at some point in time would have done that.

Articulating the second response was the Assistant Superintendent for Curriculum in Trade City, who pointed to the variety of extra services presently available to children who aren't "making it" in the regular classroom setting:

> If there's a need in the school, then it's the principal who addresses that need immediately with the teacher. And then the principal can ask for additional help. That's why you have a Title I person, who helps to insure that the child is going to make it. . . . We [also] have social workers, we have psychological examiners, we have community relations workers, we have all kinds of people to do that.

The third kind of response—that schools are limited in their capacity to meet the needs of "culturally deprived" children—is particularly interesting. It often appeared in conjunction with one of the other two responses ("classrooms are as good as we can make them" and "we have many additional programs for low achievers"). The White Collar Suburb superintendent, who argued that the inertia of classroom reading programs testified to their quality, went on to say:

> When we talk about the classroom setting and strengths and weaknesses and not all kids making it, the extension of that is, all kids *can't* make it. . . . If all the kids that come to school had an IQ between 95 and 105, and if they all came to school well-rested, with a good meal and a good night's sleep, and a chance to shower every once in a while, and lived with a couple of people who love them, and *then* we didn't do a good job in terms of educating 99 percent of these kids, then I'd say people would have a good basis upon which to challenge what we're doing.

A Trade City Reading Supervisor saw the persistently lower scores of economically disadvantaged children not as a warrant for changing schools, but as a warrant for encouraging change in the home:

> [Low achievers] are not getting the reinforcement and the interest and the support at home. It has nothing to do with teaching ability. . . . A lot of our kids in the city have not been well-traveled, have not gone on trips, so that when they read a book that deals with an airport, very few of them have been to an airport; they have nothing to bring, they don't have any meaning behind it. . . . I think it means that we've got to work harder, and get the parents involved. . . . The school can't do it alone.

This pattern, common to all four districts, suggests that the official's educational agenda makes it easier for him or her to blame the victim than to change the system. An educational agenda promoting system stability is necessitated by the administrator's awareness that his or her position is tenuous, ambiguous, and poorly understood. Administrators who actively support their subordinates by preserving the investments they have made in the status quo are far more likely to survive. And administrators seeking to carry out their educational agenda of stability and their political agenda of survival must cultivate *legitimacy*. Legitimacy gives officials the wherewithal to support the educational alternatives that are already in place, and officials who can provide such support are more likely to keep their jobs. Officials thus need legitimacy to pursue both their political and their educational objectives; but legitimacy is not easy to come by, and the following analysis will explain why.

ADMINISTRATIVE CONTEXTS
AND THE PROBLEM OF LEGITIMACY

That legitimacy is even in question for people at the top of the educational hierarchy may come as a surprise. The conventional picture of schooling suggests that power is a top-down affair: the voters elect a school board, which appoints a superintendent, who tells middle-level administrators what to do, who tell building principals what to do, who tell teachers what to do. In this view, position alone confers responsibility, power, authority, and hence legitimacy. But responsibility and resources are not at all the same thing, particularly in a context of diffuse and decentralized decision making. Legitimacy is not bestowed upon district officials; rather, it is a quality which must be cultivated and nurtured as a sort of precondition for influence in matters of instruction.

To begin with, administrators confront the same problems of professional uncertainty that teachers confront—not only with respect to the tasks of the classroom, but also with respect to their own tasks. These dual uncertainties mean that it is seldom clear when, how, and on what grounds school officials may "interfere" with normal school practices. For example, when the Director of Elementary Education in Blue Collar Suburb was asked why there is such an effort to coordinate Title I/Chapter 1 with the classroom program, he replied:

> Every skill that is ever given in reading is given in the classroom. Why some children don't get certain skills—I don't know, to tell the truth. I don't think anybody knows; we just wish we knew. That way we could implant in them that lack.

More than one official indicated that "there are no rights and wrongs" in reading instruction, and that educational research comes to contradictory conclusions about the merits of different instructional approaches; and they suggested that this affects their ability to insist that subordinates comply with official directives and recommendations.

Nor are the effects of official activities very clear. Even when schools improve, administrators can't explain why; they cannot point to past successes as sure predictors of future performance. A former superintendent in Blue Collar Suburb, when asked why reading achievement scores had been going up for the past three years, replied:

It's very difficult [to say]. And anybody that tells you, "This did it, that did it"—that's a lot of poppycock. To try to put your finger specifically on one thing that created this kind of interest [in reading]—I don't know what it is.

Uncertainty was also evident in the vague and hesitant response of the Curriculum Supervisor in Factory City to the more general question, "What do you do in your job that has an effect on the reading program?" She replied:

I'm not sure. . . . I guess it's first of all to monitor the program, and secondly, to maybe just be a supervisor and augment the reading program in any way that it needs to be.

Uncertainty about what does and doesn't work *in* the classroom is thus paralleled by uncertainty about what does and doesn't work *outside* the classroom. Administrators cannot confidently predict the results of any plans, programs, directives, or mandates they might issue, and this leaves the legitimacy of their attempts to influence teachers, specialists, and principals open to question.

A second contextual feature weakening officials' legitimacy is subordinate autonomy. District officials trying to "supervise" principals encounter the same problems that principals do in trying to supervise teachers. For the most part, they simply have to assume that their subordinates are doing what they are supposed to do:

In the broadest sense, you really rely on the people who are in the building every day to make certain that every youngster that is passing through the portals is getting a fair shake. . . . Basically you like to think that you have a competent, professional, knowledgeable, and efficient individual in the classroom. (*White Collar Suburb superintendent*)

Thus, the assumption that teachers and principals are doing a competent job and should be left alone, coupled with the self-described preoccupation of administrators with non-instructional matters, powerfully affects the legitimacy of any administrative attempt to intervene or issue specific mandates relative to the school reading program. The context of the district official's relationships with others in the school system, characterized by uncertainty, subordinate autonomy, and lack of proximity, means that legitimacy is something the official must pursue, rather than presuppose.

THE QUEST FOR LEGITIMACY:
THE RATIONAL-BUREAUCRATIC ROUTE

Trained in administration and management (Goodlad, 1979, p. 96), school officials are well versed in rational bureaucratic perspectives on administrative tasks like planning, programming, and budgeting. Ironically, according to Clark and McKibbin (1982, p. 670), "many contemporary theorists argue that bureaucratic models do not explain most of what occurs in schools most of the time, precisely because the level of technology in the field is insufficient." Nevertheless, the language administrators themselves use to characterize what they do is quite consistent with a Weberian world view. And it is important to see this language as a resource in the administrator's struggle for legitimate influence over subordinates.

The Language of Rational Bureaucracy

Among the aphorisms of rational bureaucracy to which many district officials subscribed was the belief that "organizations exist to attain specified goals" and that "specifying objectives improves performance" (Clark & McKibbin, 1982, p. 670). A newly hired reading supervisor in Factory City, for example, told me:

> We have reordered our goals for this department, because this is a brand-new department. Our emphasis this year is on building and improving reading scores. I focused in on teaching main idea . . . [and] building the vocabularies that the children have.

The Superintendent of Schools in Trade City reported:

> My overall responsibility . . . is to oversee the total program of the Trade City public schools. . . . I had a vision of where I wanted to go, and then I have to articulate that to the people who have to put it in place.

Goals and objectives were thus an important element in the administrator's perception of how the school district should work.

A corollary to the existence of goals and objectives in a rational-bureaucracy is organizational planning (Corwin, 1974, p. 252). District officials were enthusiastic about the benefits of planning for educational improvement. The Superintendent of Schools in Trade City was perhaps the strongest advocate of administrative planning:

Every school in Trade City now has a planning team and does write an instructional plan of improvement. I think we've put into place a master plan . . . and the superintendent is continually talking about that master plan, everywhere he goes, everything he writes. . . . And based on all the evidence we have at hand, objective and subjective, we think we're moving in the right direction.

The Assistant Superintendent of Elementary Education in Factory City provided a specific example of the process of devising and implementing a district-wide plan:

The state recommends that we have between 900 and 1200 minutes per week in language arts, in grades 1 through 3. We have been offering the students, prior to 1978, approximately 800 minutes per week. We increased that to 900 minutes a week, or 180 minutes a day. . . . Each teacher prepares a time table, and we run a check to be sure they are teaching reading a minimum of 900 minutes.

For these officials, making plans and monitoring their implementation was an important part of their "mission" as educators.

A third feature of rational bureaucracy my respondents exemplified was a belief in the merits of "coordination" (Corwin, 1974, p. 253). No one ever really explained exactly what coordination should involve, but its vague meaning did not detract from its popularity. The replication of classroom instruction in remedial reading services, for example, was justified by the "coordination" this practice afforded:

Why should the burden be on the child to learn multiple skills? If you coordinated it—if the homeroom teacher were teaching main idea and twenty words, and if [the child] went to the reading teacher [and] . . . had more practice with . . . those same twenty words, and more practice with main idea on different materials, he would get mastery. (*Factory City Supervisor of Reading*)

Several administrators described the value of their services in terms of the "coordination" of activities they could provide, both in the district as a whole and within individual schools.

I see myself as a coordinator. I work with the purchase of materials, and with suggestions to the teachers on how reading can be improved; [I conduct] meetings from time to time on how reading can be improved. (*Blue Collar Suburb Reading Supervisor*)

I came into the district in '75–'76, and . . . we were decentralized to the point of unorganized chaos. . . . The components were all over the place—some had a good in-service program, a couple of buildings had a good criterion-referenced testing program. Basically what we had to do was pull all these things together and decide upon a common system. (*White Collar Suburb Director of Instruction*)

Note that "coordination" can take on several different meanings. In some cases it can mean "doing the same thing in different places" (e.g., in different schools, in different classrooms at the same grade level, or in Title I sessions outside the classroom). In other cases it means "providing different services focusing on the same objectives" (testing programs, teacher workshops, and principal meetings). Despite these ambiguities, many administrators saw "coordination" as essential to successful reading programs; they urged it on others and practiced it themselves.

A fourth tenet of rational bureaucracy to which my sample of officials subscribed is a kind of reverence for information (Corwin, 1974; Weick, 1982). In their view, "objective data" and "sound technology" are to be properly disseminated and acted on for planning, decision making, and problem solving, at every level of the school system. The Director of Instruction in White Collar Suburb described the way information enabled the district reading program to be self-corrective (Weick, 1982, p. 673):

The first thing [was] a specific set of objectives; then the objectives were broken down into learning objectives at the classroom level; you had a set of criterion-referenced test items; you had an array of materials that teachers could use in order to move towards achieving the objectives with the kids; then you had the testing materials in order to ascertain whether the teacher had achieved the objectives or not.

A Trade City administrator responsible for supervising principals saw principals' store of technological information as the key to improvement in the reading program:

If principals take the [administrative] skill they learned [in our workshop], plus additional knowledge in reading . . . through an exposure to one of the top persons in reading—they will, a little at a time, be able to develop a competency with the teachers, which will in turn improve our reading program, as a result of the individuals being more expert and more scientific, if you will, in the way they plan.

The citation of research results further demonstrated the store district officials set by technical information. Officials' remarks were much more liberally sprinkled with references to scholarly research, educational publications, and systematic experimentation than were the remarks of previous respondents. In some cases their references were general; in others they mentioned specific studies. Most of these allusions were not intended to support or defend particular policies or programs in that district; rather, they resembled the kind of "name dropping" that often occurs in academic circles.

> If you look back and find the Rand report, which came out a couple of months ago, they have done an evaluation of Title I. Title I programs are only effective . . . [when they are used] to support, not supplant, what is happening in that classroom. . . . And I think Alan Cohen's right—and Right to Read did point out—children need two things to learn to read: the right kind of material, and time. And that's what I'm trying to get them to do in this program. (*Factory City Supervisor of Reading*)

> Some say the look-say method, some say the phonetic method—there have been many studies; I think the Carnegie study by Chall is an example of what I was talking about. (*Blue Collar Suburb Superintendent of Schools*)

> It's Maslow's hierarchy of needs; our kids come to school at the survival level, they're not anywhere near self-actualization. And our teachers have to be aware of that. (*Trade City Superintendent of Schools*)

No administrator talked at length about the uncertainty that often surrounds "objective data." For the most part, information, whether from external research, internal test scores, or other forms of continuous monitoring, was treated as inherently reliable, valid, and useful for decision making. Programs that systematically collect and "use" information were assumed to be superior to programs that don't.

The kind of information district officials mentioned most frequently is that provided by evaluation. Systematic monitoring and feedback were portrayed as the primary means of organizational problem solving (Clark & McKibbin, 1982), and officials described both the mechanisms in place for collecting feedback and what they would do with the data in the event that it indicated a problem.

> We put a testing program into effect that's really a model, a very good one, not just in terms of the testing but the follow-up, in terms of using the data. . . . We have an array of skills, a testing program, and then you match your materials and teaching techniques according to the kids' needs. (*White Collar Suburb Director of Instruction*)

We do standardized testing, once a year; after carefully reviewing that, we're looking for any weaknesses, whether in comprehension, encoding, decoding, whatever. We have a curriculum team, and once a weakness is brought to our attention, we sit together—there's about eight of us—and we do some brainstorming in terms of where the area is, whether it's peculiar to a building, or a section of town, or if it's a citywide problem. Once we isolate the problem, then we try to develop a strategy to tackle that problem. (*Factory City Curriculum Supervisor*)

District administrators, in short, described a great deal of what school systems do in rational-bureaucratic terms. They advocated Weberian practices and principles for themselves as well as for building-level administrators. In doing so, they assumed two things: that rational-bureaucratic precepts *are* being followed (albeit imperfectly) by local educators; and that they *should be* followed, because such a course is likely to produce the best possible outcomes. By specifying goals, making plans, practicing coordination, gathering and disseminating information, and soliciting and using feedback, district administrators tried to create order and rationality in a changing, complex, and uncertain context. The importance of the rational-bureaucratic framework these administrators advocated has less to do with its "success" in making "good" policy, than with its functions in the administrator's search for legitimacy. To this issue we now turn.

Access to Influence: The Functions of Rational Bureaucracy

The district official's faith in the rational-bureaucratic model of educational administration would be touching, were it not so ironic. Weber's world works, but not for the reasons he thought, and not for the purposes he advocated. Judging from these interviews, administrators do not rely heavily on the precepts of rational bureaucracy to make decisions their subordinates must follow. Rather, administrators use rational-bureaucratic principles to acquire the right and the resources to influence the decisions their subordinates will make. Rational bureaucracy aids the administrator in search of legitimacy just as the pursuit of routine aids the teacher in search of certainty. It establishes a forum within which officials have the right to exercise influence; it enhances official credibility by giving the appearance of access to information; and it assists officials in the task of symbol management by creating rewards and sanctions (Weick, 1982, p. 675). The precepts of rational bureaucracy are thus not the results of the way power is distributed in educational organizations; rather, they are tools that skilled administrators can use to gain access to power.

Rational bureaucratic principals serve first to establish a forum for the exercise of official influence. The articulation of goals and objectives, for example, provides a common language for officials and subordinates to use in evaluating reading program practices and results. Officials who establish the language a district uses to indicate failure or success help to create meaning in educational policy; subordinates end up debating administrators on the administrators' terms. For example, the Director of Early Childhood Programs in Factory City indicated early in our interview that a basic goal for the city reading program was to raise average achievement scores. The program emphasized "movement" in reading instruction, measured by progress in the lessons, and this emphasis afforded the official an opportunity to intervene when teachers appeared not to be reaching district objectives:

> I do a lot of checking. . . . We have progress sheets coming in to keep track of where the kids are, so that if a specific teacher hasn't moved along very far, I can pay her a visit and say, "Are you having trouble with this group?" So they know somebody's watching and that they have to make a certain amount of progress with these kids.

The existence of goals legitimates the use of data gathered for purposes of "feedback," as this official went on to illustrate:

> I was in a room March 1 and the teacher was on a certain lesson. I copied the lesson down, came back to my office and checked the record from six weeks ago. She had only moved those kids six lessons for one group and four lessons for another group. So I wrote a memo to the principal, and I said, "Look, I think you should be aware of the fact that this teacher only did six lessons and four lessons in six weeks; what's she doing with her time? I want more progress!" And I think he was upset by it, but it made him aware that people are actually looking at it.

A White Collar Suburb official echoed her sentiments:

> If you have a set of objectives, and you want teachers to move through this sequence of objectives based upon your testing program, it's very difficult for a teacher to escape that. . . . Prior to the implementation of that accountability system, the teacher just wouldn't have bothered to teach that skill.

Planning and coordination also help to legitimate officials' attempts to influence subordinate behavior. When subordinates consent to a plan, they confer on administrators the right to monitor it, to ascertain whether it has been "properly implemented," and to take corrective action when necessary. Officials and subordinates may disagree about whether the plan was a good one, whether it was well or poorly implemented, and what to do if a subordinate fails to follow it; but the existence of a plan gives officials the right to challenge subordinate behavior—that is, to encroach upon their autonomy:

> We have a five-year plan for the school district. . . . We hope to be a grade-level school system in five years. Every school has been given its own five-year plan, based on objective test data, [indicating] the kind of improvement we have to see. Every year, we're going to be sitting down with those principals and looking at the scores this year, the scores next year—"Where were you? Where have you come?" No one is suggesting that if you haven't moved your school from X to Y, you're going to be removed. But we're suggesting that if you haven't moved your school from X to Y, [we will ask] what are the problems? How can we help you? What kind of support services do you need? With the full understanding that there's a limit to how many years we're going to be able to do that until someone begins to ask a question—maybe the problem is with the leadership in the school. (*Trade City superintendent*)

Plans need not be influential in themselves, but a skilled administrator can use them to gain access to influence.

Coordination complements planning by enlarging an official's "turf," giving him or her the right to exercise influence over a wider range of activities. For example, the Director of Early Childhood Programs in Factory City was officially responsible only for supervising a pre-kindergarten program, a K–3 compensatory program, and a parent-child program for children with special needs; but the pressure to "coordinate" compensatory education with the classroom reading program gave her access to classrooms as well:

> I'm on an awful lot of committees city-wide, and I'm on the curriculum team, and we monitor for the whole city. That's really been helpful to me, because not only do I see what *my* programs are like, but I get into classrooms all over the city. . . . So because of tying in and being helped on so many committees, I think it can help me moderate what's going on in the program, too.

Similarly, the Director of Instructional Programs in White Collar Suburb was able to extend his sphere of legitimate influence to include in-service training once it was "coordinated" with the district-wide "Scope and Sequence" reading program:

> You just can't put in one of these [multiple series] systems without tying it to a very, very efficient and effective in-service program. We had to have in-service on some of those areas that we felt the teacher had some liabilities.

Still another rational-bureaucratic resource that officials can turn to is information; skillfully used, it enhances administrators' credibility with their subordinates. Their citation of research results was one way of demonstrating their technical knowledgeability and thus their credibility; so was their use of evaluation data. No official described the institution of a change or the development of a program as having followed the precepts of rational decision making (examine all the alternatives, gather data predicting their consequences, and choose the "best" alternative according to the organization's goals and resources). Instead, information and evaluation data were called upon *after* decisions had already been made. By using data to promote past successes or to explain away past failures, district officials enhance their credibility with their subordinates, laying a foundation for the future exercise of policy-making rights. Information may be produced in accord with rational-bureaucratic precepts, but its effects have more to do with establishing legitimacy than with choosing among policy options.

A final function of rational-bureaucratic language is the "management" of symbols in order to create subordinate rewards and sanctions—which can then become resources for official influence. Weick (1982, p. 675) describes this task most clearly:

> The effective administrator . . . makes full use of symbol management to tie the system together. . . . Diverse ideas about the school's mission are common under conditions of loose coupling. This very plurality makes for successful local accommodation. But people also need some shared sense of direction for their efforts. . . . Articulating a theme, reminding people of the theme, and helping people to apply the theme to interpret their work—all are major tasks of administrators in loosely coupled systems.

Earlier we saw that administrators use goal-oriented language to help establish a forum for legitimate influence. Goals and objectives can also assist in the kind of symbol management Weick advocates, and district officials described a variety of activities that helped them to articulate themes and values associated with district goals. The effect of these goal-promoting activities was to enhance officials' legitimacy in their attempts to influence subordinates.

Memos and newsletters were one means of symbol-management district administrators described.

> Our emphasis this year is on building and improving reading scores. . . . I have a newsletter which I put out, and in it I'm trying to convey a unified philosophy about the teaching of reading.

> I had my mind set on the business of respect, discipline, and the basic skills. . . . It was a constant pounding away; I was constantly sending out memos to principals telling them not to forget the business of basic skills—reading and so forth. (*Blue Collar Suburb superintendent*)

Workshops and in-service programs were another important context in which goals and objectives helped officials to manage symbols. Most officials focused on the usefulness of workshops for building shared values and perceptions of the school's mission, rather than for the specific training and information they provided.

> Under the leadership of the supervisor of elementary education and the superintendent, we are trying to in-service our principals and . . . make them realize "You are responsible for the education of six hundred children; that's your number one priority. Do you know the curriculum guide? Do you know what the reading objectives are? Do you know how to transition a child from bilingual education? (*Factory City Director of Developmental Programs*)

> The philosophy of the [multiple-series] reading program is that it is to be a highly personalized program, in that basically you take the youngster from where he or she is and you bring that youngster along according to his or her skills potential. . . . You have to do a lot of in-service with teachers who have been brought up or trained—not educated, trained—to deal in mass education. So you really have to deal with that different type of attitude, that different approach toward teaching. (*White Collar Suburb Director of Instruction*)

District committees provided still another opportunity for articulating goals and providing a needed sense of direction. The newly appointed reading supervisor in Factory City told me:

> I have organized an advisory committee, made up of principals, parents, teachers, and staff—I have about fifty some-odd people on that committee. We meet every fourth Thursday and we are now in the process of deciding what reading skills we will teach for mastery. . . . It's

been a spiral but without any goals, so this is our next step, to really decide on our goals so you can have everybody working for the same goals.

The White Collar Suburb Director of Instruction also relied on committee settings to help gain consensus on values and goals, in this case articulated within the multi-series "Scope and Sequence" reading program:

When I got into the school district . . . I resurrected a committee system that had fallen by the wayside for a number of years, about fifteen or sixteen curriculum advisory committees. One of these happened to be the Reading Curriculum Advisory Committee, and that became the group that sparked the program that pulled these components together.

Committees, workshops and memos all serve as channels through which district officials may communicate a sense of personal and institutional direction to their subordinates. While these forms of communication appear to follow the rational-bureaucratic tenet of disseminating information in order to promote coordination and optimum decision making, the information they communicate is often more symbolic than substantive. Goals like raising average reading scores, stressing basic skills, maintaining accountability, personalizing education, and achieving continuous progress—all described in the examples above—are not specific enough to guide subordinates in their day-to-day activities. They *can*, however, serve other integrative functions by helping administrators gain subordinates' consent to the themes and values the school district supports. Even if those themes and values are not closely connected with the majority of the daily routines subordinates follow, they can still become a source of rewards when subordinates consent to them and use them to interpret at least some of their work. Thus, for example, teachers may find the laborious task of student record-keeping less painful (perhaps even rewarding) when they connect it with district-wide goals of "personalizing education" (as in White Collar Suburb) or "mastering skill objectives" (as in Trade City):

I think the Individualized Pupil Monitoring System [of testing] is better than just teacher judgment. It's a more accurate diagnosis, and I can pull [the children] out for skill teaching—using commas, alphabetizing, or silent consonants. It helps us do a lot of individualizing. (*White Collar Suburb teacher*)

A city-wide committee got together and they set up this kind of checklist of goals for each grade. Now we have a form where, say, you're going to teach the vowels, you check off when each kid knows them. That really helps—it keeps you organized, you know where you are and what you're doing during the year. (*Trade City teacher*)

If wisely selected and managed, then, district symbols can become a useful resource for administrative influence. Like symbol management, the setting of goals and the disseminating of information may look like rational-bureaucratic activities that assist in decision making; but in fact they are more useful for enhancing official credibility and establishing "turfs" over which officials claim the right to exercise influence, often before they make any policy decisions at all. These functions of rational-bureaucratic precepts thus serve to set the stage for the persuasion and bargaining that characterize official attempts to exercise influence over subordinates.

EXERCISING POWER AND INFLUENCE

Achieving legitimacy and establishing credibility is only part of the battle district administrators wage. The other part consists of their attempts to make an impact on the school system, either by gaining subordinates' consent to administrative plans or by influencing subordinates' perceptions and behaviors in some noticeable fashion. Both kinds of results require administrators to rely on persuasion and negotiation rather than command or threat. These strategies, in turn, hinge on the administrator's ability to establish a trusting relationship with his or her subordinates. It is this trusting relationship that puts disadvantaged children at risk, an argument I shall advance in the concluding section of this chapter. For now, I will illustrate the operation of persuasion and negotiation and examine the establishment of trust between official and subordinate that seems to precede any influential interaction.

Many of the general forms of communication already described— memos, newsletters, and so forth—may be viewed as official attempts to influence subordinates through persuasion. Written communications help to shape subordinate thinking and to gain subordinate consent to specific district plans, such as the implementation of a new series or a cutback in compensatory education staff. Other examples of persuasion at the administrative level abounded in my interviews, appearing most often in the context of official problem solving. When administrators chose to intervene in subordinate decision making, they tried to gain cooperation through consensus. That persuasion is necessary in an uncertain educational context was apparent to many district-level respondents. A Trade City official saw both

building-level and district-level administrators as "sellers" of their suggestions:

> At one time, if an administrative or supervisory figure walked into the
> classroom, or into a school, you'd find that everybody would be on
> their toes. That's not the attitude today. It's "Show me!" or "Who are
> you to tell me?" And consequently there's got to be more of a salesman-
> ship job done by principals . . . a give and take, being diplomatic and
> humanistic, pointing out to the individual that they have a strength—
> "That was terrific!"

A Factory City official saw persuasion as not only necessary but also as
more desirable in its long-run effects:

> A lot of us feel that you get your best results if you don't impose your-
> self on someone. There's an implication that if I come to you and talk
> to you about a child in your room that's having difficulty, and I pro-
> ject the image that I know what the difficulty is and I'm here to tell you
> how to fix it, you don't get as much done as when you inquire in a sub-
> tle way, "Are you having some problems?" or "Can I give you a hand?"
> That turns it around a little bit differently. That opens up the door to
> [the teacher] saying, "Yeah, you can help me; here's the problem I'm
> having." I think [persuasion] works better whatever you do.

Part of the reason officials rely on persuasion is the absence of sanctions—
short of writing bad evaluations or terminating employment—that they
have at their disposal. But part of it is clearly a belief that effective persuasion gets good results.

The means officials can use to persuade subordinates vary. Several
discussed the use of evaluation data to provide evidence that a particular
program or behavior is warranted. Clark and McKibbin have observed that
evaluation is not so much a way to change policy, as it is a way for schools
"to sort out what they have done, decide what they do well and enjoy doing,
and rationalize continuing to do it" (1982, p. 671). The officials I interviewed certainly substantiated this claim. One justified the installation of the
district's new reading series:

> We made a board presentation and our statistics show that we are com-
> ing up to where we should be on grade level. A year ago, and a year
> before when we instituted the Holt program, children were reading
> below grade level by a large percentage. Now we're coming up to
> where we should be. That shows me that we are going in the right di-
> rection. (*Factory City Director of Developmental Programs*)

Another responded to my observation that Title I program participants remain low achievers by pointing to positive evaluation results:

> I don't think there's a simple answer to that. . . . Why are there some Title I kids who improve achievement? We have to take a look at the positive—what happens with those kids who are able to perform admirably in the Title I program? Learn from that. (*White Collar Suburb assistant superintendent*)

Information and evaluation, then, are resources for persuasion that skillful administrators can use to gain access to influence.

Administrators also used suggestions and recommendations to persuade subordinates, and they did so with a view to the individuals and contexts involved:

> Just as you have to accept individual children and where they are at, you have to accept where teachers are and *what works for them*. . . . You can't go in and impose, make edicts saying, "For this group of children you're going to use. . . ." You can suggest, but you never leave them with "You're going to do this," or "You should use that." You work toward that, but you have to have them along with you or it's not going to work. . . . You could go on a scale from 0 to 10 and there are some teachers that are very receptive, and they're the ones you work with. Then there are some that are receptive when *they* see a need, and there are some you have to run after.

The purpose of offering suggestions, according to the Assistant Superintendent for Programs and Personnel in White Collar Suburb, is to help subordinates establish "ownership" of the need for a change.

> We're talking about the whole change process, and we're no different than any other organization. If you want a person to change his or her ways, the person has to make a decision that "I'm going to change." And if the person's going to change for the better, it means that the person understands why the change is needed. And that's a whole process in terms of internalizing and understanding and what have you. . . . A person's got to own that particular problem. Once that ownership is there and they begin to understand it, then there's a chance of a change.

This same perspective characterized officials' descriptions of a third kind of persuasion—workshops and other forms of in-service training. By establishing the legitimacy of the district mission, workshops can serve as a forum to shape people's thinking and hence to alter their behavior. Workshops are clearly intended to do more than increase educators' knowledge or skills; they provide opportunities for persuading teachers and principals to think in particular ways about the district's goals, to acquire a particular set of tools for meeting those goals, and to see both the tools and the goals as the preferred expression of the district's mission in education. This became even more clear to me after I observed a workshop for principals in Trade City, intended to improve their skills in observing teachers. The speaker, a principal from a California school district, was advocating a particular model of teacher observation, and his task was clearly not just to inform the principals about the model but to persuade them to use it. Before describing the approach, he talked about the similarities between his school district and Trade City; he discussed his increased self-confidence as an observer of instruction and his improved relationship with his teachers; he emphasized the quantities of research "proving" the effectiveness of the model ("There's not a shadow of a doubt about it anymore—it's been researched to death!"); and he described it as a usable, "practical" (as opposed to "theoretical") set of tools. He concluded his presentation by saying, "Thanks for your attention—I've had more hostile groups!" This workshop was a plea to principals to get involved with instruction and to do so in a particular way; the speaker assumed that he would meet with resistance, and he spent as much time justifying his approach as he did describing it. In short, persuasion thus characterizes many of the interactions between district officials and subordinates, whether those interactions take place on paper, in group settings, or one-on-one.

A second strategy for wielding influence is negotiation. Officials' descriptions suggested that bargaining and negotiation are usually invoked for purposes of conflict resolution. Some conflicts involved different priorities in setting agendas. The Director of Developmental Programs in Factory City described his interaction with the new district Reading Supervisor, who was accountable to him, and who entered the district with a fairly lengthy agenda of changes she wanted to make, programs she wanted to initiate, and goals she wanted to reach:

> The first five months of her tenure, I met with her every week. I wanted to know where she was going, I wanted her to justify what she was doing. She's a very dynamic woman and strong individual, and we wanted to sweep clean but we didn't want to hurt too many people either. . . . I might have put the brakes on something that she wanted to implement immediately. She came from a system that has shown some success, and it's smaller than Factory City. So I might have told her, "Please back off on this a little bit; let's work on this goal for a

while. Reevaluate those five goals; maybe we can put two on the back burner and work on three." She wanted to do too many things at once.

Other officials described negotiations over the means people use to implement district goals. The Director of Instruction in White Collar Suburb, while anxious to preserve the goals of the district's "Scope and Sequence" reading program, was nevertheless willing to negotiate the ways different schools chose to implement the program:

> Can a principal say, "I want to deviate from the reading program?" That depends on what they're deviating from. If they're talking about the use of all kinds of alternative materials . . . to arrive at the objectives, fine. But we do insist that the mandate is the Scope and Sequence of Reading Skills. . . .The process is pretty open. I would say there are schools that . . . are still committed quite a bit to basals, and that's not the route we want to take. But we have not forced that down the throat of that school.

The key to successful negotiation and bargaining in a school district, like negotiation and bargaining in an individual school, is the creation of an atmosphere of trust. District officials believe that demonstrating their trustworthiness to subordinates is an essential precondition for the exercise of power and influence. For the most part, these officials showed themselves trustworthy by articulating their empathy with subordinates. The presumption seemed to be that officials who care about teachers and principals, who understand their working conditions and the paradoxical demands they struggle to meet, can be counted on to help preserve subordinates' confidence, sense of professionalism, and autonomy, even as they persuade or negotiate with them:

> [Reading consultants] have a particular set of pressures and strains because you're dependent on a good working relationship with everyone. It's not the kind of situation where possibly you could . . . close the door and that's it. . . . That isn't easy, when you're very dependent on being able to work with all kinds of people and to be responsible to parents and the administration. (*White Collar Suburb Reading Director*)

> Our principals now have very, very little time to spend with instruction. . . . They're so bogged down in required paperwork that must be done for us, because of the federal problems and state problems, doing evaluations of teachers, PPT meetings, and reports that are due in here . . . they're so bogged down they just don't have the time. (*Factory City Assistant Superintendent for Elementary Education*)

This pattern was most apparent in the way officials described their interactions with teachers. Their remarks sounded very much like those of principals and reading specialists; they tried to give teachers as much support as possible, acknowledging their autonomy and precluding the necessity of invoking more drastic sanctions (transfers or terminations).

Teachers have to feel the pressure of doing a good job, but they also have to have that reinforcement. I was a classroom teacher; I know how hard it is to be in that classroom with kids that are off the wall, day after day, eight hours a day. I know it's rough. I think teachers have to feel the positive reinforcement of [district curriculum consultants] coming around and making constructive criticisms or suggestions or giving ideas—actually going out and getting the books for a project, or filmstrips, or whatever, that the teachers don't have time to do.

I think the basic, bottom line, is that before you terminate anybody you should try to provide as much support as possible to the person, to help them become better at what they're doing, or to correct whatever they're deficient in.

In this respect, officials participate in the ideology of supportiveness that building-level educators adopt in their dealings with classroom teachers. They encouraged specialists and principals to develop a trusting relationship with teachers by actively supporting what teachers are doing:

The biggest part of the [Title I teacher's] job is . . . to offer support and aid wherever it's needed. If you go into any given situation where a teacher needs certain materials, or they need to have any one of the other supervisors come in to assist them in programming, then . . . you serve as the liaison person, to set that up, to arrange it. Because the teacher doesn't have time to chase down materials and human resources.

Officials thus were concerned to demonstrate trustworthiness both directly and indirectly: in their own contacts with teachers, principals, and specialists, and in the approach they encouraged principals and specialists to take with teachers. They also demonstrated their trustworthiness in still a third way, by supporting school-level educators in their conflicts with parents:

[There was] a parent who had a child in kindergarten, and who [felt] that there [was] not enough formalized reading instruction [because] she has a child who's really ready to go. The teacher and I talked to the parent, saying, "Well, there are other things, there are children who aren't ready, and that has to be a consideration." And she said, "I'm not talking about *those* children, I'm just talking about my own, who is. I think we give too much time to these others." This was early in the year. I talked to the principal at the school, and then we talked about the program there, and that child, and the makeup of the class, and what could be done, and *was* there anything which should be done? And we really felt a child is better off with focusing the program as the kindergarten teacher saw it. It worked out that the parent was able to see that, too; when the child got the first report card, she was feeling so much better about things.

Some parents feel that their children should be reading better than what they are, and I would say that very seldom is it true—truthfully, now—very seldom is it true that the parent's assessment of their child is what they expect it to be. If the parent has a concern, then we would check on it; we would give them the courtesy. I get assessment from the principal, I get assessment from the teacher on how the child is doing; you look over the records; with that we would discuss with the parents what the child is doing. . . . A lot of parents just don't understand the process, the actual process of learning to read. It's very difficult. So you give them a Russian book and say, "Read it." And this is what it looks like to the children—symbols, that's all.

Both these examples suggest that officials are more concerned with maintaining the confidence of their subordinates than the confidence of parents, despite their persistent pleas for parent "involvement."

Lacking significant control over subordinates' rewards and sanctions, school officials must clearly rely on bargaining and persuasion to "lead the horses" toward the maintenance of stability and security. The energy officials invest in the cultivation of legitimacy has important consequences for the role district administrators can play in promoting equality of opportunity, and the remainder of this chapter will explore that issue.

THE PURSUIT OF LEGITIMACY AND THE MOBILIZATION OF BIAS

By now a familiar pattern in the relationship between power and opportunity in public schools has emerged. The "rational" activities of planning, monitoring, and evaluating do not testify to the presence of administrative influence, but rather to its absence. Lacking certainty about their mission and effectiveness, and hampered by subordinate autonomy and distance, officials lack the wherewithal to enforce their decisions. Instead, they must turn to persuasion and bargaining, and rational-bureaucratic activities help to create a forum within which they can develop and maintain these forms of influence. Planning, monitoring, and evaluating help to create a legitimate context and a set of resources for the exercise of influence, but what happens after that depends on the skill, will, and circumstances of the administrator attempting to persuade and negotiate with subordinates. Even when the conditions are such that district officials can move toward change—when school officials succeed in "selling" a new plan or articulating a new direction—they do so only *after* successfully demonstrating their support for the school's mobilization of bias and showing their empathy for the people who work within its parameters. This sharply constrains the kinds of changes administrators are likely to advocate. Thus, the official's pursuit of legitimacy, credibility, and trust helps to maintain the school's mobilization of bias.

The evidence for this conclusion has been offered in the preceding discussion. The demands of survival require officials to pursue stability, resolving conflicts within the parameters of the alternatives schools already provide. Officials' responses to the problem of unequal school outcomes, as described earlier in this chapter, clearly reflect a commitment to the present structure of educational opportunities. I believe the explanation for this parallels the patterns described in Chapter 5: what we have here is not so much an attitude problem as an ecological problem. Officials' views of children's capabilities are shaped in important ways by the means schools use to promote equal opportunity. Their attitudes spring from system-wide patterns of behavior they must endorse in order to create and preserve their influence. Widening or redefining the range of opportunities available to children in classrooms is for the district administrator an extremely risky business, and few officials have the wherewithal to undertake it. I believe this may account for the prevalence among educators of the "deficit" perspective which depicts low-income and minority children as culturally and educationally deprived, a view which persists in the face of a rising tide of criticism from the social scientific community. The failure to change behaviors toward low-income children and the inertia of programs which assume deficiencies instead of differences promotes a belief that these children *are* in crucial respects deficient. This in turn justifies present patterns of behavior in the school's mobilization of bias; if children are deficient, educators conclude, clearly the problem is with the child and not the classroom.

Perhaps the greatest constraint administrators face in effecting change in the school's mobilization of bias in the problem of goal displacement. The official's struggle for legitimacy focuses attention on the acquisition of influence, rather than on its exercise for the purpose of school improvement. The rational-bureaucratic activities that the official uses to create a forum for the exercise of influence become ends in themselves, rather than means

(Corwin, 1974, p. 255). Thus, as Weick (1982, p. 673) observes, "administrators [are] more concerned with documentation than with tangible results," and we saw this to be the case in officials' descriptions of teacher evaluations reported in Chapter 4. Likewise, evaluation becomes a rationale for program continuation rather than program change; this is apparent in the way administrators adroitly used the discouraging results of Title I evaluations to justify maintaining current practices ("The kids do better than they would without it."). Since district officials can't control results, they encourage activities. Those activities may not further the school's goals, but they may further the official's influence over subordinates. Both of these circumstances encourage officials to pay more attention to activities than to outcomes:

> We've made a strong emphasis on reading in the past several years. [We've had] workshops for teachers; [we encourage] more time spent with reading; a greater awareness by central office staff at meetings [of] the importance of reading; greater emphasis on the first-grade teachers. . . . I don't know if there were any actual changes [in classrooms].
> (*Factory City official*)

The same activities that help structure the official's pursuit of legitimacy also help to satisfy the subordinate's desire for certainty. Teachers and principals can rely on the tests and texts administrators supply to help order a complex and confusing world. They, too, participate in goal displacement, and this reinforces the official's tendency to see activities as ends in themselves rather than as a means.

Under these circumstances, it would be surprising indeed to see an official advocate a significant change in school activities to further the goal of equal opportunity. An administrative challenge to the status quo risks the resources for power and influence officials must work so hard to acquire. The present mobilization of bias paves the rational-bureaucratic path to legitimacy; thus, school district officials will continue to "lead the horses" in the same general direction they have always traveled, without worrying too much about what the horses are drinking. In the end, those who look to the district level for school reform must clearly look elsewhere.

7

From the Mobilization of Bias to the Mobilization of Change

Strategies for School Improvement

The descriptive task of this book is essentially complete. While I have explored only a small piece of schooling for the poor—the power and opportunity structures surrounding school reading programs—the implications of this exploration are substantial. Relationships of power and influence between people in schools affect dramatically the kinds of opportunities available to low-income children learning to read. Under some circumstances, people outside the classroom—reading specialists, principals, parents, and district officials—can help children make better use of the opportunities the school provides; but rarely, if ever, do they alter the classroom mobilization of bias. As a result, any policy option designed to increase the kinds of opportunities children have to learn to read, especially options intended to make educational interactions more "appropriate to the child," must include strategies which alter the structure of power and influence in schools; the incentives for stability within present power contexts are likely to overwhelm even the most carefully constructed and faithfully implemented innovation.

On this analysis, the question educators must face is not simply "Where do we go from here?" but equally important, "*How* do we go from here?" In fact, in this chapter I will pay equal attention to the latter question, because the substance of any change is inevitably shaped by the process of change a school follows. Certainly the findings reported in this book support several specific policy recommendations; Chapter 2, for example, suggests quite clearly that the three-reading-group approach to reading instruction has a deleterious effect on low achievers and ought to be abandoned. But *how* schools abandon this arrangement and replace it with something else is at least as important as what they choose to do instead. In this chapter, then, I will summarize the findings of the preceding chapters and suggest their implications for school improvement strategies.

SCHOOL ECOLOGY
AND PROSPECTS FOR EQUAL OPPORTUNITY

The preceding chapters have suggested several important analytic conclusions about schooling for the poor that must shape any strategy for egalitarian change. Inequality appears to lie less in educators' attitudes toward poor children and their parents than in the ways they cope with the paradoxes of education in its social and societal contexts. Furthermore, the perpetuation of inequality is due not so much to educators' lack of imagination or concern, as it is to their struggle to maintain a semblance of order, control, and predictability in a complex and uncertain setting. Reform agendas which fail to account for these patterns are bound to disappoint their proponents and to render educators all the more resistant to future innovations—an ironic, if understandable, result.

Specifically, the findings of this book suggest the following:

1. The most important feature of schooling for the poor is the classroom mobilization of bias. Strategies for change must therefore be targeted at changing what goes on at the classroom level.

For the majority of poor children, school-based opportunities to learn to read are confined to the classroom. Furthermore, the learning experiences of those children who do receive additional services outside the classroom are keyed to the structure of opportunities inside the classroom. If the past is any guide, we can expect that the addition of more programs or materials intended to improve the achievement of economically disadvantaged children will "supplement, not supplant" their classroom experiences in the same fashion as Title I/Chapter 1 services; and as we have seen, this approach tends to result in "more of the same." A change in the achievement levels of poor children thus requires a change in the classrooms that structure their opportunities.

2. The classroom mobilization of bias restricts the range of opportunities teachers can provide all their students, harming poor children more than non-poor children.

The classroom mobilization of bias does not result from teachers' attitudes toward poor children but rather from their attempts to cope with the paradox of collective instruction ("teach everyone but meet individual needs"), the problem of professional uncertainty, and the complexities of power and influence. Teachers' coping strategies hamper their ability to provide opportunities that are appropriate to each child's particular strengths and weaknesses. According to the findings of Chapter 2, the pursuit of routine and control severely limits the means teachers use to pay attention to individual differences among their students and to the criteria they use to evaluate their own efforts. The classroom mobilization of bias is likely to impose definitions of educational "needs" and "abilities" in ways which make poor children appear needier and less able than their non-poor peers. It also prevents teachers from seeing educational merit in the pre-school training and experiences of the economically deprived.

    3. Teachers are currently the preeminent wielders of power in public schools.

Teachers exercise the greatest degree of influence over educational plans and the creation of meaning in the classroom. Children, parents, specialists, and administrators certainly *influence* teachers' plans by providing or withholding cooperation, support, and tangible resources; but in the final analysis, it is the teacher's agenda which predominates. Educators outside the classroom, and children within it, are rarely successful in substituting their own plans for those of the teacher or in gaining sufficient consent for the implementation of their preferred alternatives.

    4. Power and influence resources in public schools are exercised primarily through bargaining and persuasion.

The limitations of in-service programs, district directives, and "effective" principal behaviors demonstrate that rewards and sanctions in public schools are often inaccessible or difficult to manipulate with consistent success. Autonomy, insulation, skewed dependency relationships, and intangible incentives require that influence be exerted through bargaining, negotiation, compromise, and persuasion. This pattern prevails at all levels of the school system, from the complex and occasionally chaotic world of the classroom, to the more predictable rational-bureaucratic world of the district superintendent. Although bargaining and persuasion are not inherently weaker or less effective than rewards and sanctions, they do exert influence differently; the picture of public schools as dynamic systems of mutual adjustment (Lindblom, 1965), rather than as top-down, static, command-and-control organizations, is certainly different than the picture many people—including those in schools—carry with them. Strategies for change that assume negotiation are very different from strategies that assume the simple giving and taking of orders; reformers must recognize that negotiation and persuasion are the rule, not the exception, both inside and outside the classroom.

5. In their bargaining and negotiations with teachers, other adults in the school system consent to the teacher's exercise of power and influence, thus supporting the classroom mobilization of bias.

The emphasis on "coordination" between remedial reading services and the classroom reading program serves to subordinate specialists' preferences and practices to those of teachers. The principal relies on the teachers to set the principal's agenda for supporting classroom strengths and addressing classroom weaknesses. Likewise, parents who extend their "cooperation" to the teacher effectively consent to the teacher's classroom plans. District officials also accept the classroom mobilization of bias and the teacher's essential autonomy as a given in their transactions with individual schools and the people who work in them. In short, not only do classroom teachers have more resources for the exercise of power and influence, but adults at every level of the school consent to and cooperate with classroom teachers' plans. Certainly educators outside the classroom exert influence by modifying teacher plans and preferences through bargaining and persuasion but they seem willing to let teachers remain the primary planners.

6. Despite their actual power, teachers feel surprisingly powerless.

As we saw in Chapter 4, teachers recognize that they have a bigger effect than anyone else on what happens in a classroom. But they do not see this as an indicator of power, largely because they tend to confuse power and control. Their struggle for control in the classroom blinds them to the resources and strategies for influence already at their disposal; their attempts to win children's consent on the day-to-day issues, such as how long to continue a reading lesson or when to grant permission for free reading time, overshadow the larger issues to which the children have already given their consent, such as whether to work in groups or how to demonstrate their abilities. Teachers are encouraged to think of power in terms of control both by the dynamics of the classroom experience and by the external institutional ethos. After all, within the ecology of the school power structure, the teacher's loss of classroom control and predictability threatens not only the teacher, but also others in the school whose choices depend on what teachers do. It is no wonder that teachers are more likely to see the world of schooling outside the classroom as a source of demands and pressures rather than of support and cooperation. Given the external expectation of teacher control, it is not surprising that teachers are generally unaware of the extent to which parents, reading specialists, and administrators defer to teachers' preferences in offering support or suggesting changes. The teachers in my sample who did recognize this pattern did not see it as evidence of their power but rather as evidence of their isolation or aloneness. Ironically, then, the people whose plans matter the most for the classroom mobilization of bias seemed least likely to exercise their power resources consciously. What is new here is not the finding that teachers feel powerless—others have certainly described this as part of culture of the school (McPherson, 1972; Sarason, 1982)—but rather that this feeling stands in contradiction to the actual distribution and exercise of power in the school.

7. The dynamics of education in the classroom, the teacher's sense of powerlessness, and the teacher's structure of incentives make significant, systemwide, teacher-initiated improvement efforts unlikely.

Most teachers recognize the skewed distribution of reading scores according to race and income. But in their struggles to provide instruction for everyone, in their attempts to avoid any behavior that might increase their uncertainty, and in their isolation from sources of support for innovation, teachers are led to focus their energies on maintaining routine and control while providing instruction and materials in sufficient amounts. Innovation threatens their already tenuous sense of control and instructional effectiveness; and since their incentives are so centered on what happens in the classroom, teachers are unwilling to risk what little stability and sense of accomplishment the status quo can give them. Innovations initiated by teachers thus tend to be highly localized (i.e., restricted to their own classrooms) and are relatively minor adjustments (e.g., the use of supplementary texts or worksheets); teacher autonomy and isolation makes it unlikely that innovations will spread spontaneously.

8. Other adults in the educational system—parents, specialists, and administrators—are also unlikely to promote significant changes in the classroom mobilization of bias.

Educators outside the classroom—including parents—take their cues from classroom teachers. They reinforce the classroom mobilization of bias by deferring to the teacher's preferences, priorities, and policies. They identify children's "needs" and "abilities" in the same ways teachers do, and they tend to support the teacher's interpretation of appropriate instruction. Even when teachers and other educators disagree, the autonomy of the classroom experience generally permits teachers to filter the comments or contributions of people outside the classroom and maintain their usual patterns of behaviors. This conclusion casts doubt on reform proposals that require building principals, reading specialists, or district officials to "crack down" on classroom teachers in an attempt to enforce higher standards.

Reformers who exhort principals to "get in there and observe" and to "stay on top of things" fail to comprehend the myriad constraints on any principal's influence and the enormous investment principals must make in preserving stability and easing uncertainty. "Improved coordination" between reading specialists and classroom teachers, as well as "increased parent involvement," are similarly limited by the teacher's fear of uncertainty in developing educational plans. Rational-bureaucratic "fixes" at the district level, like "better planning" or "more communication," confront the same obstacles; they cannot overcome teachers' incentives to preserve stability, or the autonomy that makes this pursuit of stability possible—and necessary. In short, people outside the classroom depend on teachers more than teachers depend on them, and the result is that suggestions from "outside" are selectively received, interpreted, and implemented according to the discretion of each classroom teacher; moreover, the kinds of suggestions "outsiders" offer are heavily influenced by the classroom teacher's preferences and policies.

Taken together, these observations suggest a final conclusion:

9. Changes in the classroom mobilization of bias require changes in the perception and distribution of power in public schools.

We cannot hope to develop strategies for meaningful improvement in equality of educational opportunity without coming to terms with the fundamental relationship between the distribution of opportunities and the distribution of power and influence. In one sense, this conclusion is a specific instance of the more general claim currently being made by many policy analysts—and not just those concerned with educational policy—that successful policy design must be predicated on a solid understanding of the implementing institutions. But the findings of this book go beyond this now-conventional wisdom. Opportunity and power in public education are connected in special ways that are not immediately obvious to the casual observer, largely because *the creation of meaning is at the heart of both power and education.* It is no accident that the current discussion of "empowerment" has finally permeated the public debate on education. What this book highlights is the need for people in schools to recognize the special connections between power and education residing in the creation of meaning. Educators need to be more self-conscious about the ways in which the resources of power and influence are currently distributed and exercised in the public school, and then they need to find ways of changing the structure of power to enhance equality of educational opportunity.

This is a big agenda, one that requires far more data and experience with public schools than this book alone provides. Nevertheless, the preceding chapters do suggest promising directions for change. In the next section I will sketch out a few proposals for change that are consistent with the findings I have summarized. These proposals are intended to be suggestive, not exhaustive; my hope is that others will respond to my analysis and conclusions by creating their own agendas for reform, agendas that address the concerns raised in this book, yet which grow out of sustained reflection on particular local needs and resources (Fullan, 1982). The suggestions which follow take the challenges posed by continued educational inequalities seriously, yet they are also sensitive to the obstacles educators face in effecting meaningful change.

DIRECTIONS FOR CHANGE

The preceding analysis contends that the classroom mobilization of bias will not change without significant changes in the perception and distribution of power in the public school. Improved equality of opportunity requires educators to be far more deliberate in the appropriation and application of power and influence resources. The following suggestions are intended to help achieve these changes.

1. Educators need opportunities to reflect together on the needs and abilities of their students, unconstrained by the classroom mobilization of bias.

The preceding chapters contended that the ways educators think about their students' educational strengths and weaknesses are conditioned by the means schools use to deliver educational services. Under these circumstances, low-income and minority students suffer disproportionately; when judged against the backdrop of the classroom experience and the skills it requires for success, economically deprived children look educationally deprived as well. Educators need opportunities and resources to question their assumptions about the needs and abilities of *all* students, but especially those of poor and minority children.

Among the most persuasive arguments for reflection as a route to improvement is that offered by Karen Kepler Zumwalt (1982). Believing that "good teaching is good deliberation," she advocates a model of teacher education that stresses reflection and deliberation:

Teaching [is] a process of constantly making choices about means and ends—choices that can be informed by process-product research, descriptive research, experience, intuition, and one's own values. Research data

> . . . are used to help teachers develop their thinking and decision-making capacities and to help them reflect on and learn from their own experiences. . . . Rather than promulgating truth embodied in a teacher "should" list, . . . the deliberative approach . . . allows for a diversity of views about teaching, teacher education, and the education of children, since the aims as well as the means of education are subject to deliberation (pp. 226, 241).

Zumwalt's model of teacher education is equally attractive as a model for ongoing dialogue in the school setting; it provides both the opportunities and the resources for educators to reflect on the needs and the abilities of the students they serve in a context of constant choice making. It avoids the kind of technological orientation that tends to reinforce the classroom mobilization of bias, rather than challenging it; it is sensitive to the value of the educator's own experiences as a guide to "practical" changes (Doyle & Ponder, 1977); it is alert to the ways experience can constrain educators' assumptions about the present and visions of the future (Sarason, 1982); and it appropriately focuses attention on meaning and diversity—both of which are at the heart of educational power and opportunity. If Zumwalt is right, a deliberative orientation, especially one that includes good description of the classroom experience, may help educators to transform the mobilization of bias. Educators who are conscious about *what* they are doing can become critical about *why* they are doing it. And it is on this foundation that a transformed structure of power and opportunity may be built.

What I am suggesting here is that educators adopt Zumwalt's model and begin to question their assumptions about the opportunities they provide students, particularly in reading instruction. In the school setting, this means that educators must take time regularly to reflect together on what they are doing and why, examining their perspectives on students' needs and abilities and how these perspectives are shaped by the classroom mobilization of bias. An agenda for sustained reflection consistent with the concerns raised in this book might include the following:

> Is it true that disadvantaged children come to school with "no experience"? What are the consequences of assuming they do?
>
> How can educators learn more about the extra-school lives of disadvantaged children and process what they learn independent of the mobilization of bias?
>
> What do different families do to educate their children, and how can school educators learn from that (Leichter, 1978)?
>
> Do social development and cognitive development occur the same way in all children (contra Tanner, 1978)?

In what ways do children's varied responses to the school setting make sense to them and help them to cope (McDermott, 1977, p. 210)? How might this knowledge change educators' assessments of educational needs?

What are the "schemas" different children bring to the task of learning to read (R. C. Anderson, 1984)? How do the materials and interactions of reading instruction activate—or fail to activate—these schemas?

What alternative competencies do disadvantaged children bring with them to the school setting (Schultz, Florio, & Erickson, 1982)?

What student behaviors in the classroom are *really* necessary for learning to occur?

How might different behaviors promote learning for different kinds of children?

Why do educators think ability grouping is necessary? In what ways does it serve the needs of educators rather than students?

What alternatives to homogeneous ability grouping might exist? What assumptions about children's learning needs and diverse capabilities do these alternative models represent?

Should classrooms offer the same reward structures to all students? If not, what alternatives might be appropriate, and why (Webb, 1982)?

These are only some of the many questions educators might consider. They grow out of the analysis of the classroom mobilization of bias offered in the preceding chapters, and they assume a willingness to risk raising complex and difficult issues. Furthermore, if this deliberation is carried out successfully, I believe it can help to promote a second desirable change:

2. Teachers must begin to recognize their power and use it to transform the classroom mobilization of bias.

Teachers need to recognize the extent to which their educational plans shape the agendas of every other participant in education—children, parents, specialists, and administrators. They also need to reflect on the meanings they create in the process of carrying out their plans and gaining others' consent to them. Certainly the deliberative orientation proposed above can help teachers to achieve this awareness. Once they have come to terms with the real power resources they already have, they can free themselves from the struggle for classroom control—a control which will forever elude them, and which is in any case antithetical to the liberal and liberating intentions of American education. They can then turn their energies to changing the mobilization of bias and engaging others outside of the classroom in support of those changes. Teachers who are free from the struggle for control are free to pursue innovations that enhance equality of opportunity. At its best, deliberation that enhances each teacher's awareness of his or her own power can promote a shared willingness to tolerate ambiguity. Teachers can pursue innovations with uncertain consequences knowing that they don't have to be in control in order to be powerful.

Professional uncertainty that is acknowledged and discussed rather than denied and buried can ultimately enlarge the range of opportunities schools provide to children. The fact that educators don't know what "works" must be treated as a justification for diverse plans and multiple planners. In the end, with a consciously cultivated institutional toleration for ambiguity, the problem of professional uncertainty can become an incentive, not only for innovation inside the classroom, but outside as well. Teachers need not carry the burden of identifying and meeting individual needs in isolation; they need not be "all things to all people" in a context where ambiguity is shared and tolerated. This also frees them to enlarge their understanding of educational needs and capabilities. Teachers who no longer feel the need to control everything that goes on in classrooms can afford to examine alternative conceptions of need and ability, knowing that they will be supported by others in their attempts to respond to these new understandings. They can tolerate the discovery of additional needs as well as the redefinition of needs they already recognize.

It is here that parents can make new kinds of contributions to their children's education. Parents whose agendas were not dictated by teachers, whose independent perceptions of their children's abilities and present limitations were taken seriously, and who had a share in making educational plans for their own children, could surely help give new meaning to concepts like "ability" and "development." They also could help teachers who are striving to provide education "appropriate to the child"; a parent's experiences with her child can help to indicate which treatments and transactions are likely to be appropriate. Teachers who recognize the power they already have will be less likely to interpret independent parental contributions and assessments as threatening; they will be less compelled to solicit only the kinds of information that support the classroom mobilization of bias.

3. Changes in the classroom mobilization of bias will require a reduction in teacher isolation.

The isolation of the classroom teacher clearly contributes to the teacher's "psychic dependence" on the classroom as a source of rewards

(Lortie, 1975). This structure of incentives makes the prospect of change, with the additional instability change inevitably produces, all the more threatening. Teachers are understandably unwilling to risk losing even the modest success they enjoy within the current mobilization of bias. As frustrating, painful, and confusing as teaching can be, few teachers are likely to court failure by changing significantly the context that provides them with virtually all their rewards. Teachers who are isolated from other supportive adults have no protection from classroom disasters. The more far-reaching an innovation, the more it represents a departure from the status quo, and the greater the chances of experiencing a "disaster." The radical changes necessary to expand the alternatives available to children in the classroom—changes like abandoning ability groups—are the very ones teachers are least likely to implement on their own. Isolation makes innovation far more fearsome; a reduction in isolation may promote the kind of risk-taking necessary for innovations to work (Zumwalt, 1982).

In some respects this theme is not a new one. Certainly it is consistent with the findings of the Rand Change Agent Studies (Greenwood, Mann, & McLaughlin, 1975). Almost a decade later, in proposing guidelines for school improvement informed by the growing literature on school change, Lieberman and Miller (1984) arrived at similar conclusions. Identifying a close connection between collegiality and experimentation, they emphasize that successful staff development and school improvement efforts will be built on a foundation of "collaboration and cooperation, involving the provisions for people to do things together, talking together, and sharing concerns" (p. 16). What is perhaps not so obvious in these recommendations—recommendations that my own analysis affirms—is that this kind of collegiality represents a change in the school power structure. A reduction in isolation may reduce teachers' autonomy, making them more susceptible to influence by other teachers, specialists, principals, and possibly even parents. Furthermore, collegiality can promote changes in the teacher's incentive structure; in experiencing rewarding contacts with their colleagues, teachers may come to rely somewhat less on the classroom setting as the source of all their professional rewards. Released from the structure of rewards currently provided by the classroom mobilization of bias, teachers are freer to experiment with innovations. A change in the teacher's incentive structure may not in itself promote an expansion of reading program opportunities; teachers may decide to innovate in other classroom-level policy arenas. Still, while not sufficient, changes in incentives are clearly necessary, and a reduction in teacher isolation can help to produce such changes. It can also ease the tensions that might accompany my final proposal:

4. The responsibility and capacity to plan must be extended to educators other than classroom teachers.

Educational planning is at the heart of the school power structure. It is the teacher's capacity to plan that allows him or her to set the agenda others in the school will follow. Yet the mobilization of bias restricts the opportunities teachers can offer children in the context of the classroom plans they attempt to carry out. It also restricts the opportunities others provide outside the classroom. If schools were to encourage other educators to develop and propose their own educational plans—plans that differed from those of the classroom teacher—the range of opportunities available outside the classroom may expand substantially. This change in the distribution of power may prove especially beneficial to low-income children; it enhances the likelihood that diverse learning options will be available to supplement the classroom context that presently restricts their opportunities.

This proposal is especially relevant to prospective changes in Title I/Chapter 1 and consultant services. The findings of Chapter 3 suggest that reading specialists need permission to create their own educational plans for students. "Coordination" has been costly; some creative confusion seems to be in order. Title I/Chapter 1 teachers and reading consultants might find their work far more productive if they abandoned the attempt to replicate classroom purposes and patterns. They could make substantial contributions toward widening the range of opportunities children have to learn to read, rather than simply helping children take better advantage of the structure of opportunities already available in the classroom. If specialists were encouraged to make innovative plans independent of classroom teachers' preferences, the institutional inertia against innovation might finally be shaken. This approach requires that specialists and classroom teachers stop seeing their relationship as a "zero-sum" game, in which a victory for one party inevitably comes at the expense of the other. Instead, specialists and teachers must try to build "positive-sum" games, in which both the teacher in the classroom, and the specialist in remedial reading sessions can create their own plans and work for consent to them in their own spheres. With an increased number of legitimate participants in assessment and planning, productive disagreement and multiple strategies are more likely to ensue, and educational needs are more likely to be appropriately defined and met.

School administrators can turn their bargaining and persuasive skills to advantage in encouraging this kind of independent initiative on the part of reading specialists. As reported in Chapters 3 and 4, specialists often turn to building principals for support when there is conflict with classroom teachers. When this happens in the present context, and the principal "backs" the specialist, everyone interprets this as meaning the specialist was "right" and the teacher "wrong." I am suggesting a shift in thinking—a subtle, albeit important, shift. Principals must make it clear that when they back a specialist, they are doing so not because the specialist is *right*, but because the specialist is *different*. Specialists need the support of other people in the school to depart from the classroom mobilization of bias in their treatment of low-achieving children; they need help to see themselves as independent educators whose job is to help the child, not simply to help the teacher. Principals and other district officials also must apply their bargaining and persuasive skills to help classroom teachers see the independence of reading specialists as an expansion of opportunities and a resource for innovative ideas, rather than as a threat to their power. If we have learned anything about the role of school and district administrators, it is that their skills in creating an institutional ethos are at least as important as their skills in organizing and managing material resources. In effect, what principals can do is to support, not so much a redistribution of power in which specialists win and teachers lose, but rather an expansion of power that permits *both* specialists and teachers to create plans for educating children.

A recent proposal altering Chapter 1 of the Education Consolidation and Improvement Act may help to bring such a change about. In anticipation of the 1987 reauthorization of Chapter 1 funds, both the Reagan administration and a group of moderate House Republicans have drafted a plan to convert Chapter 1 into a voucher system. Although they differ in the specific regulations they include, both versions permit parents to use federal Chapter 1 funds for "any approved program of supplementary instruction, at a public or private institution" (Hertling, 1986, p. 12). While there is sharp opposition to this plan from Congressional critics who fear that private schools will profit and public schools will suffer, nevertheless the plan is intriguing in the redistribution of power it suggests. Schools who must compete for students may work harder at diversifying supplementary services and encouraging specialists to offer remedial instruction that differs from what is offered in the classroom. And while there is some question about whether parents will take on the burden of acquainting themselves with the complete range of alternatives that may develop (Cohen & Farrar, 1977), schools will undoubtedly anticipate that at least some parents will make the effort. This proposal may disrupt the school power structure just enough to accomplish what I have suggested: extending the responsibility for educational planning beyond the parameters of the classroom.

These proposals are consistent with the findings of this book and with the recent literature on school change. They are also consistent with the responses many teachers and specialists made to the question, "What kinds of experiences have been helpful to you in learning how to do your job effectively?" Some examples will make my point:

> Learning. By that I don't mean going back to school and getting all kinds of professional degrees—I mean learning around children, other professionals, learning from reading. . . . You get ideas from other teachers—"I used this today and it worked for me." The same exact thing may not work for me, but it might give me an idea to try something. (*Blue Collar Suburb teacher*)

> For two or three years I was involved with the Teacher Center here in Trade City, which was a support group which encouraged people doing different things. . . . Also some of the educational conferences I go to, two or three conferences a year—those are all helpful, just talking with other teachers in other places. (*Trade City teacher*)

> Primarily the other teachers. We do a lot—not on a formal basis, but we talk with each other about what we're doing, how we're approaching it. . . . This kind of give and take is very effective. And we've worked together for years here, and it's a nice group of people—like a family. (*Factory City teacher*)

These teachers were clearly finding rewards outside the classroom that made them more satisfied, and possibly more effective, inside the classroom. While their experiences do not constitute the kind of sustained reflection I am advocating, they do indicate the promise of dialogue and deliberation.

What I am suggesting, then, is that teachers concentrate their deliberative energies on assessing strengths and liabilities of the classroom mobilization of bias, addressing the specific questions raised above, as well as any others they see as relevant and instructive. The goal is to reflect on the diverse needs and capabilities of low-income children in ways which are not constrained by the school mobilization of bias. Only then can teachers begin to offer education more "appropriate to the child," such that "each child would be reading to the best of his or her ability." This approach acknowledges both the strengths and weaknesses of current structures of power and opportunity. It keeps our attention focused on the creation of meaning for all the participants in educational policy making. And it may help promote the kind of multiplicity in the meanings we attach to concepts like "need" and "ability" that Greene (1984) argues is essential in a context of diversity and ambiguity. These proposals are clearly not intended to be comprehensive or exhaustive, but they are intended to spark ideas and to stimulate sustained dialogue and reflection. If there is hope for expanded opportunity in education, I believe it is here.

Appendix
Notes
Bibliography
Index
About the Author

Appendix

The purpose of this appendix is to describe more fully the procedures I followed in collecting and analyzing the data on which this book is based. I will also offer a brief assessment of the strengths and weaknesses of my research design.

As indicated in the Introduction, I interviewed a total of 101 respondents, distributed among twelve schools in four districts. In an attempt to maintain diversity among my respondents, I selected schools in very different kinds of neighborhoods. In the two urban districts, I chose the school with the largest proportion of white students, the school with the largest proportion of black students, the school with the largest proportion of Hispanic students, and a school with a fairly mixed population. In the two suburban districts, I selected two schools of different sizes in different parts of town. Within each of these twelve schools I began by talking with four classroom teachers, one from each of the first four grades (usually excluding kindergarten), about the aims and conduct of the classroom reading program and their working relationships with specialists, parents, principals, and district officials. Following these interviews I spoke with the school's reading consultant and/or Title I teacher, and then with the school principal. District administrators were interviewed after all the school-level data had been collected and analyzed.

The selection of individual respondents varied slightly from school to school. In some schools I was permitted to select the teachers myself; when possible, I did this randomly within each grade level. In other cases the principal asked for volunteers or assigned me to the participants. Two schools employed only one teacher in each of the grades of interest. Although the presence of volunteers and assigned teachers undoubtedly influenced the representativeness of my sample, the purpose of the research design was to maintain appropriate diversity in the backgrounds, working conditions, personalities, and experiences of the subjects. Judging from the responses I received, this goal was met despite the different methods used to select the participants. All the reading specialists and principals in these schools consented to an interview. The selection of district officials was determined primarily by the preliminary interviews; I asked the school-level people in each district to tell me which administrators ought to be interviewed, and began with their recommendations. If the officials selected on this basis suggested other district officials as well, I followed their advice too.

At the conclusion of the fieldwork, I had conducted 103 interviews with 101 respondents. Two teachers from White Collar Suburb were interviewed twice in the early stages of the research in order to adjust the questionnaire. While the usual pattern in each school was to select one teacher each from grades 1-4, it was not always possible to adhere strictly to this design. For example, the Factory City school with the highest proportion of black students only served students in grades K-3, so a kindergarten teacher was included in those interviews. The exact positions held by my respondents were as follows:

Position	Number of Respondents
Kindergarten teacher	1
Kindergarten–first-grade teacher	1
First grade teacher	12
Second grade teacher	12
Third grade teacher	12
Fourth grade teacher	11
Title I/Chapter 1 teacher	9
Reading consultant	6
Principal	12
Supervisor of Reading/Language Arts	4
Supervisor of Early Childhood/Title I	4
Supervisor of Administration	4
Supervisor of Instruction	4
Asst. Superintendent for Administration	1
Asst. Superintendent for Elementary Education	2
Asst. Superintendent for Instruction/Curriculum	2
Superintendent of Schools	4

Interviews were conducted on school premises at various times of the school day. The length of each session depended primarily on the amount of time each respondent was willing and able to give, which ranged from 20 to 90 minutes and averaged about 40. Nearly all the interviews were tape-recorded. Since the time available for each session varied, some of the respondents were not asked all the questions on the interview schedule; I have indicated in the text those cases where the sample on a given item was significantly different than the total number of respondents. The interview questions were entirely open-ended, which influenced the placement and exact wording of the questions as they were posed to the respondents. In each case, I tried to balance the need for reliable data with the need for responsive and adaptive questioning procedures.

Interviews at all levels of the school system were intended to elicit descriptions and reflections on two issues: how reading programs accommodate differences among children, and how the different participants in the program—teachers, specialists, parents, principals, and district administrators—work together in the delivery of services. An important feature in the design of the questionnaires was the adaptive nature of the questions I asked. Specialist questionnaires were designed and administered after about half the teacher interviews were concluded, and in each school I waited until after the teacher interviews were completed before interviewing the specialists. Principal interviews were designed and conducted after I had analyzed the data from teachers and specialists and had formulated some tentative conclusions about power and opportunity in classroom remedial programs. Finally, after all the school-level material had been compiled and analyzed, a new and very different set of questions was devised for the district officials. These interviews were even more open-ended and interactive, directly confronting my district respondents with some of the conclusions I had reached as a result of my school-level investigations. These interviews tended to be considerably more provocative than the earlier ones, and my respondents varied a great deal in their reactions to this procedure. Some found it uncomfortable and disturbing, while others appeared to enjoy the challenge. In both cases, I was provided with a rich body of description and reflection—far richer, I believe, than it would have been if I had not predicated my questions on the school-level findings. The interview schedule for each category of respondents is provided at the end of this Appendix.

The data gathered through interviews were supplemented by two additional sources of information: classroom observation and literature reviews. I observed several periods of reading instruction in different classroom and remedial settings (i.e., different grade levels, different programs, different class sizes, different neighborhoods), sometimes while interviewing the teacher (instruction being then provided by a teacher's aide) and sometimes at the conclusion of the interviews. These observations were undertaken simply as a check on the accuracy of the teachers' descriptions of the instructional programs and practices they followed, and the resulting data were therefore not independently reported and analyzed. The literature I reviewed was drawn from a wide variety of theoretical and research perspectives, ranging from government documents to scholarly literature in multiple disciplines (anthropology, economics, education, political science, psychology, public administration, and sociology predominated). These additional perspectives helped to balance the necessarily parochial view of schooling that inevitably emerges from a grassroots investigation of the kind I had undertaken. The attempt was to blend the "subjective realities" portrayed by my respondents with the "objective realities" portrayed in a diverse body of literature and in my own observations. The interview results were examined for patterns of similarity and dissimilarity (Babbie, 1986; Miles, 1983) in the respondents' perspectives (Sharp & Green, 1975) on several issues: the ways in which educators assess and respond to learning differences among students both in and out of the classroom; the causes of success and failure in reading; the problem of fairness in the delivery of services in reading instruction; and the nature of the working relationships between the respondent and other "street-level bureaucrats" in the school system.

This research design, like any other, is limited in a number of respects. There is, as suggested above, a great risk of parochialism and tunnel vision; those who are caught up in the day-to-day projects of an organization are not always the best judges of their own behavior and its consequences. I believe this limitation is partially offset by the breadth I tried to establish in the additional research I reviewed, but the very strength of this research design—its reliance on the voices of those who actually deliver services to children—is nevertheless, by definition, its greatest weakness as well. For that reason, this work must be seen as a complement to existing research employing quite different methodologies, not as a substitute or replacement. Following Eisner (1977), my purpose is to "render . . . the range, richness, and complexity of educational phenomena" (p. 349). A rendering of complexity is not without risk in matters of reliability and replication; but no method of analysis is risk-free, and my hope is that the issues raised here will provoke further research using different designs with a different set of possibilities and pitfalls. Additionally, I have attempted to live up to Sarason's injunction that ecological investigations be conducted in as "value-free" a manner as possible (1982, p. 131). The standards I used to describe and assess how schools provide equality of educational opportunity were based on the goals school people themselves articulated and defended. Similarly, my description of the power structure characterizing school reading programs was not based on my own preconceived notions of how power ought to be distributed and exercised, but rather on the information school people provided describing how the system actually operates. I cannot claim value-free interpretation of the data I gathered—no case study author can—but the initial gathering of data was a serious attempt to describe behavior rather than to evaluate individuals.

While my research design was not overtly ethnographic, relying as it did on interviews rather than observations (Fetterman, 1982), my research purposes were nevertheless consistent with many of the fundamental principles of ethnology. Following Mehan (1982), the analysis of the interviews was intended to explain the rules and principles organizing behavior in the "practical circumstances" which constitute reading programs. The interview format permitted me to explore the formal and informal rules people in schools perceive, how they perceive these rules, and the rationale they rely on to justify both the rules and their consequences. A second ethnographic feature is the interactive/adaptive research process I employed, particularly with respect to school administrators (Heath, 1982; Hymes, 1982). The flexible, open-ended interview procedures permitted me to maintain a number of the research values which Fetterman argues that good ethnography is intended to support: phenomenology, which "requires that investigators be guided by the insider's viewpoint"; holism, which "commands our attention to the larger picture and to the interrelated nature of the minute to the whole cultural system"; a nonjudgmental orientation, which "prevents the social scientist from making some of the more obvious value judgments in research"; and contextualization, which "demands that we place the data in its own environment so as to provide a more accurate representation" (1982, p. 18).

This research design was uniquely suited to the theoretical and practical problems in education policy that I wished to explore. Both opportunity and power are concepts whose existence is partly determined by the participants of the social organization in which these concepts are given shape and substance. The fundamental role of meaning in education and its governance requires that we pay close attention to the subjective realities which contribute to public education policy. Power, opportunity, and education itself are all, at least in part, rooted in people's perceptions of their transactions with others, and the research design I employed helps to elicit those perceptions in ways that other designs simply cannot replicate. The view of schooling reflected in this book is thus partial in both senses of the word; but its partiality is, I believe, a necessary and valuable contribution to a fuller understanding of educational policy and its consequences for the children who are its intended beneficiaries.

TEACHER QUESTIONNAIRE

Children come to school with different interests, abilities, and backgrounds, yet schools are supposed to provide them all with a basic set of skills and accomplishments in reading. I am interested in finding out how reading programs in schools work, particularly in light of this problem.

All your responses to my questions will be treated confidentially and will only be reported as coming from anonymous sources. No one's name will ever be revealed or identified with any particular conversation, locally or elsewhere. You are free to discuss this interview after I have finished all the interviews I am conducting at your school.

1. *Concerning the reading program*
   a. In what ways do the children in your class differ from one another in their struggles to learn how to read?
   b. How do you identify the different kinds of reading needs your students have?
   c. How do you divide up your time among your students with respect to reading instruction?
   d. What do you think your job is with respect to teaching reading?
   e. In any reading program, there are some things teachers have to do, and others they do by choice or preference. Can you tell me about each?
2. *Concerning parents*
   a. What kinds of discussions do you have with parents about the reading program?
   b. Are there suggestions you make to parents? That parents make to you?
   c. What do you learn from parents that helps you in teaching their children how to read?
3. *Concerning reading specialists*
   a. How would you describe the working relationship between yourself and the (Title I teacher) (reading consultant)? What are some of the advantages of having him/her here? What are some of the complications or pressures?
   b. Are there specific things that the (Title I teacher) (reading consultant) wants you to do? How do you respond to his/her suggestions?
4. *Concerning principals*
   a. Are there specific things the principal has expressed an interest in, or wants you to do, in teaching reading?
   b. What does/can the principal do that is helpful or supportive concerning the reading program?
5. *Concerning school officials*
   a. What decisions, either district- or state-mandated, seem to make a difference in what goes on in your classroom during reading instruction?
   b. What mechanisms exist for teacher input into decisions about reading? Does that input make a difference in the kinds of decisions that get made? Does it affect what happens in the classroom later?

   c. Are there decisions made at the district level which affect reading, even though they are not directly related?

   d. Who has the most influence over reading in your classroom?

6. *Background*

   a. How long have you been a teacher? How long have you taught at this school?

   b. What has been helpful to you in learning how to teach?

READING SPECIALIST QUESTIONNAIRE

Children come to school with different abilities, interests, and family backgrounds, yet schools are supposed to provide them all with a basic set of skills and accomplishments in reading. I am interested in finding out how people in schools—teachers, reading specialists, principals, and local officials—cope with this situation. All your responses to my questions will be treated confidentially, and will only be reported as coming from anonymous sources. No one's name will ever be revealed or identified with any particular conversation, locally or elsewhere.

1. *Concerning the reading program*

   a. How are students selected to receive your services?

   b. How do the children you work with differ from one another in reading?

   c. How do you identify the different kinds of reading needs they have?

   d. How do you divide up your time among the various tasks you have? How do you divide up your time among the different schools to which you have been assigned?

   e. What do you think your job is with respect to reading?

2. *Concerning teachers*

   a. How would you describe the working relationship between yourself and the classroom teachers? What pressures do they bring to bear on you as you do your job?

   b. When teachers initiate conversations with you about the reading program, what concerns do they voice? What suggestions from teachers have you acted on? Are there ways they misunderstand your job?

   c. Do you approach the teachers with suggestions? What happens afterward?

3. *Concerning parents*

   a. What kinds of discussions do you have with parents about reading?

   b. Are there suggestions that you make to parents? That parents make to you?

    c. What do you learn from parents that helps you to be more effective?

4. *Concerning principals*
   a. When do you talk with the principal about the reading program? What do you talk about? What concerns does he or she voice?
   b. What does the principal do that is helpful or supportive?
   c. Have your contacts with the principal affected your working relationship with the classroom teachers? If so, how?

5. *Concerning school officials*
   a. What decisions, either district- or state-mandated, seem to make a difference for you in the reading program?
   b. Who has the most influence over what happens in reading?

6. *Background*
   a. How long have you been a reading specialist? How long have you worked at this school?
   b. What has been helpful to you in learning how to be an effective specialist?

PRINCIPAL QUESTIONNAIRE

Children come to school with different abilities, interests, and family backgrounds, yet schools are supposed to provide them all with a basic set of skills and accomplishments in reading. I am interested in finding out how people in schools—teachers, reading specialists, principals, and local officials—cope with this situation. All your responses to my questions will be treated confidentially and will only be reported as coming from anonymous sources. No one's name will ever be revealed or identified with any particular conversation, locally or elsewhere.

1. *Concerning the reading program*
   a. How was your school's reading program chosen?
   b. I understand that many principals "make rounds" of the classrooms. How often do you observe the children in reading lessons? What kinds of things do you look for or notice?
   c. What do you want to know about what happens in classrooms? Why?
   d. What do you think your job is with respect to reading?
   e. Even though children come to school with different interests, abilities, and readiness to read, you have basically one curriculum to teach them all the same basic skills. If some children work very well with that curriculum, but others don't, how can schools try to make sure that every child has a fair chance to learn to read?

2. *Concerning parents*
   a. What kinds of contacts do you have with parents concerning the reading program? What kinds of things do you discuss?
   b. How do these contacts affect the way you do your job with respect to reading?
3. *Concerning teachers*
   a. What comes up in your discussions with teachers about the reading program? How does this compare with the discussions you have concerning other school activities?
   b. Some people say that part of the principal's job is to monitor reading instruction in classrooms and to take action based on that. How does that claim fit in with the way you do your job with respect to reading?
4. *Concerning reading specialists*
   a. How would you describe the working relationship that exists between the reading specialist(s) and the classroom teachers? What are some of the benefits? What are some of the problems?
   b. What kinds of things do you do to help keep that relationship working smoothly?
5. *Concerning school officials*
   a. What decisions, either district- or state-mandated, seem to have a bearing on reading lessons here?
   b. Are there district decisions that you are responsible for enforcing in this school? How much latitude do you have as an enforcer? Are there some decisions that you have more discretion over than others?
6. *Background*
   a. How long have you been an elementary school principal? How long have you been working at this school?
   b. What has been helpful to you in becoming an effective principal?

DISTRICT OFFICIAL QUESTIONNAIRE

I am interested in finding out how schools work in view of the diversity of the children who attend them. All your responses to my questions will be treated confidentially, and will only be reported as coming from anonymous sources. No district's name will be used in my final report. No one's name will ever be revealed or identified with any particular conversation, locally or elsewhere.

1. Where does reading fit into your job? Into your daily activities? What do you do in your job that has an effect on the reading program?

2. How do you find out about problems in the reading program? What sorts of things do you find out about? (Can you give me a specific example of a time when that happened? How often does that occur?)

3. One of the problems that I've been wrestling with while I've been looking at schools and talking with teachers and principals is that fact that children are very different. They come to school from different home backgrounds, with different interests, different abilities, and different readiness to read. And somehow schools are supposed to teach them all to read.

   a. How do schools in your district try to make sure every child has a fair chance to learn to read?
   b. How does what you do affect that?
   c. The children who seem to have trouble in the classroom setting often appear, almost systematically, to be the children who come from a less economically advantaged background. Why is that?
   d. What do schools try to do to rectify the skewed distribution of reading achievement with respect to economic background?

4. In many districts, Title I teachers and reading consultants rely heavily on classroom teachers to help them figure out what a child needs in order to read better. But by depending so heavily on teachers, extra services sometimes seem to give the children more of what they got in the classroom in the first place.

   a. Is this a fair description of what happens?
   b. Is this a good thing or a bad thing? Why?
   c. (If respondent claims special services are different) How are special services different?
   d. Even when the services are different, the point seems to be to better equip the child to function in the classroom. Why is that approach taken, if the child was not functioning well in the classroom in the first place?
   e. Teachers and specialists tell me that the children who receive extra services still remain on the low end of the scale in terms of reading achievement. Why is this so?
   f. Why are services set up as they are?

5. In many of the schools I visited, principals spent a lot of time paying attention to problems connected with the reading program. I noticed that most of them did not actively seek out problems to solve—they waited for teachers to tell them what troubles they were facing and what they wanted the principal to do for them.

   a. What is your perception of what is going on?
   b. What about teachers who are not willing to tell the principal they are having trouble?

c. What can a principal do to effect change in the classroom, once he or she sees a problem? How does that change what happens in the classroom?

6. The districts I have visited provide a variety of services to help children learn to read. Most group children by ability in the classroom; many have Title I teachers and/or reading consultants to work with individual children who are having trouble; principals are directed to get involved by helping teachers out with suggestions and materials; district administrators try to set policies that create a supportive environment for reading. But as I looked at the activities of people outside the classroom— Title I teachers, principals, specialists, and administrators—it appeared that their main effort was to reinforce what was already happening in the classroom.

   a. Is my assessment right?

   b. What's the rationale behind the system?

   c. Does it make sense in view of the fact that not all children can succeed in the classroom in the first place?

   d. Are there any alternatives?

   e. It appears that people outside the classroom really try to support the teacher's efforts. But that means the weaknesses as well as the strengths of the classroom are supported. What is your view of that?

7. If you were going to do an interview like this with a superintendent or one of your superiors, what sorts of questions would you want to ask them about the reading program?

8. Is there anything I've left out of this interview, particularly about the ways schools are set up to provide services in reading instruction?

Notes

INTRODUCTION

1. Caroline Persell (1977) provides an excellent review of the controversy over the relationship between educational outcomes and life outcomes in Chapter 10 of *Education and Inequality: A Theoretical and Empirical Synthesis.* For more recent, although less detailed, reviews, see Oakes (1985, especially Chapter 10).

2. This is the almost universal justification for the continued funding of compensatory education programs, from the teacher in the classroom to the federal bureaucrat at the Department of Education. For example, an ED spokesperson testifying at the 1985 Congressional budget hearings admitted that "although Title I gains have been significant, they were still not great enough for its participants to catch up with non-disadvantaged, non-compensatory students." Nevertheless, he urged increased funding for compensatory education because "most Chapter 1 students do a lot better than they would have done if they hadn't had the program, and most of the kids were so far behind anyway" (U.S. Congress, House, March 1984, pp. 149–50).

CHAPTER 2

1. A search through some of the literature on reading instruction produces a long list of the various ways in which children may differ from one another in the process of learning to read. Children may differ in the order in which they acquire various reading skills (Carroll, 1984); in their language and vocabulary patterns (Hodges, 1976); in their rate of learning (Good & Stipek, 1983); in the "schemas which organize their knowledge of the world" (R. C. Anderson, 1984, p. 243); in their preschool experiences (Ruddell, 1976); in their motivation to read (Harris & Sipay, 1980, p. 31); in their development of perceptual and motor skills (*ibid.*, pp. 23–25); in their social and emotional development (*ibid.*, pp. 30–31); in their ability to work well in a group (Tanner, 1978); and in their cultural values (Labov, 1982).

2. As Osborn reports (1984, pp. 51, 53): "During the period allocated for reading instruction, the adopted basal materials—readers, teachers' guides, charts, workbooks, and other supplements such as practice cards and audio-visual material—were used almost exclusively. . . . Although other books were in the classroom, typically they were on the shelves and not in use, at least during the reading period."

3. It is possible that the combination of a different group of children could change the effect of the group context on the individual child's learning (Eder, 1981); but the very ad hoc and temporary nature of these arrangements makes it difficult to determine if either routines or outcomes will be significantly affected in the long run, especially since these groups are so clearly subordinate to the students' ability groups.

4. Both functions of intimacy between teachers and students have been noted in general research on classroom contexts, but not much attention has been given to the role of intimacy in reading instruction. Philip Jackson (1968) and Dan Lortie (1975) were among the first to note that the psychic rewards of teaching are rooted in positive transactions between teacher and student; House and Lapan (1978) affirm their observations. The most compelling recent case is made by Cohen and Murnane (1985) in their analysis of merit pay. They observe (p. 21): "When we asked teachers what motivated them to do good work, their answers were all consistent with what one woman in Virginia Beach told us: 'Every once in a while a light bulb goes on in a kid's head.' . . . Another teacher summed up these ideas nicely when he told us that 'student support is the biggest motivation. The harder they try, the harder I try.'" These "light bulb" experiences are closely tied to the personal relationships teachers establish with their students.

5. An excellent review of the assumptions that underlie intelligence and achievement tests and the many critiques leveled against them, including those of Jencks (1972), Bowles and Gintis (1976), and a host of others, is available in Chapter 5 of Caroline Persell's *Education and Inequality: A Theoretical and Empirical Synthesis* (1977). She concludes: "Because of their content and their administrative procedures, standardized IQ or aptitude tests are extremely inappropriate means of ascertaining the 'ability' of lower-class and minority children. The prevalent use of test scores for educational decisions has resulted in the misclassification and mislabeling of thousands of minority students, with the apparent additional consequences of undereducation, lower teacher expectations, diminished self-esteem, and increased rates of dropout" (p. 72).

6. A helpful review of the literature debating "appropriateness" in reading materials for black children is provided by Williamson-Ige (1984), who sorts the variety of approaches into no fewer than ten models. One view, for example, argues that black language patterns are linguistically deficient and that black children should use only instructional materials written in standard English. Another view notes the discontinuity between black language and the language of school, suggesting that black children use texts written in informal and familiar (although not necessarily dialectic) language. Still others advocate the use of nonstandard texts as a means of "transition" into standard English. This debate extends beyond the scholarly community to include the parents of black students, some of whom worry that the latter options would "institutionalize a low-prestige dialect in the school" (R. Williams, 1975, cited in Williamson-Ige, p. 25).

CHAPTER 3

1. This problem has persisted since the inception of Title I, partly because there has always been an incentive to separate program description from achievement effects (McLaughlin, 1975). Small gains in the achievement scores of disadvantaged and minority students who receive compensatory services—for example, 3.5 percentage points in a recent ED summary (J. Anderson, 1983)—still leave participating students well below national norms; the federal data cannot specify which features of Title I/Chapter 1 may be responsible for post-test improvements. While some narrowing of the "achievement gap" was reported in the 1980 National Assessment of Educational Progress (Murnane, 1985), the mean NAEP scores of nine-year-old black children attending schools in disadvantaged urban communities fell short by 9.9 percentage points (NAEP, 1981). Furthermore, NAEP data collection "precludes identification of the school district or even the state in which any individual student lives. As a result, the NAEP data cannot be used to evaluate whether specific policies or educational programs affect children's test scores" (Murnane, 1985, p. 118).

2. In wealthier districts, each school may have its own consultant; more often, consultants are "shared" by two or more schools. The districts I sampled varied in the availability of consultant services. In Blue Collar Suburb, a single consultant served the entire district. In Trade City and Factory City, consultants were shared by three to five schools. In White Collar Suburb, each consultant served only one school.

3. At the time the field research for the study was conducted, Title I of the 1965 Elementary and Secondary Education Act (ESEA) had not yet become Chapter 1 of the 1981 Education Consolidation and Improvement Act (ECIA). For the sake of simplicity, I will refer to the compensatory programs and personnel I actually sampled as "Title I," since that is what they were called when I studied them. When I make generalized claims about past and present compensatory programs, I will refer to them as Title I/Chapter 1 services, which reflects both the continuity of the practices characterizing compensatory education and the terminology many educators currently use in referring to these services.

4. The practices of the districts I sampled were representative of national practices as well. Gaffney and Schember (1982) report that 92 percent of Title I school districts "use a pullout design for part or all of their Title I program" (p. xi).

5. The relative effectiveness of in-class and pull-out designs is a subject of intense debate, not only among my study participants but nationally as well. Interestingly, Gaffney and Schember (1982) note that while research on the merits of each design is inconclusive, nonetheless "teachers and local administrators hold strong views on this subject, not just in favor of their own designs but against other approaches" (p. 23).

6. The literature on the expertise of Title I/Chapter 1 teachers in reading instruction is somewhat inconsistent. For example, in the compensatory education study mandated by the 1974 Education Amendments, the NIE (1977) compared the "types" of teachers working in classroom and Title I reading and language arts instruction. Based on data from twelve demonstration districts, the researchers noted that "differences between classroom teachers' and specialists' educational levels and years of experience vary substantially among districts. In some sites, the

position of specialists appears to be one of leadership based on training and/or experience. In others, specialists have less experience than teachers and either approximately the same or only slightly higher educational levels" (pp. 44, 48). More recent research on the qualifications of Title I/Chapter 1 teachers presents similarly contradictory findings; see, for example, the nationwide District Practices Study (Advanced Technology, 1983).

7. These observations are very close to those of the District Practices Study (Advanced Technology, 1983, pp. 5–30): "Only 19% of the regular classroom teachers surveyed reported any problems in teaching the Title I students or the rest of the class because of the way Title I instruction was arranged. The most frequently mentioned problems were scheduling, helping students make up missed work, students missing classwork, and interruptions in the middle of a lesson for pullout."

CHAPTER 4

1. Despite apparent consensus, this research is not without its critics. For example, Ralph and Fennessy's (1983) careful review of the evidence cited by proponents of the effective schools model (of which "effective principals" are an integral part) finds substantial observer bias, failure to measure relevant and important variables, and failure to distinguish cause from effect. Given these limitations, my purpose in this chapter is not to identify certain principals as effective and certain others as typical; nor will I attempt to establish causal relationships between certain types of principal behaviors and certain kinds of school-wide achievement outcomes. Instead, I take the effective schools/effective principals research in the spirit in which Ralph and Fennessey argue it should be taken: as a set of propositions most educational practitioners say school principals should try to live by. My intent is to highlight differences in the ways these principles did their jobs, the better to analyze the common constraints they faced and common patterns in their responses to public school reading programs.

CHAPTER 5

1. Since this was the only parent I spoke with at that school, I cannot judge how representative her responses were of the opinions of other parents. I decided to include this material, however, partly because her perspectives were so consistent with my interpretation of the data collected from school respondents, and partly because her perspectives were shaped by a high degree of involvement and awareness relative to other parents in the school. Her responses reflect the consequences of very successful attempts by the school to encourage parent involvement; they are not the result of apathy, hostility, or lack of awareness.

2. Only 36 of the 51 teacher interviews included this question. The first ten interviews were conducted in White Collar Suburb and I had not yet added the question to the interview schedule. Because of time pressures, four teachers in

Factory City were not asked to describe what they learned from parents. However, many of these 14 interviews included information about what teachers learn from parents without my asking a specific question.

3. Admittedly, the White Collar Suburb teachers were not asked to describe what they learned from parents that helps them to teach reading, so this may account in part for my observation. Nevertheless, their remarks were peppered with descriptions of other things they learned from parents—mainly home problems and children's interests—and they were asked to describe what suggestions parents had made to them about reading instruction. Thus, White Collar Suburb parents either did not engage in home instruction, said nothing to teachers about their home instruction activities, or said nothing that the teachers viewed as salient or useful. Given the allusions by several White Collar Suburb teachers to the "pressure" some of their students felt from home to progress rapidly in reading, it is doubtful that White Collar Suburb parents did not engage in home instruction or that they avoided discussing their activities with teachers.

4. The lack of agreement among researchers as to the causes of the "achievement gap" poses an interesting contrast to the near-unanimity of my respondents. It is helpful to group the wide variety of research perspectives into four types. One, which is not widely shared but is widely known, argues that people of color are genetically inferior to their majority, non-poor counterparts (Jensen, 1969). A second perspective uses the language of class structures to explain the same patterns (Bowles & Gintis, 1976; Keddie, 1977), arguing that differences in school achievement reflect concepts of ability and knowledge that elites use to maintain social control. A third view, often described as the "cultural difference" theory, emphasizes competing value structures espoused by home and school (Gilmore & Smith, 1982; Labov, 1982); some point to differences in the "schemas" poor and minority children use to organize experience and information (R. C. Anderson, 1984; Bransford, 1984); some emphasize linguistic differences between home and school (Taylor, Payne, & Cole, 1983); and some describe a variety of social-organizational differences (Au & Mason, 1982; Cazden, 1982; Schultz, Florio, & Erickson, 1982). A fourth view—the one to which my respondents subscribed—suggests that poor children lack important skills and capabilities necessary for success in school and ascribes their failure rate to their cultural deprivation or deficiencies, not their intellectual ones. Some adherents focus on vocabulary and linguistic deficiencies (Becker, 1977; Hunt, 1982), others on the lack of social skills and preschool experiences (Harris & Sipay, 1980; Tanner, 1978). While the cultural difference theory implies that schools should be changed to accommodate the alternative cultures of poor children and turn them to educational advantage, the cultural deficit theory suggests that poor children should be changed (compensated) to accommodate the demands of schooling.

Bibliography

Advanced Technology. (1983). *Local operation of Title I, ESEA 1976–1982: A resource book*. Reston, VA: Advanced Technology.

Alexander, K. L., Cook, M., and McDill, E. L. (1978). Curriculum tracking and educational stratification. *American Sociological Review, 43*, 47–66.

Anderson, J. I. (1983). *ESEA Title I grants to local education agencies. A summary of state reports for 1979–80, 1980–81, and 1981–82*. Washington, DC: U. S. Department of Education.

Anderson, R. C. (1984). Role of the reader's schema in comprehension, learning, and memory. In R. C. Anderson, J. Osborn, and R. J. Tierney (eds.), *Learning to read in American schools: Basal readers and content texts* (pp. 243–57). Hillside, NJ: Erlbaum.

Au, K. H., and Mason, J. (1981). Social organizational factors in learning to read: The balance of rights hypothesis. *Reading Research Quarterly, 117*, 115–72.

Babbie, E. (1986). *The practice of social research* (4th ed.). Belmont, CA: Wadsworth.

Bachrach, P., and Baratz, M. S. (1962). The two faces of power. *American Political Science Review, 56*, 947–52.

———. (1963). Decisions and non-decisions. *American Political Science Review, 57*, 632–42.

Baratz, S. S., and Baratz, J. C. (1970). Early childhood intervention: The social science base of institutional racism. *Harvard Educational Review, 40*, 29–50.

Barnett, B. G. (1984). Subordinate teacher power in school organizations. *Sociology of Education, 57*, 43–55.

Barriers to excellence: Our children at risk. (1985). Boston: National Coalition of Advocates for Students.

Becker, W. C. (1977). Teaching reading and language to the disadvantaged—What we have learned from field research. *Harvard Educational Review, 47*, 518–43.

Bowler, M. (1978). Textbook publishers try to please all, but first they woo the heart of Texas. *The Reading Teacher, 31*, 514–19.

Bowles, S., and Gintis, H. (1976). *Schooling in capitalist America*. New York: Basic Books.

Bransford, J. D. (1984). Schema activation and schema acquisition: Comments on

Richard C. Anderson's remarks. In R. C. Anderson, J. Osborn, and R. J. Tierney (eds.), *Learnng to read in American schools: Basal readers and content texts* (pp. 259–72). Hillside, NJ: Erlbaum.

Brookover, W., Beady, C., Flood, F., Schweitzer, J., and Weisenbaker, J. (1979). *School social systems and student achievement: Schools can make a difference.* New York: J. F. Bergin.

Burton, N. W., and Jones, L. V. (1982). Recent trends in achievement levels of black and white youth. *Educational Researcher, 11*(4), 10–17.

Carew, J. V., and Lightfoot, S. L. (1979). *Beyond bias: Perspectives on classrooms.* Cambridge, MA: Harvard University Press.

Carroll, J. B. (1984). The nature of the reading process. In A. J. Harris and E. R. Sipay (eds.), *Readings on reading instruction* (pp. 30–34). New York: Longman.

Carter, L. F. (1984). The Sustaining Effects Study of compensatory and elementary education. *Educational Researcher, 13*(7), 4–13.

Cazden, C. (1982). Four comments. In P. Gilmore and A. A. Glatthorn (eds.), *Children in and out of school: Ethnography and education* (pp. 209–26). Washington, DC: Center for Applied Linguistics.

Chall, J. S. (1967). *Learning to read: The great debate.* New York: McGraw-Hill.

Clark, D. L., and McKibbin, S. (1982). From orthodoxy to pluralism: New views of school administration. *Phi Delta Kappan, 63,* 669–72.

Cohen, D. K., and Farrar, E. (1977). Power to the parents?—The story of education vouchers. *The Public Interest,* No. 48, 72–97.

Cohen, D. K., and Murnane, R. J. (1985). The merits of merit pay. *The Public Interest,* No. 80, 3–30.

Coleman, J. S., Campbell, E. Q., Hobson, C. J., McPartland, J., Mood, A. M., Weinfeld, F. D., & York, R. L. (1966). *Equality of educational opportunity.* Washington, DC: U. S. Government Printing Office.

Corwin, R. G. (1974). Models of educational organizations. In F. N. Kerlinger and J. B. Carroll (eds.), *Review of research in education* (Vol. 2, pp. 247–95). Itasca, IL: Peacock Press.

Costa, A., and Guditis, C. (1984). Do district-wide supervisors make a difference? *Educational Leadership, 41,* 84–85.

Cremin, L. A. (1976). *Public education.* New York: Basic Books.

Dahl, R. A. (1984). *Modern political analysis* (4th ed.). Englewood Cliffs, NJ: Prentice-Hall.

Davy, J. (1983). Teaching competence and teacher education: The fundamental issues. *Teachers College Record, 84,* 553–56.

Doyle, W., and Ponder, G. A. (1977). The practicality ethic in teacher decision making. *Interchange, 8*(3), 1–12.

Duffy, G. G. (1982). Response to Borko, Shavelson, and Stern: There's more to instructional decision-making in reading than the "empty classroom." *Reading Research Quarterly, 17,* 295–300.

Durkin, D. (1978–1979). What classroom observations reveal about reading comprehension instruction. *Reading Research Quarterly, 14,* 481–533.

———. (1984). Poor black children who are successful readers: An investigation. *Urban Education, 19,* 53–76.

Eder, D. (1981). Ability grouping as a self-fulfilling prophecy: A micro-analysis of teacher-student interaction. *Sociology of Education, 54,* 151–62.

Eder, D., and Felmlee, D. (1984). The development of attention norms in ability groups. In P. L. Peterson, L. C. Wilkinson, and M. Hallinan (eds.), *The social context of instruction: Group organization and group processes* (pp. 189–208). Orlando, FL: Academic Press.

Eisner, E. (1977). On the uses of educational connoisseurship and criticism for evaluating classroom life. *Teachers College Record, 78,* 345–58.

Erickson, F., and Schultz, J. (1976). When is a context? Some issues and methods in the analysis of social competence. *Quarterly Newsletter of the Institute for Comparative Human Development, 1*(2), 5–10.

Farr, R. (1984). Reaction to "Do basal manuals teach reading comprehension?" In R. C. Anderson, J. Osborn, and R. J. Tierney (eds.), *Learning to read in American schools: Basal readers and content texts* (pp. 39–44). Hillside, NJ: Erlbaum.

Felmlee, D., and Eder, D. (1983). Contextual effects in the classroom: The impact of ability groups on student attention. *Sociology of Education, 56,* 77–87.

Fetterman, D. M. (1982). Ethnography in educational research: The dynamics of diffusion. *Educational Researcher, 11*(3), 17–22, 29.

Fullan, M. (1982). *The meaning of educational change.* New York: Teachers College Press.

Gaffney, M. J., and Schember, D. M. (1982). *The effects of the Title I Supplement-Not-Supplant and Excess Costs provisions on program design decisions: A special report from the Title I District Practices Study.* Reston, VA: Advanced Technology.

Gilmore, P., and Smith, D. M. (1982). A retrospective discussion of the state of the art in ethnography in education. In P. Gilmore and A. A. Glatthorn (eds.), *Children in and out of school: Ethnography and education* (pp. 3–18). Washington, DC: Center for Applied Linguistics.

Good, T. L., and Stipek, D. J. (1983). Individual differences in the classroom: A psychological perspective. In G. D. Fenstermacher and J. I. Goodlad (eds.), *Individual differences and the common curriculum* (Eighty-second yearbook of the National Society for Study of Education, Part I, pp. 9–43). Chicago: University of Chicago Press.

Goodlad, J. I. (1979). *What schools are for.* Bloomington, IN: Phi Delta Kappa Educational Foundation.

———. (1984). *A place called school: Prospects for the future.* New York: McGraw-Hill.

Gowin, D. B. (1981). *Educating.* New York: Cornell University Press.

Greene, M. (1984). "Excellence," meanings and multiplicity. *Teachers College Record, 86,* 283–97.

Greenwood, P. W., Mann, D., and McLaughlin, M. W. (1975). *Federal programs supporting educational change, Vol III: The process of change* (R-1589/3-HEW). Santa Monica, CA: Rand.

Hallinan, M. (1984). Summary and implications. In P. L. Peterson, L. C. Wilkinson, and M. Hallinan (eds.), *The social context of instruction: Group organization and group processes* (pp. 229–40). Orlando, FL: Academic Press.

Harris, A. J., and Sipay, E. R. (1980). *How to increase reading ability: A guide to developmental and remedial methods* (7th ed.). New York: Longman.

Heath, S. B. (1982). Ethnography in education: Defining the essentials. In P. Gilmore and A. A. Glatthorn (eds.), *Children in and out of school: Ethnography and education* (pp. 35–55). Washington, DC: Center for Applied Linguistics.

Hertling, J. (1986, February 12). Rejecting Bennett voucher bill, House G. O. P. goes own way. *Education Week, 5*(22), p. 12.

Hodges, R. E. (1976). Reactions to language acquisition and the reading process. In H. Singer and R. B. Ruddell (eds.), *Theoretical models and processes of reading* (2nd ed., pp. 39–41). Newark, DE: International Reading Association.

Hoffman, J., and Rutherford, W. (1984). Effective reading programs: A critical review of outlier studies. *Reading Research Quarterly, 20*, 79–92.

House, E. R., and Lapan, S. (1978). *Survival in the classroom: How to negotiate with kids, colleagues, and bosses.* Boston: Allyn and Bacon.

Hunt, J. M. (1982). Toward equalizing the developmental opportunities of infants and preschool children. *Journal of Social Issues, 38*(4), 163–91.

Hymes, D. (1982). What is ethnography? In P. Gilmore and A. A. Glatthorn (eds.), *Children in and out of school: Ethnography and education* (pp. 21–32). Washington, DC: Center for Applied Linguistics.

Jackson, P. (1968). *Life in classrooms.* New York: Holt, Rinehart, and Winston.

Jencks, C., Smith, M., Akland, H., Bane, M. J., Cohen, D., Gintis, H., Heyns, B., and Michelson, S. (1972). *Inequality: A reassessment of the effect of family and schooling in America.* New York: Basic Books.

Jensen, A. R. (1969). How much can we boost I. Q. and scholastic achievement? *Harvard Educational Review, 39*, 1–123.

Keddie, N. (1977). Classroom knowledge. In A. A. Bellack and H. M. Kliebard (eds.), *Curriculum and evaluation* (pp. 286–316). Berkeley, CA: McCutchan.

Labov, W. (1982). Competing value systems in the inner-city schools. In P. Gilmore and A. A. Glatthorn (eds.), *Children in and out of school: Ethnography and education* (pp. 148–71). Washington, DC: Center for Applied Linguistics.

Leichter, H. J. (1978). Families and communities as educators: Some concepts of relationship. *Teachers College Record, 79*, 567–658.

Leithwood, K. A., and Montgomery, D. J. (1982). The role of the elementary school principal in program improvement. *Review of Educational Research, 52*, 309–39.

Levin, H. M. (1984). About time for education reform. *Educational Evaluation and Policy Analysis, 6*, 151–163.

Lieberman, A. (1982). Practice makes policy: The tensions of school improvement. In A. Lieberman and M. W. McLaughlin (eds.), *Policy making in education* (81st yearbook of the National Society for the Study of Education, Part I, pp. 249–69). Chicago: University of Chicago Press.

Lieberman, A., and Miller, L. (1978). The social realities of teaching. *Teachers College Record, 80*, 54–68.

Lieberman, A., and Miller, L. (1984). School improvement: Themes and variations. *Teachers College Record, 86*, 4–19.

Lightfoot, S. L. (1978). *Worlds apart: Relationships between families and schools.* New York: Basic Books.

Lindblom, C. E. (1965). *The intelligence of democracy: Decision making through mutual adjustment.* New York: Free Press.

Lipsky, M. (1980). *Street-level bureaucracy: Dilemmas of the individual in public services.* New York: Russell Sage.

Lortie, D. C. (1975). *Schoolteacher: A sociological study.* Chicago: University of Chicago Press.

Lowi, T. (1964). American business, public policy, case-studies, and political theory. *World Politics, 16,* 677–715.

McDermott, R. P. (1977). Social relations as contexts for learning. *Harvard Educational Review, 47,* 198–213.

McLaughlin, M. W. (1975). *Evaluation and reform: The Elementary and Secondary Education Act of 1965, Title I.* Cambridge, MA: Ballinger.

McPherson, G. H. (1972). *Small town teacher.* Cambridge, MA: Harvard University Press.

Mehan, H. (1982). The structure of classroom events and their consequences for student performance. In P. Gilmore and A. A. Glatthorn (eds.), *Children in and out of school: Ethnography and education* (pp. 59–87). Washington, DC: Center for Applied Linguistics.

Miles, M. B. (1983). Qualitative data as an attractive nuisance: The problem of analysis. In J. van Maanen (ed.), *Qualitative methodology* (pp. 117–34). Beverly Hills, CA: Sage.

Murnane, R. J. (1985). An economist's look at federal and state education policies. In J. M. Quigley and D. L. Rubinfeld (eds.), *American domestic priorities: An economic appraisal* (pp. 118–47). Berkeley: University of California Press.

National Assessment of Educational Progress (NAEP). (1981). *Three national assessments of reading: Changes in performance, 1970-1980* (Report No. 11-R-01). Denver: Education Commission of the States.

National Commission on Excellence in Education. (1983). *A nation at risk: The imperative for educational reform.* Washington, DC: U.S. Government Printing Office.

National Institute of Education (NIE). (1977). *Compensatory education services.* Washington, DC: NIE.

Nyberg, D. (1981). A concept of power for education. *Teachers College Record, 82,* 535–51.

Oakes, J. (1985). *Keeping track: How schools structure inequality.* New Haven: Yale University Press.

Osborn, J. (1984). The purposes, uses, and contents of workbooks and some guidelines for publishers. In R. C. Anderson, J. Osborn, and R. J. Tierney (eds.), *Learning to read in American schools: Basal readers and content texts* (pp. 45–111). Hillside, NJ: Erlbaum.

Pauly, E. (1980). Teachers control students, students control teachers. Unpublished manuscript, Yale University, Institution for Social and Policy Studies, New Haven.

Persell, C. H. (1977). *Education and inequality: A theoretical and empirical synthesis.* New York: Free Press.

Ralph, J. H., and Fennessey, J. (1983). Science or reform: Some questions about the effective schools model. *Phi Delta Kappan, 64,* 689–94.

Ruddell, R. B. (1976). Language acquisition and the reading process. In H. Singer and R. B. Ruddell (eds.), *Theoretical models and processes of reading* (2nd ed., pp. 22–38). Newark, DE: International Reading Association.

Sarason, S. (1982). *The culture of the school and the problem of change* (2nd ed.). Boston: Allyn and Bacon.

Schattschneider, E. E. (1960). *The semisovereign people: A realist's view of democracy in America.* Hinsdale, IL: Dryden Press.

Schultz, J. J., Florio, S., and Erickson, F. (1982). Where's the floor? Aspects of the cultural organization of social relationships in communication at home and in school. In P. Gilmore and A. A. Glatthorn (eds.), *Children in and out of school: Ethnography and education* (pp. 88–123). Washington, DC: Center for Applied Linguistics.

Shannon, P. (1983). The use of commercial reading materials in American elementary schools. *Reading Research Quarterly, 19,* 68–85.

Sharp, R., and Green, A. (1975). *Education and social control: A study in progressive primary education.* London: Routledge and Kegan Paul.

Silvernail, D. L. (1979). *Teaching styles as related to student achievement: What research says to the teacher.* Washington, DC: National Education Association.

Simpson, C. (1981). Classroom structure and the organization of ability. *Sociology of Education, 54,* 120–132.

Stodolsky, S. S. (1984). Frameworks for studying instructional processes in peer work-groups. In P. L. Peterson, L. C. Wilkinson, and M. Hallinan (eds.), *The social context of instruction: Group organization and group processes* (pp. 107–24). Orlando, FL: Academic Press.

Stonehill, R. M., and Anderson, J. I. (1982, March). *An evaluation of ESEA Title I—Program operation and educational effects: A report to Congress.* Washington, DC: U.S. Department of Education.

Tanner, L. N. (1978). *Classroom discipline for effective teaching and learning.* New York: Holt, Rinehart and Winston.

Taylor, O. L., Payne, K. T., and Cole, P. (1983). A survey of bidialectical language arts programs in the United States. *Journal of Negro Education, 52,* 35–45.

U.S. Congress, House, Committee on Appropriations. (1984). *Hearings Before the Subcommittee on the Departments of Labor, Health and Human Services, Education, and Related Agencies of the Committee on Appropriations* (98th Congress, Second Session, Part 6: Department of Education). Washington, DC: U.S. Government Printing Office.

Weatherley, R., and Lipsky, M. (1977). Street-level bureaucrats and institutional innovation: Implementing special-education reform. *Harvard Educational Review, 47,* 171–97.

Webb, N. M. (1982). Student interaction and learning in small groups. *Review of Educational Research, 52,* 421–45.

Weick, K. E. (1976). Educational organizations as loosely coupled systems. *Administrative Science Quarterly, 21,* 1–19.

———. (1982). Administering education in loosely coupled schools. *Phi Delta Kappan, 63,* 673–76.

Williamson-Ige, D. K. (1984). Approaches to black language studies: A cultural critique. *Journal of Black Studies, 15,* 17–20.

Wise, A. M. (1979). *Legislated learning: The bureaucratization of the American classroom.* Berkeley: University of California Press.

Zigler, E., and Kagan, S. L. (1982). Child development knowledge and educational practice: Using what we know. In A. Lieberman and M. W. McLaughlin (eds.), *Policy making in education* (81st yearbook of the National Society for the Study of Education, Part I, pp. 80–104). Chicago: University of Chicago Press.

Zumwalt, K. K. (1982). Research on teaching: Policy implications for teacher education. In A. Lieberman and M. W. McLaughlin (eds.), *Policy making in education* (81st yearbook of the National Society for the Study of Education, Part I, pp. 215–48). Chicago: University of Chicago Press.

Index

About the Author

Jo Michelle Beld Fraatz is Assistant Professor of Political Science at Saint Olaf College in Northfield, Minnesota. She received her Ph.D. in political science from Yale University in 1982. Her interest in education politics and policy began in graduate school, sparked by a teaching assistantship in the politics of education with Edward Pauly, then of the Yale Institution for Social and Policy Studies, and by a research assistantship on equality of opportunity with Robert A. Dahl, Sterling Professor of Political Science. Dr. Fraatz is also the author of "Policy Analysts as Advocates" and "Participation, Power, and Public Schools."